GENERAL PSYCHOLOGY
—FOR—
CHRISTIAN
COUNSELORS

GENERAL PSYCHOLOGY —FOR— CHRISTIAN COUNSELORS

RONALD L. KOTESKEY

✣

Abingdon Press / Nashville

GENERAL PSYCHOLOGY FOR CHRISTIAN COUNSELORS

Copyright © 1983 by Abingdon Press

Library of Congress Cataloging in Publication Data

KOTESKEY, RONALD L., 1942–
General psychology for Christian counselors.
Bibliography: p.
Includes index.
1. Counseling. 2. Christianity—Psychology.
3. Psychology. I. Title.
BF637.C6K67 1983   150   82-13848

ISBN 0-687-14044-7

MANUFACTURED BY THE PARTHENON PRESS AT
NASHVILLE, TENNESSEE, UNITED STATES OF AMERICA

To Bonnie

P R E F A C E

At least once in my college general psychology course when we are discussing physiological psychology, sensation, perception, or learning, some student asks, "What does this have to do with psychology?" Of course, this is because that student sees psychology as synonymous with counseling—and he or she wants to learn counseling without learning psychology. Other students, when presented with my Christian perspective on psychology, say, "So what?" There seem to be similar sentiments among students in counseling, pastors who counsel, and Christian counselors in general.

Because of these sentiments, I have written this book as a companion to my previous book, *Psychology from a Christian Perspective,* which was a theoretical approach to psychology with little application. The present book extends that position into the applied area of counseling and shows how all areas of general psychology are relevant to abnormal psychology and counseling. It shows how a Christian perspective brings unity to psychology and emphasizes the interconnectedness of all areas of general psychology. It is not just a presentation of secular psychology. Rather it points out several important areas ignored in secular general psychology, discusses these areas from a Christian perspective, and applies them to disorders and treatment.

This is not a general psychology textbook, but it takes material selectively from general psychology and shows how it can be applied. Because of limited space, I have omitted much subject matter of general psychology. This is not a critique of secular psychology. Several fine critiques are available, so this book deals with putting the pieces together after such critiques have been made. Readings are suggested at the end of each chapter because I hope that the book will inspire further reading.

This book is for general psychology students who are interested in counseling, for clinical and counseling psychologists who forgot (or never learned) their general psychology, and for pastors and others involved in counseling. It will also interest the educated layman who has had some psychology.

Each chapter builds on previous chapters, so they should be read in order. Most of the chapters are in three sections. The first section gives a brief summary of relevant knowledge in a given area, the second section discusses disorders in that area, and the third section discusses treatments based on making changes in that area.

Many individuals have contributed to making this book a reality. Bonnie, my wife, keyed the manuscript into the computer. Ian Layton and Bill Toll got it from Asbury's computer to Abingdon's. Students in two classes read previous versions of the manuscript. Philip Captain, Annette Fisher, Marty Seitz, and Randi Timpe all read the first draft and made invaluable comments. Richard Sherry commented on the final draft. Asbury College granted a one-quarter work leave during which material used in the first draft was originally developed. Finally, my children, Keith, Cheryl, and Kent, were very understanding in giving me time to work on the manuscript.

C O N T E N T S

INTRODUCTION TO PSYCHOLOGY

It would seem logical to think that material in general psychology would progress from more basic knowledge in the first chapters of the book to the application of that knowledge in later chapters. However, such is not the case. Evidence that basic knowledge of psychology is unnecessary for the "application" of psychology is found in the fact, that in many courses, the applied chapters are studied before the basic facts chapters. Apparently, one can apply techniques whose bases one does not know.

Although most textbook writers do not say that such is the case, Mischel and Mischel (1980) suggest that for a "personal-social focus" course, one should turn immediately to their four chapters on personality after their introductory chapter. Hutt, Isaacson, and Blum (1966) went even further when they wrote their introductory text *Psychology: The Science of Interpersonal Behavior.* After an introductory chapter, they go immediately to chapters on complex topics; such as personality, conflict, anxiety, maladjustment, testing, and therapy. Thus, one does not apparently need to know anything (at least not anything taught in general psychology) about physiological psychology, sensation, perception, emotion, learning, memory, motivation, or thinking to understand the complexities of the human personality or to change it.

This approach appeals to many prospective counselors who

want to learn counseling techniques without going through the drudgery of learning so much of the "irrelevant" in general psychology. This especially appeals to many who are interested in pastoral counseling or Christian counseling and who do not want to "waste time" learning about statistics, experimental design, animal experiments, and so forth. As appealing as this approach seems to be, it simply is not logical. Who would want to go to a physician who only knew how to give injections and write prescriptions, but never wanted to study biochemistry and pharmacology? This physician could write many different long drug names and put the needle in with little pain, but would not think it was worth the time to learn about the general effects of that drug on the body and the various side-effects. How can one expect to help the "mentally ill" and never study mental processes, or to help the "emotionally disturbed" and never study the emotions?

The thesis of this book is that truth is a unity and that a Christian perspective will allow us to see that unity in psychology. Rather than being irrelevant, general psychology (when placed in a Christian perspective) can provide a framework around which abnormal psychology and clinical-counseling psychology can be organized. When psychology is organized in this framework, we can see relationships between various disorders and treatments that are not apparent without it. We can also see that facts from general psychology and Christianity give us insights that aid us in helping others.

Now let us turn to topics usually covered in an introductory chapter of a general psychology text and see how they are related to Christian counseling. Introductory chapters usually cover the topics of history, systems, definitions, goals, and methods of psychology, so we will consider these here.

History and Systems of Psychology

What could be further removed from the counseling room than the study of the history and systems of psychology?

Almost anything, because the counselors' basic assumptions about the people they are working with, what is thought to be wrong with those people, the goal of counseling, and the method of reaching that goal are all determined by the system the counselors hold. Although there have been half a dozen or more schools or systems of psychology during psychology's century of existence, we will consider only three of them here, because they have been major forces in American psychology and have made the greatest impact on counseling. Behaviorism and psychoanalysis dominated the American psychological scene during the first half of the twentieth century, and humanistic psychology has emerged as a third force during the second half.

Psychoanalysis

Although psychoanalysis was not developed as a part of psychology, it has influenced psychology greatly, especially that part of psychology concerned with counseling. Therefore, we will consider it here as a system of psychology, realizing that it was developed in the context of medical practice. Psychoanalysis was developed by Sigmund Freud in his attempts to treat people called neurotics. As Freud worked with his patients, he gradually developed a theory of personality and a method of treating such disorders.

Assumptions. Any system of psychology must begin with a set of assumptions: unproven, plausible, noncontradictory statements taken at face value. They are the starting point for building a system. What assumptions did Sigmund Freud make about people? First, let us look at his assumption about good and evil. For Freud the most basic structure of personality is the id; in fact, it is the only structure present at birth. The id essentially urges people to take what they want without being concerned about the consequences to self or others. If we are to talk in terms of good and evil, the id would have to be considered as basically evil. Furthermore, the id is unchangeable. We must simply learn to rechannel its expression so that we can live with it.

Second, Freud saw human actions as being completely determined by forces deep within each person. In this psychic determinism, nothing happened by chance. Every "mistake" was really an expression of the deepest motives of the person. For example, a boy wrote to a girl, "I would like to kill you tonight." Even if he meant to write "kiss" instead of "kill," Freud would say that boy really did want to kill the girl. Usually such deep desires are kept in check, but occasionally they slip through as "accidents" (but they are not really accidents).

Third, Freud saw humans as basically irrational. Although the ego does exist as the rational part of the personality, it always remains subservient to the irrational id. The ego strives to control the impulsive, self-centered id, but it has no energy of its own, depending on the id for all of its psychic energy. The ego tries to allow the id to express itself in such a way that the safety of the person and others will not be endangered.

Finally, Freud saw the unconscious part of the mind as being much more important than the conscious. Although he talked about three levels of consciousness, the unconscious is by far the largest, most important part of the mind. Freud likened the mind to an iceberg in that most of it is below the surface. Events in the unconscious are of utmost importance in determining the behavior of the individual. "Neurotic" behavior is caused by unconscious conflicts, and such people are totally unaware of the causes of their irrational behavior.

Freud made many other assumptions about people, but it should be obvious that if you see the individuals sitting before you as being basically evil, determined, irrational, and unaware of why they behave as they do, you will engage in a very different type of counseling than you would if you saw them as basically good, free to choose, rational, and aware of themselves.

Definition and Goals. Freud never wrote a systematic psychology, so we need to gather his psychology from the twenty-four volume set of *The Standard Edition of the Works of Sigmund Freud* (1886-1939). Freud's major goal was to find some method of treating his patients who suffered from a variety of neurotic symptoms. Although Freud was educated as a physician and practiced as a clinical neurologist, he gradually came to adopt nonmedical methods of treating his patients. He was always trying to develop a treatment for neurosis and did not feel bound by existing methods.

Psychoanalysis became both a method of treatment and a system of personality. It can best be defined as the study of unconscious motivations, conflicts between them, and the effects of such conflicts on behavior. Freud gradually became convinced that the causes of his patients' problems were to be found in the unconscious, so he spent much of his time attempting to find out what was happening there.

Methods. Although Freud did not originate the concept of the unconscious, he did emphasize it to a greater extent than anyone had done previously. No methods existed for its systematic study, so Freud gradually adopted the "talking cure" or "catharsis," what has come to be called the technique of free association. In this method patients lie on a couch and talk freely about every thought they have, no matter how socially unacceptable, unimportant, embarrassing, or foolish it is. Freud believed that as patients do this, they gradually reveal what is in their unconscious. In the relaxed state and with the analyst's encouragement, the ego gradually lowers its guard, so that more and more unconscious material enters consciousness, is spoken, and can be interpreted by the analyst.

A second method of getting at the unconscious is dream analysis. Freud's reasoning was similar here. While people are asleep, their rational egos are less on guard so material from the unconscious id gets into their dreams. Since the ego is still somewhat on guard, the material remembered in the conscious recall of the dream will be disguised. However, the analyst then interprets what the patient has recalled to get at the deeper meanings of what is happening at the unconscious level.

As patients went through several years of such treatment, most would gradually improve. Freud believed that as he was getting at the unconscious causes of their problems and bringing them to consciousness, he was effecting a cure. Notice how Freud's methods follow from his assumptions about people. If people are evil, determined, irrational, and not conscious of their problems, then some methods must be found for getting at the unconscious aspects of personality. Although psychoanalysis has been very influential in psychology, let us now consider an approach to psychology that begins with a different set of assumptions.

Humanistic Psychology

Humanistic psychology is a relatively recent development that is more of a movement than a well-developed system. Humanistic psychologists generally focus on the experiencing person, emphasizing distinctively human qualities, such as choice and creativity. They are concerned with the dignity and worth of individuals and want to develop human potential. Thus they are more concerned with studying meaningful problems than with using "correct" research procedures. Although there was no clearly defined founder, Carl Rogers (1951) and Abraham Maslow (1954) were major early leaders in this movement.

Assumptions. With their emphasis on human freedom and dignity, humanistic psychologists begin with a different set of assumptions about people. First, rather than seeing humans as being basically evil, humanistic psychologists see them as being basically good. Although human beings can be very cruel, destructive, and antisocial, humanistic psychologists contend that (at the deepest levels) each person strives for a positive, healthy, creative fulfilling of the person's potential. Culture may suppress this inherent goodness in people, but this positive potential will reveal itself in the life of the individual if given the opportunity. This goodness may be relatively weak compared to the cultural forces that make people bad, but the goodness can never be obliterated.

Second, humanistic psychologists see human beings as fundamentally free to make their own decisions, and thus as responsible for their own behavior. Of course, people do not have absolute freedom to do anything, but they can actually see different paths open to them and really make a choice of which one to take. Most humanistic psychologists would say that as individuals mature, they become more free to actualize the potential they have as human beings. This assumption that people are free and responsible is quite different from Freud's deterministic assumption.

Third, although humanistic psychologists agree that humans are somewhat irrational, they believe most human behavior is governed by rational forces. Humanistic psychologists place little emphasis on animal research because they see people as being quite different from animals, rational rather than irrational. When given the chance, most individuals can give valid reasons for their behavior.

Finally, although humanistic psychologists agree that the unconscious does exist, they see people as being primarily aware of themselves. The unconscious has relatively little influence on behavior as compared to that of the conscious. Most people are aware of why they behave the way they do. In contrast to Freud, humanistic psychologists see the unconscious as having good as well as bad aspects. Buried in the unconscious are creativity, love, tenderness, self-acceptance, and understanding.

Think of the difference it makes in your counseling if you see the person sitting before you as basically good, free, rational, and conscious, rather than evil, determined, irrational, and unconscious. Of course, you may decide to assume that the person has all of these characteristics to some degree.

Definition and Goals. Like Freud, the humanistic psychologists have no systematic psychology, so we must gather their psychology from the pages of the *Journal of Humanistic Psychology* and some of the "official" statements of the

Association for Humanistic Psychology. The general goal of humanistic psychologists is the development of the potential in every person. They want to develop a complete description of what it means to live as a human being. They study all aspects of human experience to the end of helping people become all that they can become. Rather than trying to make "sick" people "normal," humanistic psychologists are interested in taking "normal" or "average" people and helping them to become "actualized" or "fully functioning."

Although no specific definition of humanistic psychology is agreed upon, humanistic psychology usually is the study of normal or exceptional human beings. If we want to know how fast humans can run, we do not study crippled runners. If we want to know the intellectual feats humans can perform, we do not study the mentally retarded. Likewise, humanistic psychologists would say that if we want to know human potential psychologically, we should not study the mentally ill. They would contend that the study of the sick, crippled, and immature will lead to a sick, crippled, and immature psychology.

Methods. Humanistic psychologists place little emphasis on method. They believe that the goal is the important thing and that they should use any method that enables them to reach the goal. Rather than stating how psychologists should "do psychology," they emphasize the goal of helping people reach their potential, using any method available. Of course, the methods emphasize conscious, rational, verbal interchange with the person. The psychologist may use anything from directive counseling to allowing the client to decide what should be talked about. Now that we have examined systems which take extreme positions on the issues, let us consider another major force in American psychology.

Behaviorism

Behaviorism is that system of psychology founded by John B. Watson (1913/1968) and currently represented by B. F.

Skinner (1971). It emphasizes an objective, experimental, scientific approach to behavior. Watson's behaviorism was a psychology in which all behaviors, no matter how complex, could be reduced to a series of stimulus-response connections. The behaviorists were reacting against the subjectivity found in the psychology of the early twentieth century. They set out to study only what can be observed. Behaviorists view human beings as essentially complex machines or complex animals. People are quantitatively different (more complex) from animals and machines, but not qualitatively different.

Assumptions. With this mechanistic view of people, many of the assumptions psychoanalysts and humanistic psychologists made about persons become irrelevant. First, since humans are not qualitatively different from animals and machines, they are neither good nor evil. The whole question of good and evil is quite irrelevant here, because machines are neither good nor evil. From the behavioristic perspective, human beings may learn actions that result in good or bad for others, but they are intrinsically neither good nor evil.

Second, behaviorists see human action as being determined. Humans are stimulus-response mechanisms who behave in response to some input or stimulus. Human beings do not have the power to make actual choices, since they just respond to stimuli present in the environment. Theirs is an environmental determinism in which behavior is determined by external factors; as contrasted to Freud's psychic determinism in which internal, unconscious factors determine behavior.

Third, behaviorists see people as being neither rational nor irrational. This whole dimension does not really apply to a behaviorist's approach to people, because behavior is seen as a function of past rewards or of stimulus-response relationships. Finally, the conscious-unconscious dimension is also not relevant to a behavioristic approach. In a mechanistic approach, it does not make sense to talk about humans as being conscious or not conscious of themselves.

Again, consider the difference it makes in counseling if

counselors assume this mechanistic view of the individuals sitting before them. If the behavior of the counselees is seen as determined and the other three dimensions (good-evil, rational-irrational, and conscious-unconscious) are seen as irrelevant, the whole emphasis will be on changing the environment in an effort to change the behavior of the counselees, rather than attempting to make some change inside them.

Definition and Goals. Watson (1913/1968) defined psychology as the "science of behavior," and said that he would never have to go back on his definition, never use terms like consciousness, mind, mental state, imagery, and so forth. Psychology was to be the science of overt, objectively observable responses; only those that could be observed and recorded by someone else. It was to be a purely objective branch of natural science.

The goal of behavioristic psychology was the prediction and control of behavior. Watson wanted to reach the point where he had completely worked out all stimulus-response connections so that given the response, he could tell what the stimulus had been; and given the stimulus, he could predict what the response would be.

Methods. Watson (1913/1968) would allow only objective methods to be used in the investigation of behavior. He specifically stated that observation, conditioned reflexes, verbal reports, and testing methods could be used. Although it sounds like he was allowing subjectivity into behaviorism, one must understand that in verbal report, words were to be regarded like any other responses, such as a knee jerk or an eye blink. Verbal responses were simply overt responses, and did not indicate anything in one's "mind" or "thoughts." Tests did not measure intelligence or personality, but simply were a series of stimuli that elicited responses from people.

Summary

The assumptions, goals, and methods for the three major forces in psychology are shown in Figure 1:1. Notice that psychoanalysis and humanistic psychology take opposite positions on these assumptions, have different goals, and have different methods. Behaviorism does not take strong positions on these issues (except for determinism) because of its mechanistic view of humans. Of course, today most counselors would not call themselves pure psychoanalysts, behaviorists, or humanistic psychologists. However, even psychologists who do not accept a full system of psychology still must have some position on these issues. Later on in the chapter, we will present one Christian position on these issues.

Before moving on to other topics, let us consider how theological positions may also influence counseling. One Christian taking a theological position emphasizing human capacity for choice may tell counselees that God wants to save them. Another (Adams, 1970) taking a position emphasizing God's sovereignty may say that a counselor cannot tell counselees that God wants to save them, because he does not know. Thus, not only do our philosophical assumptions influence our counseling, but so does our theology. Different Christians will take different philosophical and theological positions, and it is important to be aware of the positions we, and others, are taking.

Methods of Research

Most general psychology texts include a section on research methods in psychology. Although many different methods are usually discussed, they can usually be classified into two categories.

Descriptive Methods

First are the descriptive methods, including all those in which the researcher does not exercise experimental control. Sometimes psychologists have a tendency to consider these methods "second-rate," because it is extremely difficult to

21

Figure 1:1 A comparison of the major assumptions, goals, and methods of the three major forces in psychology and the Christian perspective taken here.

	Psychoanalytic	Humanistic	Behavioristic	Christianity
ASSUMPTIONS ABOUT HUMAN BEINGS	Evil Determinism Irrational Unconscious	Good Freedom Rational Conscious	Neither Determinism Neither Neither	Both Both Both Both
GOALS OF PSYCHOLOGY	Therapy for neurotics	Realize potential	Predict and control behavior	Know world, made like God
METHODS OF PSYCHOLOGY	Free Association Dream Analysis	All Methods	Objective Methods	All Methods not antithetical to Christianity

prove cause-effect relationships with them. However, these are acceptable methods of research.

The most basic of these descriptive methods is naturalistic observation. In fact, it is the most basic method of science, since all of science begins with the scientist's observations. In this method, the scientist simply observes and records behavior in its natural setting without attempting to intervene at all. Sometimes this method is the only one that can be used. For example, it is the only method available to astronomers, since they cannot insert and remove galaxies or stars, or even planets. Likewise, in many instances psychologists cannot maintain experimental control over everything happening to the subject during research, so they must be content with observations. This is true of psychologists interested in the influence of spiritual forces on individuals. They cannot completely control the effect of the Holy Spirit or of Satan on individuals, so they must use naturalistic observation. Naturalistic observation is also a valuable source of hypotheses about the causes of behavior.

Another descriptive method is correlation, going one step beyond that of naturalistic observation. It results in a number that tells the researcher not only that there is a relationship, but whether the relationship is positive or negative, and how great the relationship is. The correlation method also allows us to predict how well a person will do on future, related tasks. To be admitted to college, one must pass before admissions committees, who may use correlational techniques to predict whether the prospective student can succeed, based on high school grades and admission test scores.

Experimental Methods

The second major method of research is the experimental method. Since the main objective of research is to discover cause-effect relationships, the experimental method is used whenever possible. The basic idea of the experimental method is to take two groups of subjects (or one group under two different conditions) and treat them exactly the same in every way but one. If they behave differently after the treatments, the researchers conclude that the different treatments caused the difference in behaviors.

For example, an experiment is recorded in the first chapter of the book of Daniel in the Old Testament. Daniel and the other Hebrew captives did not want to eat the rich foods provided for them, so they proposed an experiment. All the young men were treated the same except that the Hebrews ate vegetables and water for ten days, while the others ate the king's rich food. At the end of the experiment the Hebrews looked healthier and better nourished than the others, so it was concluded that vegetables and water were better for them than the rich food.

All Christian counselors should be skilled in both types of research. They need to use the descriptive methods to observe people carefully so that they can develop new methods of counseling. Many Christian counselors seem to be content simply to take the same methods of therapy used by secular counselors and tack on a Bible verse so that it can be called Christian counseling. As Christians we need to be developing new approaches to counseling that grow out of a Christian set of assumptions. This does not mean that we will all use the same methods of counseling, because Christians take different philosophical and theological positions. Different Christians need to make their unique contributions by developing approaches to counseling based on their own individual scripturally derived assumptions.

Christian counselors also need to know how to use the experimental method to evaluate both their own approaches to therapy, and therapies proposed by others. Many times therapies are accepted without any evaluation of their effectiveness. Since the majority of people being counseled would get better even without professional counseling, counselors must be able to show that their counseling brings better results than this existing rate of "spontaneous" cures. The fact is that many people get better spontaneously (without professional help), so it should come as no surprise that many get better no matter what counseling techniques are used. For a method to be proven effective, we must be able to show that more are helped when given counseling than when they are not treated. For example, if seventy percent improve with no treatment, and only seventy percent improve when we treat them, we have not shown that we are doing any good. Too often we are more interested in learning new techniques than in evaluating their effectiveness. Christians are not alone in doing this, but we should be more discriminating in our use of new techniques, insisting on evidence of effectiveness.

A Christian Perspective

At this point, let us consider the particular Christian perspective used as a framework to organize a Christian psychology. Christians also make assumptions about the nature of human beings and we should be aware of the assumptions we make.

God

First, we assume that God exists and is the source of all else in existence. He is independent of nature. There is nothing to limit his sovereignty. He is both infinite and personal. He has revealed himself to us in several ways. Of course, we first think of his special revelation as recorded in the Bible. In this revelation, God spoke through individuals who recorded what he had said, the history of the nation of Israel, the life of Christ, and the history of the early church. All Christians emphasize this revelation, but we must not forget that this special revelation tells us that a general (natural) revelation also exists. Psalm 19 and Romans 1 give the strongest statements about this natural revelation. The Romans passage explicitly states that God has revealed enough of himself in his creation to make his eternal power and divinity evident, and even people who have not heard God's special revelation are without excuse.

Nature

The universe is the creation of God. He created it and sustains it. Although God is immanent in the world, it is not identical with him nor a part of his being. He also transcends the world. Since God's creation was made by a rational being, it is real, it was created good, and it is orderly. Furthermore, since humans are made in God's image, they can discover these patterns and regularities by examining the world. Some of the best methods we have for learning about God's creation are the scientific methods used by psychology and other sciences.

Humans

The last part of Genesis 1 tells us that humans are created in God's image. That is, we are created beings like animals, plants, and inorganic creation. However, we are special in that we are made in God's image. Humans are a composite unity of spirit and matter. We must remember that we are a unity, but that we may look at ourselves from different vantage points, sometimes emphasizing how we are like the rest of creation and at other times emphasizing how we are like God. This is diagrammed schematically in Figure 1:2. This figure will serve as a basis for the rest of the book. As each new topic in psychology is introduced, it will be placed in this perspective so that you will have a unified reinterpretation of secular psychology from a Christian perspective. Now let us briefly discuss some of the implications of saying that humans are like animals in some ways and like God in others.

Humans Like Animals. A little reflection will lead to the conclusion that humans are more like animals than they are like anything else in creation. They are more like animals than like plants or inorganic creation. As created beings we are finite creatures, like animals. We are similar to animals anatomically and physiologically. We are also similar to them in some of our behaviors.

Figure 1:2   A Christian perspective into which psychology can be placed.

HUMANS

Created.........................in the....................Image of God
LIKE ANIMALS   LIKE GOD

Some passages of Scripture refer to the fact that humans are like animals in some ways. Psalm 49 points out that humans must die like any animal. Ecclesiastes 3 notes that humans are similar to animals; both breathe the same air, both die, both are made of the dust of the earth, and both must return to it. Like the rest of creation, humans depend upon God for everything, even their continued existence.

That humans are like animals in some ways has implications for counseling. We find that some techniques for treatment were originally developed through research on animals and were directly applied to helping humans. Before leaving the topic of the similarity of humans and animals, it should be noted that saying similarities exist does not mean that humans are merely animals. Even scientists who spend most of their time studying the similarities between animals and humans come to recognize the differences as well.

Humans Like God. God created humans male and female in his own image. Some theologians maintain that the fall of humanity into sin has shattered that mirror, but others interpret Scripture to indicate that the image remains. When God prohibited murder, he said that to kill a human being is to kill one made like himself—and that was after the Fall (Genesis 9). In New Testament times, the apostle Paul wrote how we can be mirrors that reflect God's glory and that we become more like him as his Spirit works in us (II Cor. 3:18). James, likewise, noted that we use the tongue to bless our Father, God, and we use the same tongue to curse our fellow human beings who are all created in God's likeness (James 3:9, 10).

Although some Christians speak more of how evil people

are, Christianity declares both how evil and how lofty humans are and can become. Psalm 139 speaks not only of Jehovah's glory, but of humans' being wonderfully made. Psalm 8 talks about the majesty of God and goes on to say that he made humans only a little lower than God himself. Humans are crowned with glory and honor and given dominion over God's creation; over mammals, birds, and fish. God saw humans as being important enough to send his Son to die for them.

That humans are like God in some ways has implications for counseling. As we are counseling, we must remember that we are not just working with machine-like objects or animal-like organisms, but with beings who have capacity for love, mercy, and other God-like attributes. Of course, all this does not mean to imply that there are no differences between humans and God. God is sovereign, omniscient, infinite, omnipotent, and so forth. Humans can never have these attributes of God, but we are commanded to be like him in some ways.

Humans Unique. Finally, we must remember that humans are unique, different from both God and animals. God gave humans the capacity to make choices for which they would be held responsible. Humans chose to disobey God, and this sin then came between God and humans. We are thus in a fallen state.

That humans are affected by sin also has implications for counseling. We must not ignore sin and its effects in the lives of our counselees. However, we must be careful not to make sinfulness the distinguishing characteristic of humanness. Before the fall into sin, humans were still human, but without sin. Jesus himself was fully human as well as divine, but he never sinned. He was tempted just as we are, but he never yielded to those temptations and sinned (Heb. 4:15).

Psychology from a Christian Perspective

Now that we have considered our basic Christian perspective, let us see how psychology can fit into it. Let us begin by placing things already discussed in the perspective, then continuing to add to it throughout the book.

Definition

As we have seen, psychology has had a number of definitions. At its beginning scientific psychology was the study of consciousness or the mind. Then this was abandoned in favor of psychology as the study of behavior. Currently, Hilgard, Atkinson and Atkinson (1979, p. 12) define it as the study of "behavior and mental processes." This definition takes in the whole range of psychology and fits into our Christian perspective, as shown in Figure 1:3. Note that when concentrating on observable behavior, we are looking at the aspect of humans that is very similar to animals. We can study the overt behavior of humans in the same ways as we do that of animals. The study of animal behavior will also have implications for the study of humans. However, when we study humanity's mental processes, we are studying beings quite different from animals and much more like God.

Figure 1:3 The definition of psychology from a Christian perspective.

HUMANS

Created......................... in the....................Image of God
Like Animals   Like God
OVERT........................ DEFINITION........ MENTAL
BEHAVIOR   PROCESSES

There is one danger in using this schematic diagram of the Christian perspective. That danger is that we may see it as strongly implying a dualism, when we want to emphasize the unity of human beings. You may ask, "Is a person really like animals or really like God?" Such a question is inappropriate because we are *both* like animals and like God. The question is not, "Should psychologists study overt behavior or mental processes?" They should study both. A study of overt behavior that ignores mental processes will give a distorted view of human behavior. Likewise, studying mental processes without considering overt behavior will give a distorted view.

This definition has implications for our counseling. We must consistently be concerned about both the animal-like *and* the God-like aspects of humans. If counselors concentrate only on overt behavior or only on mental processes, they are ignoring a whole dimension of people that must be treated. As Christian counselors we must not restrict psychology to only one of its aspects, as some secular counselors have done.

Goals

We discussed the various goals of three systems of psychology, so we need to look at the goals of a Christian psychology. These goals are presented in Figure 1:4. Note that one basic goal is to understand God's creation and control it (have dominion over it) to a greater degree, especially the behavior and mental processes of living beings in that creation. As Christians we are interested in learning not only about God's creation, but about God himself. Although this is not one of the primary goals of psychology, it may well be that as we understand more about human behavior, we will understand God better, since humans are made in his image.

Figure 1:4 Goals of psychology from a Christian perspective.

HUMANS

Created........................ in the....................		Image of God
Like Animals		Like God
Overt Behavior...............Definition..............		Mental Processes
UNDERSTAND.............GOALS................		MAKE PEOPLE
CREATION		LIKE GOD

Another major goal of Christian counselors is to help humans become as God-like as possible. We must always keep this goal in mind. We are not just trying to make people "not sick" or help them adjust to the world, but to make them like God (like Christ). As we study the factors in the development of Christ-like traits, we can use our knowledge to help immature Christians become more like God. Applied psychology becomes a matter of promoting Christian maturity rather than helping people conform more to whatever society considers normal. The first step in this process is to introduce people to Christ and to do this in such a way that they will want to make a commitment to him. Then we are commanded to go beyond this—in the Great Commission, when we are told to make disciples. We cannot produce spiritual life or growth, but we can bring about conditions that will encourage such growth.

Systems

Although there have been at least six major systems of psychology and even more minor movements in its one-hundred-year history, we are considering only the three major ones most relevant to counseling. If we review the assumptions given in Figure 1:1, we will be able to see how these major systems fit into this Christian perspective. Since the major assumptions of psychoanalysis are that people are evil, determined, irrational, and not conscious of their inner motives, we will place psychoanalysis under the animal-like aspects of humans as shown in Figure 1:5. Although many Christians would not consider animals evil, animals are determined, irrational, and not conscious, at least as far as we know.

Since the major assumptions of humanistic psychology are that humans are good, free, rational, and conscious, we will consider humanistic psychology as studying the God-like aspects of humans, as shown in Figure 1:5. (Humanistic psychologists themselves may disagree with this.) Finally,

Figure 1:5 Systems of psychology from a Christian perspective.

HUMANS

Created............in the...........Image of God
Like Animals		Like God
Overt Behavior..........Definition...........Mental Processes
Understand...........Goals............Make People
Creation		Like God
PSYCHO-...........SYSTEMS..........HUMANISTIC
ANALYSIS		PSYCHOLOGY
BEHAVIORISM

behaviorists assume that humans are determined and much like animals. In fact, Watson (1913/1968) stated that behaviorists recognized no dividing line between "man and brute."

Since these (and other) major systems of psychology can be subsumed under our Christian perspective, we will not take extreme positions on these issues. As shown in Figure 1:1, our perspective places us in the center of all of these assumptions. That is, we believe that humans were created good, but that they fell into sin (Gen. 3); therefore, they are both good *and* evil. In some respects human behavior is determined, but many Christians believe that God made us actually capable of choosing whether to follow him or not. As created in God's image we are rational beings, but we also find that we act irrationally at times. Finally, much of the time we are conscious of our motives, but there are times when we are quite unaware of why we act the way we do. Making these assumptions about our counselees does not simplify our approach to counseling, but makes it more complex. The major approaches to counseling try to simplify things, usually to the point of excluding some major aspect of people. From our Christian perspective, we will try to consider the animal-like, the God-like, and the unique aspects of the unified human being.

Methods of Research

Finally, let us consider how the methods of research fit into this Christian perspective. Since the experimental method involves a great deal of experimental control, it is most appropriate for studying animals, and those aspects of humans that are most similar to animals, as shown in Figure 1:6. In most experiments the subjects are viewed as reacting, noninitiating organisms. The experimental method is particularly well-suited to study these aspects of humans.

Figure 1:6 Research methods from a Christian perspective.

HUMANS

Created	in the	Image of God
Like Animals		Like God
Overt Behavior	Definition	Mental Processes
Understand Creation	Goals	Make People Like God
Psychoanalysis Behaviorism	Systems	Humanistic Psychology
EXPERI- MENTAL	METHODS	DESCRIPTIVE

Although the experimental method is very powerful, it cannot always be used. For example, we read in Daniel 1:17 that *God* gave the four Hebrews great ability to learn—and we cannot control what God does. In situations where he is working in some special way, the experimental method may lead to wrong conclusions. From the perspective taken here the descriptive methods are particularly well-suited to study the God-like aspects of humans as shown in Figure 1:6. In some respects humans are active, initiating agents who direct their own behavior, and the descriptive methods are appropriate for studying these aspects of humanity.

Conclusion

We have seen that psychology can be reinterpreted from a Christian perspective. The definition, goals, systems, and research methods of psychology can all be placed in our perspective of viewing humans like animals in some respects and like God in others. The rest of this book will be concerned with adding the subject areas of general psychology to this perspective, considering the types of problems that can arise in each area, and considering how these problems can be treated.

Suggested Readings

"Introduction" and "Methods" chapters in general psychology textbooks are recommended. Also recommended are History and Systems of Psychology and Experimental Psychology textbooks. Hjelle and Ziegler (1981), Koteskey (1980), Lundin (1979), Matheson, Bruce, and Beauchamp (1978), Schultz (1981), and Wertheimer (1972) expand on material discussed in this chapter.

PHYSIOLOGICAL PSYCHOLOGY

Since psychology is the science of behavior and mental processes, psychologists look everywhere for influences on both. One obvious place to begin is to look at the organism itself, at its anatomy and physiology. It is obvious that removing an eye will interfere with a person's vision. It is not as obvious what a change in the brain or the chemical balance of the body will do to a person. Physiological psychology is the study of the anatomical and physiological bases of behavior and mental processes.

Physiological psychology can be placed in our Christian perspective as shown in Figure 2:1. As human beings we have a physical structure similar to that of animals, as shown in the lower center of the figure (Physiological—Structure). This means we are looking for causes of behavior and mental processes in the physical, animal-like aspects of humans. Since humans are like animals in that both are created beings, the use of animals for research is understandable in physiological psychology. Although some data come from humans who have been hurt and brought in for treatment, most data come from animals and are then generalized to humans. Humans cannot be used in many experimental studies for ethical reasons.

Students frequently think that the data gathered from animals have little to do with counseling. It is hard to see how a change in the secretion of a gland, or the sodium-potassium

Figure 2:1 Physiological psychology and organic disorders from a Christian perspective.

HUMANS

Created .... in the .... Image of God
Like Animals .... Like God
Overt Behavior .... Definition .... Mental Processes
Understand .... Goals .... Make People
Creation .... Like God
Psychoanalysis .... Systems .... Humanistic
Behaviorism .... Psychology
Experimental .... Methods .... Descriptive

(DISORDER)
ORGANIC DISORDERS .. PHYSIOLOGICAL .... STRUCTURE ....
(ORGANIC MENTAL DISORDERS)

balance of the body, or the chemicals in the synapses between neurons could be related to behavior in any important way. Even though they seem far removed from behavior, anatomy and physiology underly *all* behavior and mental processes because humans are a unity. Changes in anatomy and physiology cause changes in behavior and thinking, and Christian counselors must be aware of the kinds of changes that occur. Even though they cannot treat such changes, they must be able to recognize them and refer their counselees to physicians for treatment.

Humans as Physical Beings—Like Animals

Before we can talk about the anatomical and physiological bases of behavior, we must know something about anatomy and physiology. Let us begin with a discussion of the nervous system.

The Nervous System

The basic unit of the nervous system is the neuron, a single nerve cell. Some neurons conduct impulses from receptors toward the brain, others from the brain toward muscles and glands, and still others from one neuron to another. The neural impulse is an electrochemical process involving changes in the amount of sodium and potassium inside the neuron. Anything that affects the sodium-potassium balance in the body will affect the nervous impulse.

These neurons are organized into the nervous system, connecting all parts of the body. The peripheral nervous system includes all neurons except the brain and spinal cord. One part of it (the somatic) conducts impulses to and from the brain and is involved in our "voluntary" movements. The other part (the autonomic) conducts impulses from the brain to glands and smooth muscles and is usually not under voluntary control.

The central nervous system consists of the brain and spinal cord. Fortunately, this part of the nervous system is well-protected, because damage to it is usually permanent. The spinal cord generally conducts impulses to and from the brain and contains many reflexes. The brain is the most important and least understood neural structure. Some parts of it control vital processes, such as heart rate, breathing rate, blood pressure, and so forth. Other parts coordinate movements, control motivation and emotion, relay sensations to higher centers, and so forth. The most important part of the human brain is the cerebral cortex, where we become conscious of the sensations, think, and initiate movements. Christian counselors should know the major functions of all parts of the nervous system so that they can recognize signs of damage to it.

The Synapse

The synapse is the region where information is transmitted from neuron to neuron. Since the neurons do not actually touch each other, there must be some way to get a neural impulse from one to another. When an impulse reaches the end of the neuron, it causes a chemical (a neurotransmitter) to be released. This chemical travels to the adjoining neurons and, if enough of the chemical is present, starts an impulse in the next neuron.

Various chemicals are used in different parts of the nervous system. When we take other chemicals that block these chemicals (the neurotransmitters) from being released or prevent them from acting on the next neuron, we can produce great changes in our behavior and mental processes. Christian counselors should be familiar with these neurotransmitters, the chemicals that affect them, and the symptoms of disturbance.

Endocrine Glands

The endocrine glands secrete substances directly into the blood stream. These secretions are the hormones, and are carried to all parts of the body by the circulatory system. These hormones then usually have a specific effect on some other part of the body. They control everything from an individual's energy level to his or her body size. Some regulate the sodium-potassium balance in the body and thus affect neural transmission.

When hormones are undersecreted, people can usually supplement them with hormone pills or injections. Most of us know someone who takes insulin or birth control pills, both some type of hormone. When our endocrine system gets out of balance, it can affect our behavior and mental processes. We need to be aware of symptoms of such imbalance. Now that we have briefly considered anatomy and physiology, let us consider some effects of disorders related to them.

Disorders

Throughout this book we will use the diagnostic categories provided in the latest edition of the the *Diagnostic and Statistical Manual of Mental Disorders* (3rd ed.) published by the American Psychiatric Association. DSM-III, as it is commonly called, requires diagnosis along five axes, or dimensions. Every patient is to be evaluated on each of these axes. Axes I and II include the various psychological, personality, and developmental disorders. Disorders on these two axes are the ones counselors usually attempt to treat. Axis III is for physical disorders, any medical problems that may be influencing the psychological ones. From our perspective it is important to consider these physical disorders in the animal-like aspects of people. Axis IV is related to the severity of psychosocial stress the patient is currently under. Finally, Axis V is an evaluation of the person's highest level of functioning during the past year.

On Axis I, DSM-III has a category that is relevant to the animal-like, physiological aspects of persons. This is the category of organic mental disorders, as shown in Figure 2:1. As we build on our Christian perspective, we will list the kind of disorder found in each area of psychology (Organic Disorders) and below it, give one example of such a disorder from DSM-III, below the category, and in parentheses (Organic Mental Disorders). The DSM-III categories will not always fit neatly into this Christian perspective. For example, the word "mental" in the organic mental disorders may seem to imply that they should be categorized under "like God." However, the word "mental" simply means that the person's thinking processes have been affected by organic changes. Since we are interested in getting at the cause, not the symptom, we will place organic mental disorders under "like animals."

The organic mental disorders in DSM-III include those commonly called the senile and presenile dementias, which may show delirium, delusions, depressions, or just be plain senility, all caused by deterioration of the central nervous system. They also include substance-induced disorders, in which the change to the central nervous system is caused by known substances such as alcohol, barbiturates, cocaine, hallucinogens, PCP, and so forth. Let us now consider some of the disorders that can occur when anatomical and physiological changes take place in a person.

Disorders of the Nervous System

One of the classical examples of nervous system disorders results from the venereal disease, syphilis. If it is untreated, about five percent of the time it invades the central nervous system and the person develops a disorder called *general paresis*. The first symptoms may appear anywhere from two to forty years after the first infection, but they usually appear about ten to fifteen years later. The individual first becomes careless and begins to make mistakes. Comprehension and judgment suffer so that the person evades problems. A blunting of the emotional life occurs. Speech and writing become disturbed. Motor coordination deteriorates so that the individual develops a shuffling walk. Personality deterioration takes place and memory problems occur. Finally, the individual leads a vegetative life. All of these behavioral and mental changes are caused by an infection in the nervous system.

Brain tumors can also lead to behavioral and mental changes. The nature of the changes is determined primarily by the location of the tumor, its rate of growth, the personality of the individual, and the person's tolerance for stress. Symptoms include memory impairment, headaches, depression, listlessness, drowsiness, irritability, indifference, restlessness, anxiety, apprehension, and loss of inhibitions. Personality change is common, but may be minimal if the person previously had a well-integrated personality. Again, all of these behavioral and mental changes are caused by damage to the nervous system.

As the organs of the body deteriorate, the brain is not spared. The behavioral and mental changes that accompany this deterioration with aging are called senile and presenile dementias. Individuals usually gradually withdraw from social contacts, mental alertness diminishes, and they become intellectually rigid so that they resist changes or new ideas. They become self-centered and preoccupied with their own bodily functions. Memory deteriorates while disorientiation, insomnia, and failure of judgment increase. These changes in behavior and mental processes are caused by general brain deterioration.

Disorders at the Synapse

Acetylcholine (ACh) is a chemical used by neurons involved in moving the skeletal muscles. Acetychloinesterase (an enzyme) which is present in the synapse breaks down the ACh almost immediately. Anything that interferes with this chemical activity will change behavior. For instance, physostigmine inhibits the activity of acetylcholinesterase so that ACh accumulates in the synapse where it can cause violent muscular contractions. However, used in small quantities, physostigmine can be used to treat myasthenia gravis, a disease that produces very weak muscles.

Norepinephrine is a chemical used in various areas of the brain and in neurons going to some organs of the body. It has been strongly implicated in affecting mood and motivation, so drugs which interfere with it will affect motivation and emotion. For example, although reserpine is used to treat high blood pressure, it also causes depression.

Dopamine is found in the brain, especially in neurons involved in the control of movement. Benzotropine inhibits the re-uptake of dopamine and is used in the treatment of Parkinson's disease, characterized by movement disorders. Drugs that increase transmission at dopamine synapses increase schizophrenic symptoms. Sometimes patients being treated for Parkinson's disease develop psychotic symptoms.

Therefore, it is important for counselors to know the effects, especially the "side effects," of drugs their counselees are taking. As we have seen, medication for high blood pressure may not only lower blood pressure, but bring on depression. Medication for Parkinson's disease may not only reduce tremors, but produce psychotic symptoms as well. Whenever counseling a person, one should be sure to ask about any drugs being taken, then check the side effects. Counselors should know what is happening in various synapses and how drugs can change the chemical activity there. The general public is becoming more aware of such effects because popular magazines are printing articles on the side effects of drugs. Every Christian counselor should have a recent copy of the *Physician's Desk Reference* (PDR) which lists available drugs and their side effects (published yearly). If a counselee is taking any drugs, even nonprescription drugs, the PDR should be checked to see if the drugs could be altering behavior and mental processes.

Disorders of the Endocrine Glands

The thyroid gland affects the general amount of energy, motivation, and alertness a person has. Overactivity of this gland results in an individual who is hyperactive or "nervous," has a huge appetite but cannot gain weight, sleeps little, is irritable, and is unable to concentrate. In its most severe form, it is called Grave's disease, and may include great apprehension, severe agitation, excessive motor activity, and even hallucinations.

Opposite in both cause and effect is an underactivity of the thyroid. When it occurs in adults, the person becomes sluggish, cannot maintain body temperature, has reduced muscle tone, motivation, alertness, and sleeps much of the time. If it becomes severe enough, the central nervous system may deteriorate until the individual becomes mentally retarded. If the undersecretion occurs in children, there is a lack of both physical and mental growth.

The adrenal glands are a pair of glands located above the kidneys. Each gland is really two glands, and here we will consider the outer part called the *cortex*. The hormones secreted by the adrenal cortex regulate the sodium and potassium balance of the body, carbohydrate metabolism, and sexual functioning, among other things. Chronic undersecretion of the adrenal cortex is called Addison's disease, which has a variety of physical and psychological symptoms. Some affected individuals are simply moderately depressed and withdrawn, while others have depressions, great anxiety, irritability, and become invalids. The excessive elimination of sodium and retention of potassium reduces the excitability of nerves and muscles. There is also less storage of reserve blood sugar so that there is a lack of vigor, muscle weakness, and lower body temperature.

An oversecretion of the adrenal cortex is rare in humans, but quite dramatic in its effects. It may result in early sexual development in children or masculinity in women. Bearded ladies in the circus, if they are not fakes, are women with an overactive adrenal cortex. One such disorder which may arise in young women is called Cushing's syndrome. It may involve extreme fluctuations in mood, ranging from indifference to great hostility along with obesity and muscle weakness.

Other endocrine glands also have effects on behavior and mental processes. Christian counselors should know the symptoms of glandular abnormalities and consider them when trying to determine what is wrong with the counselee. They should be aware that misdiagnosis and wrong treatment may have serious consequences. For example, suppose that an underactivity of the thyroid is treated as a "neurosis," and the person's "tiredness" is thought to be caused by "psychological" problems. Such treatment is inappropriate and if the underactivity is not treated, it may progress to permanent damage to the nervous system. As physicians may be sued for malpractice, so may Christian counselors who have not taken time to learn physiological causes of abnormal behavior.

Treatment

Psychology has been accused of being long on diagnosis, but short on cure. Sometimes this is indeed the case. At times psychologists spend a great deal of time arguing about what label to place on an individual, yet the diagnosis has no influence on what treatment is chosen. The classification was done for statistical purposes so they can report how many schizophrenics, paranoids, and others they treat, but the treatment is nearly always the same by any given psychologist. Each type of treatment is presented as a cure-all for any problem.

It is the thesis of this book that general psychology has studied humans from many different aspects and that problems may develop in any of these areas. The problem of diagnosis, then, is not just one of classifying individuals, but one of deciding in which area (or areas) of the person's life the problem has arisen. Once we have determined the source of the disorder, we are in a position to treat it. A treatment appropriate to the source of the problem must then be chosen. Christian counselors must be able to use a variety of treatments so they can help people who have disorders in different areas of their lives. Since people are wholes, we must treat all aspects of them simultaneously, or at least as close together in time as possible. Curing the physical problem, even if it is the source of the problem, may not treat secondary problems that have arisen. For example, getting the person off reserpine may relieve depression but do nothing about the lowered self-esteem, marital conflict, or spiritual problems the depression brought on.

A major part of this thesis is that no one treatment is adequate for all problems, and one of the reasons for our relatively poor showing in the treatment of "mental illness" is that most psychologists use only one type, or a few types, of treatment. For example, we have talked about one area of general psychology in this chapter, physiological psychology. However, none of the methods used by any of the three major systems of psychology presented in chapter 1 is adequate to treat these disorders. If the disorder is caused by damage to the nervous system or endocrine malfunction, it will do little good to try to delve into the unconscious through free association or dream analysis. Neither will it do any good to treat the individuals as conscious, responsible beings and urge them on toward self-actualization, or to treat them as machines and reinforce different kinds of behaviors. Furthermore, it will not do any good to ask the people to repent of their sins, or cast out demons. The disorder must be treated at its source and in all its aspects. In fact, the question may not even be, "which form of treatment when?" Rather, all forms of treatment may be used to some degree; so that the question is, "to what degree do I use each treatment?" Since the animal-like and God-like aspects interact, we must always treat both.

Of course, one problem is that counselors are not able to treat most physiological problems. People with physiological problems must be referred to competent physicians. However, psychologists should be aware of these physiological problems, aware of what can (or cannot) be done about them, and willing to refer when unable to help. Every Christian counselor should have a good working relationship with a psychiatrist or other physician who can treat such disorders. Referral may not be all that is needed. For example, a person who has had a physical problem may be angry at God for the illness, and may have fallen into temptation, so that the God-like aspects may need treatment as well. Let us now consider what can be done for the disorders discussed in this chapter.

Nervous System

As a general rule, damage in the central nervous system (brain and spinal cord) is permanent, but in the peripheral nervous system it is temporary. Although some of the functions may be recovered (apparently some other neurons take them over), the damage to the central nervous system itself is permanent. Since such damage is permanent, the best treatment is prevention, and much of this damage is preventable. For example, one can often avoid situations in which frequent blows to the head kill widespread brain cells by slamming the brain against the skull (in spite of its liquid cushion). Such concussions often occur in sports such as boxing. A large number of concussions results in the person's being "punch drunk," with sensory impairment, motor incoordination, and irrationality. These are symptoms of drunkenness, but caused by brain damage. Of course, such changes can be prevented by not allowing the head to be hit.

General paresis can also be prevented. Of course, the best way to avoid it is to abstain from sexual activity with a person who has syphilis. If one has contracted syphilis, it can often be treated, usually with penicillin, and general paresis prevented. If brain damage is not extensive, the person may show good recovery. However, usually treatment is not begun until extensive damage has been done to the brain, so all that one can do is to prevent further damage.

The results of treatment of brain tumors depend on the size and location of the tumor and the amount of brain tissue that is to be removed with the tumor. Sometimes there seems to be a complete recovery, while at other times there may be permanent symptoms, such as partial paralysis and a lowered intellectual functioning.

The outcome of treatment of senile dementia has traditionally been thought to be unfavorable because the brain damage is irreversible. However, given appropriate treatment (not only physically, but also socially), much recovery in both behavior and mental processes is possible.

Synapses

In general, if a disorder is caused by some drug that has been given to the person, simply the normal physiological processes occurring over time will result in the removal of the drug from the synapses. However, there are a few cases where this is not so. An example is the well-publicized "flashbacks" people experience months or years after using LSD.

One serious problem is caused by the use of the antipsychotic drugs (or major tranquilizers) to relieve the symptoms of psychosis. The most common of these drugs are the phenothiazines, which were first marketed in the United States in 1954 when chlorpromazine was sold under the trade name Thorazine. Within eight months of its appearance, it had been given to about two million patients. Today most of the psychotics in the United States take one of the phenothiazines daily. The problem with the phenothiazines is that one of their side effects is tardive dyskinesia, a muscle disorder in which the patients show involuntary movements of the mouth, lips, tongue, trunk, arms, and legs. It is a serious problem because it affects a large number of people and is untreatable and irreversible. Perhaps someday this may be treatable, but at the present time it is permanent. Although some drugs treat other side effects of phenothiazines, they are ineffective in preventing tardive dyskinesia. Unlike other side-effects, it does not disappear when the drug is stopped. In fact, it usually appears when the dosage is decreased or the drug is stopped altogether. If any of your counselees are taking antipsychotic drugs, they and their families should be informed of this side effect and of the fact that more than a third of the chronic patients in mental hospitals have it.

Endocrine Glands

Most disorders of the endocrine glands can be treated so that the effects do not become permanent, if the disorders are treated in time. If an individual has an overactive thyroid gland, the condition of overactivity can be cured by surgically removing part of the gland. There is usually no permanent impairment if the person has an underactive thyroid. Recovery is possible with supplementary doses of thyroxin (the hormone) when the condition is discovered in time. This is especially important in children to prevent mental retardation, which may occur if the disorder is untreated.

If the adrenal gland is undersecreting, medical treatment can restore normal functioning even in individuals who have severe cases of Addison's disease. This was the case with President John F. Kennedy, who had Addison's disease.

Thus, it is important to discover the cause of these disorders and give them appropriate treatment. From our Christian perspective, we would look for the physiological causes of disorders and try to replace the hormones, remove the tumors, and so forth, to restore the individual to normal physiological, and thus behavioral and mental, functioning. Of course, we must also be alert to secondary problems that may have developed, and treat them as well. As noted previously, treating the animal-like, physical disorders may not cure other disorders that have resulted from the original one. Before closing this chapter, we will consider other physiological treatments most often used in treatment of behavioral disorders.

Other Physiological Treatments

If we follow our original thesis of finding out what is wrong with the individual physiologically and then giving an appropriate treatment, we would not use the most popular physiological treatments available today. These methods have all been discovered accidentally. Furthermore, no one knows why they work—and there is a great deal of controversy over whether or not they do work. In addition, they have a number of side effects that are very serious.

Psychosurgery. Modern use of psychosurgery, surgery aimed at eliminating abnormal behavior, began in 1935 when the first prefrontal lobotomy was performed. The prefrontal lobotomy is a procedure in which the neurons connecting certain parts of the brain are cut. During the next twenty years (1935-1955) about seventy thousand of these operations were performed, mostly on institutionalized psychotics. Although some people improved, the side effects were extreme. Some people emerged from the surgery in a permanent vegetative state, others were childlike or had a flattened emotional life, still others had convulsions, and some died. Gross surgical techniques such as this were nearly abandoned by the late 1950s when drugs came into wide use.

Recently, however, more refined techniques of psychosurgery have begun to be used. Rather than destroying major parts of the brain, localized lesions are made in specified parts of the brain by means of radioactive particles inserted through small ceramic rods. These are still experimental techniques used only on severely disturbed patients, and have been effective in some cases, but not in others. The side-effects are not as serious, but this is a radical and irreversible treatment. Whenever neurons are damaged in the central nervous system, the results are permanent—they cannot be "undone." Such operations are not a matter of correcting a known brain abnormality.

Electroconvulsive Therapy. With electroconvulsive therapy (ECT), patients are given an electric shock that produces a convulsion and unconsciousness. When the patients regain consciousness, they do not remember the shock or the convulsion. Typically about ten such shocks are given over several weeks, although many more or fewer may be given.

Although shock treatment has been widely used, why it works when it does is still a mystery. Although it was tried on many types of mental illness when it was first used, it seems to work best on severely depressed patients.

Like psychosurgery, no one knows why ECT works, so it is not a matter of correcting something wrong with the person. Furthermore, there are a number of side effects. The most common one is amnesia for recent events, and in some cases even for events in the more distant past. Usually this amnesia disappears within a few weeks, but sometimes it is permanent. Although electroconvulsive therapy is said to be painless, patients come to fear it greatly. Many state legislatures have passed laws against its abuse (without defining "abuse" adequately). It is not unlikely that overuse of electroconvulsive shock has led to significant brain damage in some cases.

Although the use of such electroconvulsive shock is declining, a shock treatment passing the current through only one side of the brain has recently come into use. This type of treatment still produces seizures effectively and seems to have fewer side effects. Again, counselees should be aware that any brain damage is permanent. They should be aware that the brain functions on an electrochemical basis and that this massive shock will interfere, at least temporarily, with normal brain function.

Drugs. By far the most widespread current physiological treatment is the use of drugs. When first introduced, these drugs were hailed as the long-sought cure to mental illness. At last peace rather than chaos reigned on the mental hospital wards. Furthermore, mental hospital populations began to decline. As long as patients kept taking their drugs, they were able to function in society. However, many are beginning to question the widespread use of these drugs. The major question is whether they cure the disorder or merely mask the symptoms. The drugs were not developed to correct any known physiological imbalances, but were adopted because they eliminated many of the most objectionable symptoms.

There are three major types of drugs used to treat mental

disorders. Antianxiety drugs, or minor tranquilizers, are widely used to reduce tension and anxiety. Valium, an antianxiety drug, is the most commonly prescribed drug in the world. It is estimated that at least half of the households in the United States have used one of the three most common minor tranquilizers: Valium, Librium, or Miltown. Usually these drugs are prescribed by general practitioners for people who are under stress. Thus, it is likely that some of your counselees have taken, or are taking them.

These antianxiety drugs may serve a useful function when used on a short-term basis, but any long-term use should be discouraged. They have side effects of fatigue and drowsiness. They also have the effect of reducing inhibitions so that antisocial behavior may surface. When people try to stop taking the drugs, the original symptoms return with greater strength, so the drugs are taken in ever increasing doses. The use of these drugs seems to suggest that the suppression of anxiety is the best way to deal with it. This is like turning off the fire alarm rather than putting out the fire. Finally, even when used with psychotherapy, these drugs may be doing more harm than good. Learning is often state-dependent, which means that what we learn in one physiological state may not generalize to another. Thus, new skills learned for dealing with anxiety while taking these drugs may not be useable when the drugs are stopped.

The antipsychotic drugs, or major tranquilizers, are used to reduce psychotic symptoms. These drugs do more than tranquilize. While they do produce a calming effect, they reduce the major psychotic symptoms of delusions and hallucinations. The use of these drugs has transformed mental wards from places where bizarre behavior was commonplace to places where patients act much like normal people. Furthermore, patients can now be discharged from the hospital as long as they keep taking their drugs.

We have already dealt with some of the side effects of these drugs, such as tardive dyskinesia. Not only are there side effects, but patients taking these drugs do not become the alert, competent people we would hope for. Patients released on antipsychotic drugs usually make only a marginal adjustment to life. While these drugs have reduced the number of long-term hospitalizations, they may result in a "revolving door" admission policy. After being released, patients often quit taking their drugs, so the psychotic symptoms reappear. Then they have to be readmitted, only to be released and readmitted again. Like the antianxiety drugs, the antipsychotics seem to be turning off the worst symptoms without solving the problem.

The antidepressant drugs are used to elevate the mood of depressed patients. The first antidepressant (iproniazid) was used to treat tuberculosis. When it made the tubercular patients cheerful, it was then used with depressives, until it was discovered that it also caused liver damage as a side effect. Then another class of antidepressants (the MAO inhibitors) was widely used. However, these also had side effects on the liver, brain, and circulatory system. Furthermore, when combined with certain foods, especially those produced by fermentation (such as cheese or beer), they can produce illness or death. More recently a new class of antidepressants (tricyclics) has been introduced. Although they have side effects of blurred vision, drowsiness, and constipation, they do not seem to do permanent damage to the body.

In general, we must be very cautious in the use of drugs to treat disorders of behavior and mental processes. We must be clear that these drugs do not cure all of the disorders, but only relieve the symptoms. Antipsychotic drugs may be preferable to straightjackets, padded cells, and the general bedlam that was found in mental hospitals before 1950, but the patients are not cured. Taking these drugs is like taking an aspirin for a cold—it makes the disorder more bearable, but does not cure it. In fact, it may be that the use of drugs to suppress symptoms has made the task of developing better treatments seem less important.

Conclusion

In this chapter we have considered the first of the areas of psychology usually discussed in general psychology, that of physiological psychology. We have placed this in our Christian perspective in that humans are animal-like in their anatomy and physiology. Changes in anatomy and physiology can bring about disorders in behavior and mental processes. Changes in the nervous system, synapses, and the endocrine system can bring about great changes in behavior and mental processes, some temporary and some permanent. Of course, other physiological changes can also have an effect. Since we know that these anatomical and physiological changes produce disorders, we can take steps to prevent them, or to reverse them, where possible. This seems reasonable from our perspective. If something is wrong with the person's anatomy or physiology, we can treat it by taking corrective measures. This treatment is quite different from the most popular current types of physiological treatment.

Suggested Readings

"Physiological Psychology" or "Biological Bases of Behavior" chapters in general psychology textbooks are recommended. Also physiological psychology textbooks and chapters on "Organic Disorders" and "Biological Therapies" in abnormal psychology textbooks are recommended for a more thorough discussion. Bootzin and Acocella (1980), Breggin (1979), Brown and Wallace (1980), Coleman, Butcher, and Carson (1980), Garfield and Bergin (1978), Leukel (1976), and Valenstein (1980) expand on material presented in this chapter.

C H A P T E R • 3

SPIRITUAL
PSYCHOLOGY

Anyone looking at the title of this chapter will realize that it is not a typical chapter title in general psychology textbooks. This is one of the areas omitted by secular psychologists and since this is written from a Christian perspective, we add it here. Humans have nerves, muscles, and glands like animals, but they are also spiritual beings like God. This fits into our Christian perspective as shown in the lower, center of Figure 3:1 (Structure—Spiritual). We agree that humans are similar to animals in many ways. When we begin to deal with language, personality, creativity, morality, ethics, love, and so forth, we need to look more to comparisons with God than to the structure and function of the brain. God is spirit, and humans created in his image are also spiritual beings.

This means that we are looking for causes of behavior and mental processes in the spiritual, God-like aspects of humans. Humanity's animal-like physical aspects have been discussed, but its God-like spiritual ones have not. When Jesus was talking with the woman at the well in Samaria, he emphasized that God is spirit and those who worship him must do so in spirit and in truth. The apostle Paul notes that God is spirit, and in the next sentence he notes that we are changed into God's likeness by the spirit of the Lord himself (II Cor. 3). Many other passages of Scripture refer to the fact that humans are spiritual beings. Christian counselors must always

Figure 3:1 Spiritual psychology and spiritual disorders from a Christian perspective.

HUMANS

	Created	in the	Image of God
	Like Animals		Like God
	Overt Behavior	Definition	Mental Processes
	Understand Creation	Goals	Make People Like God
	Psychoanalysis / Behaviorism	Systems	Humanistic Psychology
	Experimental	Methods	Descriptive
(DISORDER)			(DISORDER)
Organic Disorders (Organic Mental Disorders)	Physiological	STRUCTURE	SPIRITUAL ... SPIRITUAL DISORDERS—SIN (PERSONALITY DISORDERS)

remember this when engaged in counseling: humans are made in God's image and can become more like him.

Humans as Spiritual Beings—Like God

Let us now consider what God is like, so that we have a clearer understanding of what it is we are trying to foster in our counselees. Theologians have been studying what God is like for hundreds of years. Of course, God is not exactly like anything or anyone we know. When humans have attempted to describe God, words have failed. Ezekiel could not adequately describe God, so he fell back on saying what God resembled. We cannot know all about God, but he has chosen to reveal certain things about himself which we call his attributes. Although volumes have been written about God's attributes, Tozer (1961) summarizes them so well that we will use his list here. He subtitled his book, "The Attributes of God: Their Meaning in the Christian Life." To keep from selecting only those seen as most relevant, we will consider implications of all he lists.

Before beginning the actual comparisons we need to consider two things. First, some people are reluctant to make comparisons between humans and God. They believe that there is such a great difference between the two that meaningful comparisons cannot be made. However, we must remember that the Bible itself, God's own special revelation to us, repeatedly makes these comparisons. We are told to be holy, perfect, loving, merciful, and so forth, like God. Most Christians say that they want to be more Christlike. What they really mean is that they want to become more like the attributes of God they see revealed in Christ. Second, when considering any one attribute in detail, we find that the other attributes are always involved. All of God's attributes are essentially one, blending into each other in his unity. In fact, his attributes really define each other. We must not overemphasize any one attribute or set of attributes to the exclusion of others.

Schaeffer (1968) refers to God as the personal-infinite God of the Bible and says that we are similar to God in his personal aspects, but different from him in his infinite aspects. As we look at Tozer's (1961) list of God's attributes, we find that over half of them are related to God's infinite aspects. Of course, we cannot be like him in these ways. Rather than discussing these, we will simply list them. God is self-existent, self-sufficient, eternal, infinite, immutable, omniscient, omnipotent, transcendent, omnipresent, and sovereign. Although we can never have these attributes, we are a bit like God even in these. For example, we are not from everlasting to everlasting (eternal) like God, but we do have life from now on (eternal life). Although we can never be omniscient, we can still increase our knowledge. Although we are not sovereign, we are still given dominion over the earth. Thus, even in these infinite aspects, we are still somewhat like God, and as counselors we have reason to urge our counselees toward growth in these areas. Now let us consider the remaining nine attributes of God listed by Tozer, attributes in which we find ourselves even more like God.

A Trinity. One of the great mysteries of the Christian faith is the Holy Trinity. Although the Trinity is three persons, he is one God and he is a unity. This doctrine of the Trinity has at least two major implications for a Christian psychology. First, God is a social being and we, created in his image, are social beings. When he created human beings, he created them male and female in his image, so that our very sexuality is a reflection of God's image in us. We need each other as beings created in the image of a social God. Second, the unity of the Trinity should be characteristic of our social relationships. Jesus prayed that we might be perfect in one. Paul repeatedly used the "body" analogy in referring to the church, emphasizing that we are many but make up one body in Christ. As Christian counselors, we must emphasize unity in the social relationships of our counselees.

Wise. God is a God of wisdom, a wisdom we cannot fully understand. In fact, it is said that his foolishness is wiser than the wisdom of humans. In his wisdom everything is in focus and in the proper relationship. Although we cannot ever have perfect wisdom, we are encouraged to seek wisdom and he promises to give it to us. It is true that humans have increased their knowledge (the number of facts they know), but they have problems increasing their wisdom (the true meaning and application of that knowledge for godly living). Knowledge without wisdom may be a very dangerous thing. Clearly, we must encourage our counselees to seek wisdom from God.

Faithful. God does not break his promises. It is impossible for God to lie, because he is the truth. Our whole hope for the future lies in God's faithfulness. We have seen how he has kept his word in the past and know that he will continue to keep it in the future. Since God is faithful, we are also encouraged to be faithful. Although our hearts are deceitful, with God's help it is possible to keep our covenant with him. Although the history of God's people is full of broken covenants, we must not get the idea that this is the way it ought to be. That only indicates what humans have done, not what they should do. We should encourage our counselees to be God-like in keeping their agreements.

Good. God is good. In fact, goodness is defined by his very nature. He is kind and benevolent toward us. He is tenderhearted, sympathetic, open, frank, friendly, and likes to give us blessings and make us happy. God wants the best for us and is good to us even when we are in rebellion against him. We are to be good, like God. Jesus pointed out that although some said we should love our friends and hate our enemies, we should love our enemies as well. We should love our enemies, lend to them, pray for them, do good to them, and not criticize or condemn them. Jesus specifically points out that in doing this we will be true children of God. Anyone can do good to his or her friends, but to do good to our enemies is a very God-like attribute. Counselees should be encouraged to be good, as God is good.

Just. God is a righteous God. He judges with moral equity, and is no respector of persons. He treats everyone fairly, giving sunshine and rain to both just and unjust people. He judges according to truth. We are to be just to those under our authority as God is just to us. God commands us to do justice because his righteousness is about to be revealed. Justice and fair judgment are as important to God as sacrifice is. We are to defend the poor and the orphans and to do justice to the sick and needy.

Merciful. God is actively compassionate. Justice is often contrasted with mercy, but there is no conflict between these in God. There is nothing in God's justice that stops the exercise of his mercy. He is one God, just and merciful at the same time. God's divine pity and compassion are extended to us. His mercy is available to us now through Jesus Christ our Lord. God is a God of mercy and delights in extending it to those who call on him. We are specifically commanded to be merciful as God is merciful. If we are merciful to others, God will also be merciful to us. Our counselees should be both just and merciful.

Full of Grace. Closely related to God's mercy is his grace. His grace enables him to help the undeserving, to spare the guilty. He extends his grace, through which we are saved, to sinful humans through Jesus Christ. Everyone who has been justified has received this justification only through his grace, which is extended freely to all. We are to forgive others as Christ forgave us. Even if someone offends us repeatedly, we are to forgive and forgive and forgive, just as God forgives us when we repeatedly fall. Jesus said that when we pray, we should forgive anyone of whatever we have against them so that God can forgive us. When we pray the "Lord's Prayer," we ask God to forgive us as we forgive others.

Love. God is love. It is the very nature of God's eternal love to give. He loved us so much that he sent his son to die that we might have everlasting life. Although humans have no greater love than to lay down their lives for friends, God loved us so much that Christ died for us while we were still sinners, enemies of God. Jesus said that he had loved us as the father had loved him and that we were to continue in his love. He commanded us to love one another as he had loved us. That is, we are to be God-like in our love. We must encourage our counselees to be gracious and loving.

Holy. Only God is absolutely holy. When we see him as he really is, we are acutely aware of our lack of holiness. We are incapable of fully grasping what God's holiness means because it is not simply better than the best we know. It is unique. It is an absolute holiness that knows no degrees. However, we are told by God in both the Old and New Testaments to be holy because he is holy. We are to worship and serve him in holiness. God shares a relative holiness with us as our preparation for heaven. He has made it available to us through Christ. We must encourage our counselees to seek this holiness.

In summary, we have considered the attributes of God and seen that we are commanded to be like him with respect to many of his attributes. We must remember that although we considered the attributes of God one at a time, God is a unity. When considering any one attribute in detail, the other attributes are always involved. All of the attributes are essentially one. They all blend into each other in his unity. In our counseling, we are to bring about the conditions that will foster the development of this God-likeness in our counselees—and in ourselves.

Disorders

Since human beings are spiritual beings, sin is possible. However, the concept of sin has not been a popular one in psychology, and not even in some interpretations of Christianity. When O. H. Mowrer presented a paper on "Some Constructive Features of the Concept of Sin" in a symposium at the 1959 APA covention, it drew national attention in newspapers and magazines. Kelly (1967) was courageous enough to come right out and use the term "sin" and deal with it as a psychological term, realizing that this would make most of the psychologists and psychiatrists present shudder. The absence of much mention of the term prompted Menninger (1973) to title his book, *Whatever Became of Sin?* However, when the term was used, it was defined only in the social sense of being against people.

Sin

The concept of sin fits into our Christian perspective as a spiritual disorder (as shown in Figure 3:1). Nearly any dictionary gives at least two major definitions, the first of which is "to violate divine law," the second, "to violate human rights." From our perspective, sin is *against God.* It is primarily a matter of transgressing against God even when it is against other people. When Potiphar's wife was attempting to seduce Joseph, he asked her how he could do this great wickedness and sin *against God.* When the prodigal son returned, he said that he had sinned *against heaven* and before his father. King David was guilty of adultery and murder but when he prayed for forgiveness in Psalm 51, he said to God, *"Against thee, thee only,* have I sinned. . . ." Oates (1973) discusses the various aspects of sin: sin as idolatry, as the antithesis of faith, as destructive habit, as self-elevation, as stupidity, and as alienation.

Many writers have pointed out that the first four of the Ten Commandments are sins against God and the last six are against humans. These last six are against humans, but they are still against God because humans are made in God's image. Menninger (1973) never discussed the question of what became of the concept of sin against God, only what became of the concept of sin against other people. There were probably two reasons for the change from thinking of sin as "against God" to thinking of it as "against humans." One reason is that many people have done what Mowrer (1966) advocated. They have abandoned the"God-hypothesis" in the transcendental sense. If there is no transcendent God, there can be no sin against him. The other reason for this change in the definition of sin is that many people think of God as only a force, only infinite, and not as personal. One cannot sin against a force, only against a person; only against *the* Person. In that sense Menninger was correct; sin is against persons made in the image of the Person.

As mentioned in chapter 1, humans are unique in having been made with the capacity to sin and in having sinned. Animals do not have the capacity to sin and God will not sin. It is the image of God in humans which makes them morally responsible. God gave humans the capacity to choose between good and evil. Unfortunately, humans chose evil and continue to do so today.

This is not to say that sinfulness is inherent in humans. Adam and Eve were created fully human in the image of God, but without sin. Jesus was fully human, as well as fully divine, yet he did not sin. Although sin is not inherent in our definition of humanness, all humans (except Jesus) have sinned. Christ died for us because we are unable to handle this sin problem ourselves.

Since sinning is universal, we must consider its effects. It was sin that marred the image of God in humans and keeps us from reaching our God-like potential. Sin results in separation between the sinner and the one sinned against. It separates us from God, and from one another. The final penalty of sin is death, both physical and spiritual. Sin was the original cause of humanity's problems, but we so often continue in sin and increase our own individual problems. A partial list of forms of sin given by the apostle Paul includes adultery, fornication, impure thoughts, spiritism, hatred, fighting, jealousy, anger, complaining, envy, murder, and drunkenness. As Christian counselors, we see sin as one of the disorders in the lives of our counselees.

Guilt

Although most psychologists do not accept the concept of sin, they certainly accept one result of sin, guilt feelings. One only needs to look at an abnormal psychology text to see how often guilt or guilt feelings are mentioned as factors in the development of "mental illness." Narramore (1974) has proposed that guilt is to some degree involved in the development of all disorders.

At this point we must make a clear distinction between "guilt" and "guilt feelings," because they are often confused. When secular psychologists use the term *guilt*, they usually mean that people feel guilty about something they have done. Without the concept of God, there is no concept of sin against God, and no concept of being actually guilty before God. The guilt feelings are seen as causing the disorder, rather than as a symptom of the disorder. The guilt feelings are seen as being bad, something that must be decreased. A common response by the counselors is to try to convince the counselees that they should not feel guilty.

Christians, on the other hand, use the term guilt to refer to the objective relationship between a person and God. The person has really done something against God. This objective state of being guilty *should* give rise to feelings of guilt. Guilt feelings are not seen as a cause of the disorder, but as a symptom of the disorder (sin). Christians have a positive view of guilt feelings. Such feelings came as a result of the Fall, but they are God's gift to humanity. They keep sinners from being content to be unlike God in their sin. People cannot be talked out of their guilt, and usually not even out of their guilt feelings. Such feelings can be diminished by talking, but sin must be forgiven for the sinner's guilt to be removed. Only forgiveness by God can permanently "cure" the objective guilt and thus, the guilt feelings. As Christian counselors, we must deal not only with guilt feelings, but with guilt itself.

Of course, guilt feelings do not always indicate the presence of guilt. Some people feel guilty about their humanness, so we must distinguish between humanness and sinfulness. Jesus was human, but not sinful. He experienced sorrow, hunger, and fatigue, and he wept. Some feel guilty about their temptations, so we must distinguish between temptation and sin. Jesus experienced temptation, but he did not sin.

Although some people believe they should reach a point where they are not even attracted by temptations, Jesus never reached it. Some Christians feel guilty for violating Jewish ceremonial laws, as when Paul wrote about eating meat sacrificed to idols. Others feel guilty about sins already forgiven. Finally, some people feel guilty about violating someone else's convictions; so we must distinguish between human convictions and God's law. It seems like someone has a conviction against nearly every possible action, so we must continually bring our counselees back to God's Word.

Personality Disorders

As evidence that guilt feelings are a blessing, let us consider the case of the people who apparently have no guilt feelings. In DSM-III, the personality disorders have been put on Axis II. These fit into our perspective as shown in Figure 3:1. These people have a pattern of disrupted personal relationships and feel no responsibility for their own problems or for other people. They are manipulative, self-seeking, and feel no guilt about hurting other people or for unethical behavior. Since these people feel no remorse, they usually do not even seek help for their disturbed relationships and sinful behavior. The most extreme type of this disorder is the antisocial (or psychopathic, or sociopathic) personality. Such people are unsocialized and seem to be incapable of loyalty to individuals, groups, or social values. They are more likely to wind up confined in penal institutions than in mental hospitals, but most of them manage to stay out of institutions even though they are in constant conflict with authorities.

Demon Possession

Early writings in many cultures show that demon possession was one of the earliest explanations of mental illness. Stone Age cavemen probably cut a circular hole in the skulls of people complaining of certain mental disorders, likely those involving headaches and convulsions. Presumably this opening allowed the evil spirit causing the trouble to escape. Emphasis on demonology declined during the Middle Ages. Treatment of the disturbed was then left largely to the clergy, and the mentally ill were usually treated with considerable kindness.

However, as theological beliefs about such behavior became more fully developed and widely accepted by the secular world, even treatment by the church became more harsh. The treatment then was to make the body such an unpleasant place to reside that the demon would leave. People were whipped, starved, chained, immersed in hot water, and so forth—anything to drive the devil out of them. With the rise of modern science, attributing everything to demons declined. The maladjusted were then put in asylums where treatment was not much better. As confidence in science and medicine rose, it became very unfashionable to believe in such things as demons. Recently, however, there has been a resurgence of interest in demons.

The position taken here is that there are such things as demons, and they do influence people, but not all odd behavior is a symptom of demon possession. Let us see what scripture says about demonology, especially as it might be related to what we call mental illness. Demon possession is relatively rare in the Old Testament, although it is strongly suggested in some passages. Under the influence of a tormenting spirit, Saul was very jealous and violent, attempting to kill David and even his own son, Jonathan. However, not all odd behavior was attributed to evil spirits. Only a couple of chapters later, we find David pretending to be crazy because he was afraid of an enemy king. David drooled into his beard and scratched on doors until the king concluded that David must be mad. There is no indication that he pretended to be demon possessed, only that he pretended to be insane. For seven years, Nebuchadnezzar lived in the fields like an animal, eating grass like a cow. His hair and nails were not cut. He was driven from his throne, but when his "reason returned" (spontaneous recovery), he once again became ruler. Again, his odd behavior was not attributed to demon possession, only to the fact that God was teaching him a lesson.

Demon possession was prevalent in Jesus' time. It resulted in violence, inability to speak, blindness, falling into fire or water, great strength, uncontrolled movements, foaming at the mouth, grinding of the teeth and rigidity. Of course, many of these "symptoms" are the same as those of the mentally ill or epileptic of today. Yet Jesus distinguished between illness and demon possession. Once when two blind men came to him, he healed them by touching their eyes. Later a man who was blind and dumb was brought to him. Jesus cast out the demon and the man could see and speak. In one case blindness was caused by demon possession, in another it was not.

Insanity was not equated with demon possession by early Christians. In fact, at one time when Jesus himself was so busy that he could not find time to eat, some of his friends tried to take him home with them, thinking he was out of his mind. They did not even mention demon possession. Festus accused the apostle Paul of being insane. He did not attribute Paul's insanity to demon possession, but to long studying. The Bible distinguishes between diseases, demon possession, and mental illness. When describing those brought to Jesus, writers distinguish between those who were demon possessed and those who were lunatic (literally, "moon-struck").

Demon possession can cause behavior that is not God-like, but it is not the only cause of such behavior. Although most Christians have not previously done so, they must clearly state the differences between demon possession and other disorders. Sall (1976) has made a clinical distinction between demon possession and other disorders. He notes that demons are anti-Christ, while psychotics often fantasize religious experience. Demons are separate beings, while psychotic experiences are the result of withdrawal. Demons are rational beings, while psychotics are irrational. Demons are object-related, while psychotics suffer from a loss of object reality.

A distinction must also be made between demon *possession* and demonic *influence*. Only unbelievers are exposed to demon possession. The believer who is "in Christ," filled with the Holy Spirit, cannot be possessed by a demon. However, both believers and unbelievers are subject to demonic influence. In demon possession, the demon invades the personality and gains control over the individual. In demonic influence, attack is made from without, through temptation, suggestion, and pressure. As Christian counselors, we must at least consider that the source of a disorder may be demon possession.

Treatment

After counselors have determined that the cause of the disorder is due to a problem in the spiritual aspect of an individual, they should give an appropriate treatment. If the cause of the disorder is a spiritual problem, a physiological treatment is simply not appropriate, at least not as the sole or primary method. Too often, people plagued with guilt feelings because of unforgiven sin take tranquilizers to make them feel better, rather than seeking God's forgiveness.

Forgiveness

If counselees have unforgiven sin in their lives, they need to do several things to bring about a solution to this problem. There is a penalty for sin, but Christ has paid that for us, so we do not have to suffer the full penalty. Salvation is of God and only through Christ, but God requires several things of us.

We are to *confess* our sins. Sin must be forgiven and the way to forgiveness is through confession. The Bible shows us numerous examples of confession, including Saul, David, and Peter. Confession to each other has become rather popular today with the rise of sensitivity groups. In fact, we have gotten to the place where individuals often seem to be trying to surpass each other in their confessions. The person who does not have something to confess is seen as hiding something, as being less than honest. Although confession is good, alone it is not enough.

We are also to *repent*. To most people this seems to mean being sorry for their sins, or sorry for the penalty of sin. Although sorrow may be included in repentance, this is *not* the essence of repentance. Repentance means a change of purpose or a change of mind. We are to turn from our sinful ways to God.

We are also to accept Christ by *faith*. We are to believe in him for our salvation. Christ has paid the penalty for our sins, but we must trust in him for this. Oates (1973) notes that each aspect of sin is mirrored in an aspect of forgiveness. If sin is idolatry, forgiveness is enlargement of life. If sin is the antithesis of faith, forgiveness is an invitation to pilgrimage. If sin is destructive habit, forgiveness is the restoration of strength. If sin is self-elevation, forgiveness is restored joy in being human. If sin is stupidity, forgiveness is the gift of wisdom. If sin is alienation, forgiveness is the gift of community.

In a very real sense, every Christian counselor is an evangelist who attempts to bring the counselee to Jesus Christ. This attempt should probably not be made early in the counseling relationship. If the counselee is not a Christian, it is the responsibility of the Christian counselor to present Christ at some point before the relationship is ended. Of course, in some institutions, counselors may be legally prevented from verbally attempting a conversion. Some people contend that this witnessing is taking unfair advantage of non-Christians; "setting them up." However, if the counselees have chosen a Christian counselor or a Christian institution, there is nothing wrong with presenting Christ. Counselees should expect that.

Two things need to be emphasized. First, although Christ has paid the penalty for our sin, we must still live with its consequences. We live in a fallen world, and coming to Christ will not solve all problems. All people who have general paresis will not suddenly be given new brains just because they come to Christ. The converted alcoholic will not always be given a new liver, but may have to live the rest of his or her life with cirrhosis of the liver. After King David committed adultery with Bath-sheba and murdered her husband, his confession and repentance were followed by forgiveness, but his child still died. We must make sure that our counselees realize that forgiveness does not mean that all the consequences of sin will be removed.

Second, we must be aware of the principle of multiple causation. Counselees may have disorders in several areas of their lives. In fact, this is usually the case. Persons may have both unforgiven sin *and* cerebral arteriosclerosis, both a spiritual and a physiological problem, as well as other disorders. We must examine all areas of people's lives and not be content with an oversimplified approach of looking for only one problem. Let us now consider two approaches that have emphasized the treatment of spiritual problems.

Nouthetic Counseling. Although he has been severely criticized, Jay Adams has a great deal to say to us about the treatment of spiritual problems. He sees humanity's basic problem in terms of sin. God created humans to have authority and rule over the earth, but sin brought a reversal so that the earth gained dominion over humanity. Contrary to God's intention, the environment rules humans rather than humans' ruling the environment. He notes that the Bible talks of organically based problems and of problems that stem from sinful attitudes and behavior, but not of any third source of problems we call "mental illness." Except for organic disorders, the "mentally ill" are people with unsolved personal problems.

Adams (1970) has developed nouthetic counseling (nouthetic confrontation) to deal with these problems. Such nouthetic confrontation has three basic elements. The first is the idea that there is something wrong (some sin, obstruction, problem, or difficulty) with the person and that this need has to be acknowledged and dealt with. The second element is the idea that problems are solved nouthetically, by verbal means.

69

The contact is a personal conference and discussion aimed toward bringing greater conformity to biblical standards. Finally, the counselor's motive is always to be that the verbal correction benefit the counselee. Rather than being directed toward punishment, even disciplinary punishment, nouthesis is motivated by love and concern for the good of the counselee.

Nouthetic counseling is direct and confrontive. Adams points out that women come with tissues ready and men come with their tempers ready to flare, but the nouthetic counselor does not let such things detract from getting to the problem. For example, when a woman breaks into bawling, crying, and sobbing, one should look her in the eye and tell her to be quiet. Tell her to stop this nonsense and get down to business. Tell her that you know there is something wrong in her life and she needs to start "talking turkey." This kind of counseling can be very effective in dealing with sin in the lives of some persons, and it should be known and used by Christian counselors at appropriate times.

Spirituotherapy. Charles Solomon (1971) has also developed an approach to treating spiritual disorders. He sees a human being as a tri-unity of spirit, soul, and body. The spirit is the spiritual part, which relates to God. The soul is the psychological part of mind, emotions, and will, which relates to others. The body is the physiological part, which relates to the environment. There can be problems in any of these three areas, but the prime consideration is the person's relationship to God. The relationship to God is corrected by salvation, assurance of salvation, security in that relationship, acceptance by God, and total commitment to him.

However, Solomon notes that even after this, the self (ego, will, old nature) may still be at the center of our life, trying to control things. If this is true, it can lead to inferiority, insecurity, inadequacy, guilt, worry, doubts, fears, frustration, hostility, and even psychiatric and physical symptoms. What the counselees must do is to put Christ at the center of their lives so that Christ is in control and self is subordinate to him. When this is done, one has the attitudes of Christ, strength in Christ, all needs supplied, peace, joy, and a healthy body. This is the spirit-filled or spirit-controlled life. The purpose of all this is that we should be conformed to the image of Christ.

Spirituotherapy, like nouthetic counseling, is direct and confrontive. Also, like nouthetic counseling, it involves a rejection of all kinds of secular psychological counseling. Solomon sees psychotherapy as strengthening the self, when spirituotherapy says that self should be reduced to nothing so that Christ can be everything. Adams also rejects all other approaches to therapy, including the three major forces presented in this book. Neither Adams nor Solomon would approve of where I have placed them in the spectrum. I see their approaches as valuable in dealing with spiritual problems, but limited to these. We certainly must treat such problems, but we must treat others as well. We must not reject these approaches, but see them as fitting into our larger perspective. Other Christian psychologists have written about dealing with spiritual problems, but Adams and Solomon were chosen here because they restrict their treatment only to such problems and reject psychology as a method of treatment.

As Christian counselors, we must also deal with guilt feelings that persist even when guilt is gone. As noted earlier, we must distinguish between humanness, temptations, and convictions on the one hand, and sin on the other. We must also deal with guilt about a problem in other areas of life. For example, one person came feeling very guilty about falling asleep repeatedly during devotions. I asked him when he had devotions (6:00 A.M.), when he went to bed (2:00 A.M.) and about the presence of known sin in his life (none). From his answers, I concluded that his problem was physiological (lack of sleep) rather than spiritual, and told him to get more sleep. He did, and was no longer troubled with falling asleep during devotions. He did not need spiritual help, but physical help.

Before leaving this section on forgiveness, let us consider

the outcome of treatment of personality disorders. Remember that from our perspective, guilt is seen as a blessing because it makes us discontented with our unGod-like state—and the people with personality disorders experience no guilt. As we would expect, these individuals are usually very resistant to treatment. They usually begin teatment only because someone else is insisting on it. They do not believe that there is any need for them to change and they frequently drop out of treatment. In general, the traditional psychotherapeutic and biological treatments have not been effective.

Casting Out Demons

If the cause of the disorder is demon possession, something must be done to expel the demons. Although exorcisms were commonly practiced by the Jews during Jesus' time, neither Jesus nor his followers used any conjurations, incantations, or magical ceremonies to cast out demons. Jesus relied on his own living word of infinite power. He spoke and the demons obeyed him. The phrase "In Jesus' name" is not a magic phrase to bring about a cure, but a reliance on the Infinite behind the name.

Jesus delegated his power over demons to the twelve, the seventy, and to believers in general. His apostles cast out demons in his name. This is not to imply that casting out demons is a simple task, because even his disciples failed at times. As Christian counselors we should be in a place spiritually where we can call on the power behind the name of Jesus to cast out demons. If we do not believe we are capable of this, we should know some Christian to whom we can refer our counselee, just as we would refer someone with a physical problem to a physician.

Conclusion

In this chapter we have said that humans are spiritual beings like God, as well as physical beings like animals. As we consider how humans are like God, we must remember that our goal in counseling is to provide conditions in which our counselees (and we ourselves) will become more like him. Since humans are spiritual beings, there can be disorders in this area of life. These disorders are caused by sin, which brings guilt and guilt feelings. They may even be caused by demon possession. Our task as Christian counselors, then, is to deal with the sin problem by bringing our counselees to Christ for forgiveness or casting out the demons. Taking a tranquilizer is treatment just as inappropriate for the results of sin as nouthetic counseling is for the person with physical disorders. Our treatment must be appropriate for the disorder. It must also be comprehensive, not restricted to only the primary cause, but also dealing with related problems that have arisen.

Suggested Readings

There are few books that deal with the subject matter of this chapter in any systematic way. Adams (1970), Koteskey (1980), Oates (1973), Solomon (1971), and Tozer (1969) expand on material presented here.

CHAPTER • 4

DEVELOPMENTAL PSYCHOLOGY

Another major area of psychology is developmental psychology, in which psychologists are interested in describing and explaining changes in behavior and mental processes that result from maturation and experience. American developmental psychology has traditionally been unbalanced, in that psychologists saw "development" as something that happened primarily to children and adolescents. Most books before 1970 were written on child psychology and adolescent psychology, but even those on developmental psychology devoted about nine-tenths of the book to the first two decades of life and the remaining one-tenth to the last five decades. Fortunately, psychologists are beginning to correct this imbalance. As Christians we should take this more balanced view of development.

Developmental psychology fits into our Christian perspective as shown in the lower central part of Figure 4:1 (Immaturity—Development—Maturity). Note that immature people are more like animals, and as they mature they become more like God—at least they have that potential. As we consider different sections of developmental psychology, we will see repeatedly that people progress from animal-like to God-like. Note how closely this progression is related to our applied goal, that of making people more like God. Salvation, as discussed in the last chapter, is only the first step in making people like God, so we will discuss other steps in

Figure 4:1 Developmental psychology and developmental disorders from a Christian perspective.

HUMANS

Created..............in the..............Image of God
Like Animals   Like God
Overt Behavior..........Definition..........Mental Processes
Understand..............Goals..............Make People
Creation   Like God
Psychoanalysis............Systems............Humanistic
Behaviorism   Psychology
Experimental..............Methods............Descriptive
Physiological..............Structure..............Spiritual

(DISORDER)   (DISORDER)
Organic Disorders............Spiritual............Spiritual Disorders—Sin
(Organic Mental Disorders)   (Personality Disorders)

PHYSICAL DISORDERS..........IMMATURITY..........DEVELOPMENT..........MATURITY..........SPIRITUAL IMMATURITY
(DISORDERS APPEARING IN CHILDHOOD OR ADOLESCENCE)   (NO DSM-III CATEGORY)

this chapter. Let us now consider some of the various aspects of development studied by developmental psychologists.

Physical Development

Physical development takes place primarily during the first two decades of life. During the first year, height increases by more than a third and weight triples. Bones continue to ossify and muscles grow. Body proportions change. At birth the head is about one-quarter of the length of the body. By five years of age the child's height has more than doubled, but the head is only a little more than one-eighth of the length.

Between the ages of five and nine, children grow at a fairly constant rate. However, between the ages of ten and fifteen, puberty occurs. Great changes happen as the anterior pituitary increases its output of certain hormones. This results in a sudden spurt of growth in the bones and muscles and in sexual development. After the adolescent growth spurt, the rate of growth decreases and full adult size is usually reached by the age of sixteen or eighteen. Slight increases in height and weight occur during the next few years, but physical development is now nearly at its peak.

Although endurance increases for another twenty years, performance on tasks requiring speed and agility begins to decline slowly after the early twenties. Perhaps society places too much emphasis on this decline, because the decline between twenty and sixty years of age is very gradual, especially if people care for themselves physically. Furthermore, adults more than compensate for the physical decline by using better judgment. For example, although the reaction time of an adolescent male is faster than that of a sixty-year-old, the adolescent's traffic accident rate is more than twice as high.

The most outstanding characteristic of the psychology of aging is the sensorimotor decline. With aging, all of the senses show some changes that reduce the individual's contact with the environment. Individuals are not able to see, hear, touch, taste, or smell their surroundings as well as they once did. Responses change as well, tending to slow down. Since we are animal-like physically, from our perspective we would expect a decline of the physical as we age.

Spiritual Development

Several developmental psychologists have emphasized various stages of development, an approach we will take in this section. In general, such psychologists have found that humans develop from being quite animal-like to becoming more God-like. For example, although Freud (1888-1939) is most famous for his psychosexual stages of development, let us consider his theory of the development of the basic structures of personality. According to Freud, the child is born with only the id, the storehouse of the animal, primitive, irrational, and brutish. The next structure to develop is the ego, the cognitive or rational part of the personality. The final structure to develop is the superego, the moral and idealistic part of the personality.

Order of redemption. Although theologians usually do not use the term "stages" when talking about spiritual development, they use the same concept. Berkhof (1946) talks about the "relation between sanctification and some of the other stages in the work of redemption" (p. 536). There is little agreement among theologians on the specifics of the stages of spiritual development. Sometimes they may use the same terms, but with different meanings. However, they generally agree on broad stages of development toward God-likeness, so let us consider some of these.

First, human beings are born in a sinful state, commonly called *original sin.* This original sin is present in the life of every person from birth, and is the root of the overt sins appearing later in life. Humans can do nothing to rescue themselves from this sinful state, an unGod-like stage of development.

The second stage of development is a state of salvation.

They have been born again, justified before God, and regeneration has given them new life. Their sins have been forgiven and they are now living and growing in Christ. These people have repented of their sinful ways and are converted to Christ.

The third general stage is that of sanctification. Theologians probably disagree more about this stage of development than any other. They disagree about when it takes place and what happens in it. Some say sanctification is completed during life on earth; others, at a person's death; and still others, after death. Some emphasize its aspect of dedication, being "set apart" or consecrated. Others emphasize its aspect of transformation or being made holy.

The final general stage of development is glorification. This means life in heaven where we will be even more like God. There is more agreement on this final stage of development. Now let us consider how psychologists have studied the development of God-likenesses in humans.

Cognitive Development. Cognitive development also follows a progression from animal-like to God-like. The most influential individual in the study of this area is Piaget, who observed what he called the sensorimotor stage during the first two years of the child's life. Infants begin with little more than reflexes in the first month of life. The second stage is the preoperational stage, which lasts from about age two to seven. Children now acquire language and can manipulate the meaning of objects and events. The third stage of development is the stage of concrete operations, from about age seven to eleven or twelve. Children can now have a mental representation of a series of actions, can draw a map, and think in relational terms. The final stage of development is the stage of formal operations, in which people can finally begin to think in purely symbolic terms. They can now use abstract rules to solve a whole class of problems and can think in terms of hypothetical ideas. Note the progressive development from animal-like to God-like.

Moral Development. In recent years there has been an

increasing concern with moral development during childhood, adolescence, and adulthood. Kohlberg (1973) studied three levels of moral development. At the premoral level, individuals obey or disobey the rules to avoid punishment or to get rewards. Even animals can respond on the basis of reward and punishment. At the conventional level, people try to please and help others to get their approval or do their duty to maintain social order. At the principled level, people obey laws because those laws are a "contract" they have with others to avoid violating their rights. They also make judgments on the basis of self-accepted moral principles containing ideas of justice, human rights, and human dignity. Kohlberg has speculated on the possibility of an ontological-religious orientation in which the person deals with the question "Why be moral?" People with this orientation adopt a cosmic perspective with a sense of being a part of the whole of life, and often express themselves in theistic terms. Again, notice that we begin even our moral development with an animal-like emphasis on reward and punishment and have the potential to develop toward a God-like perspective.

It is important for Christian counselors to know the course of development in various aspects of the person because too often we expect too much of individuals. We may expect children to do some physical activity they simply are unable to do, but this is not as likely as expecting some cognitive activity or moral judgment beyond their years. For example, parents of children who are not yet even able to learn algebra in school expect them to understand that God is Spirit, or to understand about the Holy Spirit. If children are at the preoperational stage or the stage of concrete operations, we need to spend more time talking about Jesus, who was the incarnation of God, so that they can understand.

We also often expect children to make moral decisions on the basis of universal ethical principles when they are still at premoral levels. If we were more honest, we would have to admit that many of our moral decisions are made at the conventional level or even at the premoral level. Parents who expect their children to behave and think at a level beyond their capacities place them in very frustrating situations and need to be educated about the capabilities of children at different ages. Let us now consider some of the developmental disorders that can occur.

Disorders

As we think of disorders of development, we have to think of both sides of our perspective shown in Figure 4:1. We can look for disorders of development on the animal-like side of our perspective; so in this chapter we will look at some of the physiological causes. We can also look for disorders of development on the God-like side of our perspective; so in this chapter we will also consider disorders of spiritual development.

Physiological Developmental Disorders

When we consider physiological causes of faulty development, we can examine several sources of the disorder. In this section we will discuss the sources of these disorders: genetic-chromosomal factors, glandular factors, and environmental factors.

Genetic-Chromosomal Factors. Sometimes developmental disorders are caused by abonormalities in the chromosomes. One of the most common and widely known of these is Down's syndrome, often called *mongolism* because people who have the syndrome have almond-shaped eyes. There are a number of physical symptoms, such as thick eyelids, flat face and nose, large tongue, short neck, and so forth. The main change in behavior and mental processes is the mental retardation. Most such people show moderate mental retardation, but they can take care of themselves and get along well in a family or institution because they tend to be affectionate and docile. The cause of this disorder is a known physical problem, an extra chromosome at conception.

Another example is Huntington's chorea, a hereditary disorder transmitted genetically. Caused by a dominant gene passed on by either parent, it usually cannot be detected until the symptoms begin to develop at age 30 or 35. Persons with Huntington's chorea seem completely normal throughout childhood, adolescence, and early adulthood, but in their thirties they become moody and their intellectual functions deteriorate. In addition to these changes in mental processes are motor symptoms, most notably an involuntary jerking of the limbs. Again, we have a known cause of this disorder, a cause that is hereditary, definitely transmitted genetically. If the parents do not develop the disorder, they cannot have passed it on to their children.

Glandular Factors. Developmental disorders may be caused by glandular malfunctions. In chapter 2, we discussed disorders that could occur if the thyroid or adrenals malfunctioned. Cretinism will develop in infants who have an undersecretion of thyroxin. People with this problem will show both physical and mental retardation.

The endocrine gland most associated with development is the pituitary gland, located at the base of the brain. Although this gland secretes several hormones, including one to control the thyroid, we will discuss only two of them here. The anterior pituitary secretes the somatotropic hormone, which stimulates normal growth of the whole body in the developing person. The timing and extent of growth are regulated by the amount of somatotropic hormone in the bloodstream. An underscretion results in a pituitary dwarf who has normal intelligence and body proportions, but is only three or four feet tall. An oversecretion results in a pituitary giant of normal body proportions and intelligence, but very tall. If the oversecretion begins after maturity, cartilage hardens into bone and the bones become misshapen and thickened. Tissue of the face and tongue enlarges, and the abdomen protrudes so that the individual has a coarse, apelike appearance.

The anterior pituitary also secretes gonadotropic hormones, which regulate sexual development. The increased output of these hormones after puberty results in the appearance of secondary sexual characteristics. These hormones also cause the mature follicle of the ovary to rupture and release the ovum. They also stimulate the development of the sperm and ova and the development of milk in the mammary glands of the female. Since sexual behavior depends to some extent on hormones, the pituitary influences such behavior.

Environmental Factors. A person may be genetically normal but not receive essential nutrients. Protein deficiency in the mother's diet during pregancy or in the baby's diet after birth can cause lowered intelligence. Severe malnutrition not only retards physical growth, but mental growth as well. Infants who die from malnutrition during the first year of life show brain damage. Those who are malnourished but survive also have stunted brain growth—irreversibly damaged, because this is the time of most brain development. This is a serious problem when we consider that about one-third of the world's children die of malnutrition before age five, and another third lack sufficient protein.

Sometimes a combination of genetic and environmental factors causes developmental disorders. This is the case in Phenylketonuria (PKU), a metabolic disorder. Children with PKU appear normal at birth, but do not have an enzyme needed to break down phenylalamine, an amino acid commonly found in our diet. If they eat enough phenaylalamine, it increases in the blood and finally causes brain damage. Both mental retardation and motor incoordination will then result. PKU apparently is caused by a recessive gene, so that for it to develop, the child must inherit the gene from both parents.

DSM-III Categories. Both Axis I and Axis II of DSM-III have categories of developmental disorders. Axis I has a category called *disorders,* which usually first manifest themselves in infancy, childhood, or adolescence. These include mental retardation, attention deficits, conduct disorders, anxiety disorders, eating disorders, stereotyped movement disorders, and so forth. Axis II lists several specific developmental disorders with respect to reading, arithmetic, language, articulation, and so forth. Although some of these would have physiological bases, most of them are not now known to have such bases. They are just disorders that first appear in young people.

Spiritual Developmental Disorders

Volumes have been written on the concept of Christian maturity, but mostly from the viewpoint of the theologian. Christian psychologists have also explored the concept to some extent. In fact, the theme of the 1968 convention of the Christian Association for Psychological Studies was, "The Christian's Quest for Maturity." Disorders of spiritual development grow from a failure to mature through the expected stages.

Spiritual Immaturity. Individuals may be retarded in their spiritual development. Obviously many individuals have not even been converted and are still living in sin. These people make no profession of faith in Christ, and may not even be interested in repentance and the new birth.

Some people are born again, but never grow in the faith. They keep asking the same questions and are not making any spiritual progress. The writer to the Hebrews noted that they still needed someone to teach them the first lessons in the faith. Rather than spiritual meat, they needed spiritual milk. Peter told his readers the same thing. The apostle Paul also said it to the Corinthian church. We must discern the spiritual maturity of our counselees, as did the writers of the New Testament.

It is more difficult to make general statements about sanctification, because one's theology makes such a difference here. If sanctification is seen as being synonymous with growth, nothing needs to be added. However, if sanctification is seen as being completed in this life, we must consider what happens then. Wesley (1777/1921) says that after sanctification the Christian still grows in grace, in the knowledge of Christ, and in the love and image of God. This growth continues until death and perhaps into all eternity. In fact, Wesley notes that the sanctified individual "may grow far swifter than he did before."

Mental Retardation. Some individuals never develop through the stages of cognitive development to abstract thinking. They remain able to think only at some of the concrete levels, or even only at the sensorimotor level. Mental retardation is usually defined as below-average intellectual functioning along with deficits in adaptive behavior occuring before age eighteen. It is usually specifically defined in terms of scores on IQ tests, which means that we are talking primarily about a person's ability to deal with conventional academic schoolwork. The number of people diagnosed as mentally retarded increases sharply at ages five or six, peaks at age fifteen, and drops off sharply after that. This means that such people can function nearly normally at home before school age and in society after they can drop out of school, so they are not classified as retarded then.

Psychologists have used several different labels to describe different degrees of retardation. Currently the adjectives, "mild," "moderate," "severe," and "profound" are used with the words "mental retardation" to describe the behavior of the individual. "Mild mental retardation" is used to describe those who can usually live quite normal lives with little or no help. They can read, write, hold a job, and function socially most of the time, but may need occasional help or advice when facing particularly complex or stressful tasks. "Moderately retarded" people can learn to care for themselves but not learn to be fully independent. They can work in a sheltered environment, but they often appear clumsy because of poor motor coordination. "Severely retarded" people are always dependent on others for their care, although they can develop some skills necessary for personal hygiene and can do simple work and household tasks.

"Profoundly retarded" individuals usually require custodial care throughout their lives. Although they can master a few simple tasks, they are quite unadaptable and often have physical handicaps as well.

We have already seen how changes in the central nervous system or an imbalance in the endocrine system can produce mental retardation. Infections or toxic substances can also cause it. If a pregnant woman gets syphilis or German measles, her child may be mentally retarded. Carbon monoxide or lead can cause brain damage, as can an overdose of drugs in infancy. Physical injury at birth or a lack of oxygen can also lead to mental retardation. Mental retardation may also simply be a result of as yet unknown genetic problems.

As Christian counselors, we must be very careful about classifying someone as mentally retarded. We define mental retardation in terms of both academic and social performance, and neither is easy to measure. IQ tests can give low scores as a result of misunderstood instructions, language problems, lack of motivation or problems with tests themselves. A child socially well-adapted to life in rural Appalachia or in an urban ghetto may not be socially prepared for formal schooling, but not be retarded at all. Labeling children has profound effects on their self-image and how others see them. Placing them in a special education class or institutionalizing them may be totally inappropriate, but result in producing what was diagnosed.

Treatment

Once we have determined the source of the developmental problem, we are in a position to treat it. Of course, at times there is no cure, but the disorders can often be prevented. We must remember that our diagnosis is not only for statistical purposes, but is to assist us in selecting an appropriate treatment. Our general strategy for treatment of developmental disorders is first to decide which area (or areas) have stagnated development; second, diagnose where the person is in development in that area; finally, give appropriate treatment to move the person to the next stage, movement toward greater maturity. Of course, we should be sensitive to problems that may have developed in other areas as well. For example, an adolescent may be too short because of a problem with the pituitary, but increasing body size will not necessarily cure the personal-social problems that may have developed. Let us now consider treatment for both physiological and spiritual developmental disorders.

Physical Treatment

If the disorder has a physiological basis, a physical treatment is likely to be necessary, and Christian counselors should know other Christian professionals to whom they can refer people with such problems.

Genetic-Chromosomal Treatment. There is usually no treatment for disorders caused by genetic-chromosomal factors. Fortunately, these disorders can often be prevented. For example, although there is no known treatment for Down's syndrome, its likelihood increases directly with the age of the parents when the child is conceived. A woman in her forties is forty times as likely to have a Down's syndrome baby as is a woman in her twenties. A man over fifty-five years of age is twice as likely to sire such a child as one in his early twenties. If older women had fewer babies, the number of Down's syndrome babies would decrease markedly.

There is no treatment for Huntington's chorea. Children whose parents have it have no way of knowing whether or not they themselves have the disorder until they are in their thirties. Since it is caused by a dominant gene, if these people would delay having children until their mid-thirties, this disorder could be eliminated. When genetic-chromosomal factors are involved, many counselees want to know what the chances are of their having a child (or another child) with a given disorder. Christian counselors should know how such disorders are transmitted, whether they depend on dominant or recessive genes, whether the disorders are inherited or not, whether there is an inherited predisposition, and so forth. If the counselors do not know these things, they should know someone to whom they can refer their counselees for genetic counseling.

Glandular Treatment. In general, if the glandular malfunctions are detected early and treatment begun in time, the disorders can be prevented. In some cases the course of the disorders can be reversed, but this is not always so. Although Christian counselors cannot treat such disorders, they should be familiar enough with them to recognize them and refer counselees to an endocrinologist. As was mentioned in chapter 2, both the physical and mental retardation of cretinism can be prevented if thyroxin is given early enough. However, if it is not detected in time, permanent damage occurs.

If there is an undersecretion of the somatotropic hormone, dwarfism can be prevented if hormone therapy is begun soon enough. However, care must be taken to determine that normal growth has not already stopped, or the treatment to prevent dwarfism may cause acromegaly. If the person starts becoming a pituitary giant or acromegaly begins, surgery on the pituitary is possible, but very difficult because of its location. Physicians can also treat undersecretions of the gonodatropic hormones by using hormone therapy.

Environmental Treatment. Most environmentally caused disorders have obvious treatments. If the problem is malnutrition during pregnancy, we can counsel expectant mothers to eat a balanced diet, urging them to be especially careful to get enough protein. Likewise, since infants need a balanced diet, we can counsel parents in terms of feeding the basic food groups to their children. Although this is not the kind of counseling we think of ourselves as doing, we can do it to prevent retardation—a disorder for which there is no treatment.

Although we cannot replace the enzyme deficit causing the PKU, we can prevent PKU by means of a restricted diet for the infant. Methods are available to detect PKU early and if treatment is begun early, deterioration can be prevented so that intellectual functioning will be kept near normal.

Spiritual Treatment

The term *spiritual treatment* is used to refer to treatment of developmental disorders in the God-like aspects of humans. This includes cognitive aspects as well as spiritual ones. Again, our general strategy is to determine the source of the disorder and give an appropriate treatment or treatments.

Discipleship. If Christian counselors have determined that the problem is one of spiritual immaturity, their task is one of discipleship. Although salvation, discussed in chapter 3, is very important, it is of God. We were called to be witnesses and to make disciples. The process of discipling is one of teaching. Unfortunately, more attention has traditionally been paid to salvation than to discipleship. It is time we paid more attention to our assigned teaching function. Growth is a function of both the individuals' potential and their environments. Although we have little control over their potential to be like God, we can certainly influence their environment. We need to question seriously how much our worship services, Sunday schools, prayer meetings, youth meetings, and so forth, lead to the development of God-like attributes. Too often these are either nonfunctional traditions or directly adopted secular techniques that have nothing to do with fostering spiritual growth.

We must be careful not to expect too much from young Christians. Too often they compare their own spiritual maturity to that of someone who is much more mature, and in so doing they feel either guilty or discouraged. Counselees should not feel guilty for their lack of maturity unless they have voluntarily refused to grow. Maturity takes time, but time does not necessarily bring maturity. Our task is to help those who have been Christians for some time but have grown little, not to load guilt feelings on young Christians.

Our counselees also need to be reminded that growth often comes in spurts, and that Christians often remain on relatively level plateaus for some time. They should not be discouraged by lack of growth if they have been trying to grow. God does not hold us responsible for growth, only for walking in whatever light he gives us.

We must emphasize growth in Christ. People grow through the Word, by putting away childish things, by cultivating understanding, by striving to become Christ-like, by overcoming temptation, by going through trials and difficulty, and so forth. In past generations, Christians talked about "means of grace," and we should make sure that our counselees are engaging in these expected Christian behaviors. They need to engage in these with an understanding that the behaviors have no merit in themselves, but that they are a means to the end of growing spiritually, to the end of becoming more like God.

Education. Education of the mentally retarded is well established in the public school system. Treatment of the mentally retarded has varied throughout history; from allowing them to die, to accepting and supporting them in society. The movement toward institutionalization during the last century brought great optimism, but frequently resulted in warehouses of suffering and neglect. Rather than being trained and returned to their homes, the mentally retarded were soon forgotten—out of sight, out of mind. Then came a great push toward special education classes in the schools, but this resulted in the mentally retarded being isolated within the school. Currently the move is toward putting them in regular classes during much of the day. We have thus come full circle with the treatment.

As usual, the best treatment is prevention. When we know the cause of the disorder, we can frequently prevent it. Prevention of damage to the brain at birth or any other time and prevention of cretinism can reduce the number of retarded individuals. Prenatal care of the mother and reducing our use of lead in paint and gasoline can prevent more.

Conclusion

We have seen that the general course of human development is from animal-like to God-like, and that our goal as Christian counselors is to aid individuals in this development. Disorders may occur to retard either physiological or spiritual development. It is our task to determine the nature of the problem and prevent or treat it if possible. We must not get so caught up in our culture that we are unable to take a Christian perspective on developmental tasks throughout the life-span.

Suggested Readings

Developmental Psychology textbooks are suggested as good material to elaborate on material presented in this chapter. Chapters on "Developmental Psychology" in general psychology textbooks are also recommended, as are the "Disorders of Childhood" or "Disorders of Childhood and Adolescence" chapters in Abnormal Psychology textbooks. Bootzin and Acocella (1980), Coleman, Butcher, and Carson (1980), Koteskey (1980), Leukel (1976), Munsey (1980), Perry (1974), Piaget and Inhelder (1966/1969), and Schell and Hall (1979) expand on material presented in this chapter.

SENSATION

One major area of interest to psychologists has been the study of how humans come into contact with their environment, how they become aware of the world around them. As you look at the title of the chapter, you might ask why psychology looks at sensation, since psychology is the science of behavior and mental processes. Sensation qualifies in both respects. When energy strikes an appropriate receptor, the receptor initiates a neural impulse which is a response, or a behavior. These impulses usually result in other responses, but not all are as immediately obvious as those following sitting on a tack or touching a hot stove. Sensation is also a mental process, as it is the way in which we come consciously into contact with the world around us. Imagine what your mental processes would be without any of your senses. A very important reason for studying sensation is that our sensations become organized into perceptions that largely determine how people behave. If we can understand how people perceive their world, we have come a long way toward understanding their behavior.

Sensation refers to the stimulation of the receptors, the neural impulses in the sensory neurons, and the things (sounds, colors, and so forth) of which a person is consciously aware and can report to others. We are created beings, like animals, so our sensory receptors and neural connections to

Figure 5:1 Sensation and sensory disorders from a Christian perspective.

HUMANS

Created............	in the............	Image of God
Like Animals		Like God
Overt Behavior........	Definition........	Mental Processes
Understand...........	Goals...........	Make People
Creation		Like God
Psychoanalysis........	Systems........	Humanistic
Behaviorism		Psychology
	Experimental........	Methods........	Descriptive
(DISORDER)		(DISORDER)
Organic Disorders........	Physiological........	Structure........	Spiritual........	Spiritual Disorders—Sin
(Organic Mental Disorders)		(Personality Disorders)
Physical Disorders........	Immaturity........	Development........	Maturity........	Spiritual Immaturity
(Disorders Appearing in Childhood or Adolescence)		(No DSM-III Category)
SENSORY DISORDERS...SENSATION........	AWARENESS........
(SOMATOFORM DISORDERS)	

the brain are very similar to those of animals. Sensation can be placed in our Christian perspective, as shown in the lower central part of Figure 5:1 (Sensation—Awareness). In fact, a great deal of what we know about our senses was learned from the study of animals.

Since sensation is so important in our behavior and mental processes, Christian counselors should know how the senses operate and be alert to disorders in them. Odd as it may seem, people who have sensory defects do not realize it until someone else detects differences in their behavior or mental processes. If people have never had a particular kind of sensory experience, they do not even know what they are missing. Try describing what "red" is like to someone who is completely color-blind, or a great choir singing the *Messiah* to someone deaf from birth. If the individual has gradually lost sensory sensitivity, he or she may not be aware of the loss. Many people cannot see well or hear well and are not even aware that they have a problem because the change has been so gradual.

Structure

As we relate sensation to the subject areas above it in Figure 5:1, we see that our senses are very much like those of animals, anatomically and physiologically. In terms of the stimuli to which we are sensitive, we are very similar to animals. Our eyes respond to about the same portion of the spectrum as animals do, our ears to about the same frequencies as animals, our skin to about the same temperatures and pressures, and so forth.

Our receptors are very similar to those of animals. Gregory (1973) notes that various primitive eyes all have the same basic plan, that of a lens forming an image on a set of receptors that are sensitive to light. Human eyes are typical vertebrate eyes. Although the external structure of our receptors for hearing (what we call our "ear") is quite different from that of animals, the receptors themselves, in the cochlea where the neural impulses are generated, are very similar to those in animals.

The physiological responses, which take place in the rods and cones of the eyes and in the hair cells of the cochlea, are similar in humans and animals. Even the pathway from the receptors to the brain is remarkably similar. With all of these anatomical and physiological similarities, it is little wonder that sensation is a major topic in physiological psychology. We should know how the senses work and the pathways to the brain so that we can determine the origin of sensory disorders and then give appropriate treatments or refer a client to someone who can treat the disorders.

Development

The senses change over the course of human development. Newborn infants apparently have all their senses, but most of their senses are less developed than those of adults. Infants can see, but they probably see rather blurred images at first and do not have full visual capacity until about six months of age. At just a few days old, they can hear as faint a sound as most adults, but their pitch discrimination takes some time to develop. Little is known about how much infants can taste, but taste sensitivity is not fully developed until the age of puberty. Newborns can also respond to odors very well.

Birren (1964) summarizes vast amounts of data on the psychology of aging. He notes that older people cannot see as clearly or see in as dim a light as younger people can. With increasing age, in our society people suffer a general decline in hearing for all frequencies, with an even greater hearing loss in the higher frequencies. Other senses show similar declines. We must be careful not to expect too much of the older person in the areas of sensory sensitivity and discrimination.

These physical declines are nothing new. One finds a rather complete description of these in the poetic language of the first seven verses of Ecclesiastes 12. Visual problems that accompany increasing age are found in the passage where both Isaac and Jacob are described as having eyes that were dim. When the priest Eli grew old, he had visual problems and was blind at the age of 98.

Sensory Deprivation

We have noted how sensory stimulation affects our behavior, but what happens to a person who is deprived of sensory stimulation? For many years, shipwrecked sailors, arctic explorers, and even airline pilots on intercontinental flights have reported their minds' playing "tricks" on them after long periods of unchanging sensations. Their minds wander, they find it difficult to maintain attention, and some even report seeing things that are not there.

Heron (1957) reports how this phenomenon has been investigated in the laboratory under controlled conditions. Volunteer college students were paid simply to lie in bed and receive virtually no sensations. Rather than the anticipated pleasant interlude, the students experienced difficulty in concentration after a while, followed by sensing things that were not really there (hallucinations). The students had no control over this and asked to be released from the experiment after only a few days. In experiments removing even more stimuli, people could only stand it for only a few hours.

Apparently a changing sensory environment is essential for us to keep in contact with physical reality. If we do not receive the necessary input from our senses, our mind makes up perceptions of its own. Humans are a composite unity of spirit and matter, like both God and animals. If they do not receive normal input from their animal-like senses, their God-like perceptual processes seem to carry on anyway. They become increasingly removed from the physical reality around them.

Disorders

Disorders in sensation can result in marked abnormalities in behavior and mental processes. People with sensory problems may be mistakenly diagnosed as having psychological problems because they act and think so differently. We must be sensitive to the origins of such disorders so that we can give appropriate treatments. These sensory disorders can be placed in our perspective as shown in Figure 5:1.

Sensory Deficits

People who have sensory deficits are going to act differently from those who have average sensory capacities. As previously noted, sensory capacity generally declines with increasing age. However, in this section let us consider the effects of some specific types of sensory deficits.

Visual Deficits. Some visual deficits are of little consequence in our society, while others have more of an effect. For example, not being able to see in extremely dim light is not very important in our society, where quite bright light, even at night, is the rule. Nearsighted people have lenses that are too thick or eyeballs whose the retina is too far from the lens. Distant objects are blurred so that such individuals cannot see them clearly. Nearsighted people usually hold objects close to their eyes to read or work on them. Nearsightedness can bring about great changes in behavior and mental processes. These people may not be able to recognize people at a distance and may seem unfriendly. Nearsighted drivers may not be able to see oncoming cars and might pass dangerously. Nearsighted children may not be able to see work projected on a screen or written on a chalkboard and thus do poorly in school.

Farsighted people have lenses that are too thin or eyeballs in which the retina is too close to the lens. They typically hold books at arm's length to be able to read them because objects nearer the eye are blurred. Although the consequences are not as great as for nearsightedness, the abnormal stress of constant accommodation can cause fatigue and headaches. Due to a set of reflexes, the farsighted person may have a blurred image in one eye because it is out of focus. When this happens, the brain learns to suppress the input from one eye and rely on that from the other; a condition called amblyopia. We must be aware of such defects in children and refer them to ophthalmologists. If this condition is not discovered early enough, the input from one eye may be permanently suppressed, causing an irreversible partial blindness in it.

Auditory Deficiencies. Defects in hearing can also cause changes in behavior and thinking. Outer ear defects reduce the capacity to hear all frequencies. The auditory canal may become clogged with wax so that the sound waves cannot reach the eardrum. Problems may also arise in the middle ear. The eustacian tube may become infected and not be able to equalize the air pressure in the middle ear. A bony growth may form around one of the bones so that it cannot move, causing a loss in sensitivity to lower pitches. Defects in the inner ear are usually caused by damage to the hair cells or to the neurons. Such "nerve deafness" usually affects high pitches more than low. Such damage occurs when we hear sudden, very loud sounds or loud sounds prolonged for several hours. Guns, artillery, factories, and rock concerts can all do nerve damage, and such damage is permanent.

Auditory defects are even more difficult to detect than visual ones. People with these defects may seem to be inattentive, obstinate, or even retarded, when their problem is that they cannot hear what is going on around them. This happens not only with children, but also with older people who do not want to admit that their hearing is failing. We should always consider the possibility that the person we are counseling cannot hear well. We must not react with irritation at having to repeat things or overreact by talking too loudly.

Other Sensory Defects. Defects in other senses may also change behavior and mental processes. Taste receptors are not as sensitive after middle age, as gonadal hormones decrease. Some older people tend to lose interest in food, and this may be misconstrued as depression. Others add large amounts of seasonings to their food to keep it tasting the same as it did when they were younger. The extra sugar and salt they add may actually injure their health.

The sense of smell can be affected by substances in the nose. When we have a head cold or get water in our nose, our sense of smell decreases. Some air deodorants use chemicals that temporarily decrease our sense of smell. Since smell is involved in what we commonly call taste, loss of the sense of smell may result in a lack of appetite.

Damage to the cerebellum may result either in disturbances in balance or in tremors. For example, damage to one part causes intention tremor and overreaching or underreaching. The person's hand may be steady until he or she begins a voluntary movement, and then the tremor begins, along with a lack of coordination between precise movements and background movements. Such individuals should be referred to a physician to see if the deterioration can be halted.

Sensory Absence

For lack of a better term, I have called this section on the complete absence of any sensation from a given sense, "sensory absence." Any one of the senses can be completely lost, and this has an even more profound influence on behavior and thinking.

Blindness. Injury to the eyes or injury to the nervous system may cause total or partial blindness. Christian counselors should know the neural pathway to the brain so that they know where the damage has occurred and not confuse it with conversion disorders. Damage to one side of the occipital lobe of the brain will cause loss of sight in half of each eye. Damage to the optic chiasma will cause tunnel vision, with some loss in each eye. Damage to the optic nerve will affect only the one eye. Such individuals should be referred to ophthalmologists for treatment of physical problems, but counselors may help them adapt to their loss of vision.

Deafness. Since deafness is not immediately obvious to an

observer, the general public has failed to understand, and has been uninterested in, the great problems of the deaf. Undetected deafness in children may be interpreted as poor motivation, inattentiveness, or mental retardation. Children deaf from birth cannot acquire speech in the ordinary way, because they cannot hear the speech of others. This lack of language makes it difficult for such children to be integrated fully into the family and the broader society. Without common language, education is very difficult, and deaf children are usually several years behind their hearing contemporaries. Many methods exist for detecting deafness and severe hearing loss. We must always consider the possibility of deafness as a cause of the abnormal behavior we observe.

Psychological vs. Physical Disorders

Up to this point, we have discussed sensory disorders with physical causes. However, some similar disorders have no known physical causes, and Christian counselors should know enough about the functioning of the senses and the neural pathways to be able to tell the difference. Disorders in sensory functioning in DSM-III are called somatoform disorders, indicating that the person has bodily or physical symptoms for which no physical basis can be found. Some of these somatoform disorders involve feeling sensations for which there are no physical stimuli. Others involve the absence of sensations when stimuli are present and all senses are organically sound. Let us now consider the major somatoform disorders.

Conversion Disorder. Conversion disorders involve loss or impairment of some sensory or motor function. A wide range of symptoms is possible, as wide as for those of physical disabilities, except that there is no known physical problem. Conversion disorders are not "faked," but are involuntary responses, not under the person's conscious control. These disorders are different from psychophysiological (psychosomatic) disorders such as ulcers, in which the psychological factors have actually affected the physical condition.

Conversion disorders may include an amazing variety of sensory symptoms, all without any physical changes. These disorders may involve any of the senses, but blindness, deafness and loss of sensations in the skin are the most common. Loss of sensitivity, a partial loss of sensivity, or excessive sensitivity may occur. Not only may the external senses be affected, but so may a wide variety of sensations from within the body. Conversion disorders may also include motor symptoms such as paralysis or speech disturbances.

We should know enough about the senses to be able to distinguish between organic disorders and conversion disorders. For example, if people have blindness in the right half of each eye, it is likely that something is wrong neurologically. If a counselee reports numbness in the thumb and index finger and it goes part of the way up the arm, a physical problem is likely present. However, if they have a selective blindness in one eye so that, although they do not report seeing anything, they still can walk without running into things, they probably have a conversion disorder. If they report a "glove anesthesia" or a "wristband anesthesia," they have a conversion disorder, because there is no way they could have that set of symptoms from damage to the nervous system. Of course, people with conversion reactions can describe the symptoms with little anxiety, at least with much less fear than patients with organic damage. The symptoms may also be changed or removed under hypnosis or when the person is suddenly awakened from a sound sleep.

Psychogenic Pain Disorder. People with a psychogenic pain disorder report severe and lasting pain for which there is no apparent physical basis, or is much greater than would be expected from the physical damage done. The pain sensations are often located in the area of some vital organs, such as the heart, the lower back, or the arms or legs. These people go from one doctor to another trying to find someone who can find the source of the pain or at least give them some strong pain-killing drugs. Unfortunately, many of these people become physically disabled through addiction to their pain-killing drugs or through the effects of operations they have been able to persuade some surgeon to perform. Note that this is a sensory disorder in that these people keep feeling pain, even though there is no physical basis for such sensations.

Hypochondriasis. People with hypochondriasis have many complaints about physical illnesses, are preoccupied with their health, and are greatly afraid of disease. These individuals report a great many uncomfortable and unusual sensations anywhere in the body, but most often in the areas of the stomach, the chest, the head, and the genitals. These people have difficulty precisely describing their sensations. They may begin by describing them as a pain, then say that it is really not a pain, but a gnawing sensation, and so forth. Hypochondriacs often describe sensations which they believe would be symptoms of particular diseases. They frequently believe they are suffering from serious diseases, such as cancer, and may begin reporting symptoms suggested by the counselor. Although they believe they are seriously ill, they usually do not show the fear that would be expected of someone who had that disease. We should be alert for this adding of symptoms (sensations) and the lack of concern.

In all of these somatoform disorders, we have found great changes in sensations in the absence of a physical stimulus. Sensations may be increased or decreased. Since conversion disorders, psychogenic pain disorders, and hypochondriasis all involve these changes in sensations, the somatoform disorders can be placed in our Christian perspective as shown in Figure 5:1. They are not sensory disorders in the sense of being physical disorders, but they involve changes in sensations. People who have these disorders may also develop spiritual disorders when they become angry, resentful, or just confused.

Treatment

After determining the causes of the disorders, we must see that the counselee receives appropriate treatment. We must be careful to detect sensory disorders as sensory, problems to be treated by physicians or optometrists, rather than seeing these disorders as mental retardation or learning disorders to be treated by psychologists or educators. Let us now consider appropriate treatments for each of the disorders discussed.

Correction of Deficits

As people experience a sensory decline with aging, we must help them to see that this is something to be expected and that there is nothing "wrong" with these signs of aging. Some people refuse to wear bifocals or hearing aids because they believe that others will think they are getting old. They do not realize that others are even more sensitive to their deficits of poor eyesight or poor hearing.

Correction of Vision. Nearsightedness can be corrected by wearing corrective concave lenses, either in the form of glasses or in the form of contact lenses right on the cornea. Surgical correction is also possible, but not widely done. Farsightedness can be corrected in similar ways, except that the lenses used are convex to focus the light waves. It is extremely important that amblyopia be detected and treated early, so that the visual disorder will not become permanent. Since the input from one eye is being suppressed by the brain, we can force its use by partly or completely blindfolding the dominant eye for a part of each day. Of course, correction of vision is not our primary concern, but we must be sensitive to visual problems and may need to help treat behavioral or mental disorders arising from the poor vision.

Correction of Hearing. The best treatment of hearing disorders is prevention. That is, people who take care of their ears by not putting things into them, treating infections immediately, and avoiding loud sounds are not as likely to have hearing disorders. In general, transmission deafness caused by problems in the outer or middle ear can be corrected. Wax in the auditory canal can be carefully removed so that the sound waves reach the eardrum. Plastic "bones" may be used to replace natural ones in the middle ear, repairing transmission deafness. Regardless of what one reads in the popular press, nerve deafness cannot be cured. Damage to the hair cells and neurons is permanent. A prescription hearing aid corrects one's hearing like prescription lenses correct one's vision, but it does not "cure" it. Since nerve deafness cannot be cured, prevention is important. We should refer such people to physicians, but may also treat secondary problems.

Other Sensory Deficits. Although nothing can be done about the taste receptors in older persons, increasing their intake of "trace" metals such as zinc and copper seems to make the individual's sense of taste more sensitive. Furthermore, since there is sour and bitter sensitivity in the roof of the mouth, the upper plates of dentures can be designed to let the taste stimuli reach the palate. We must caution counselees about increasing their intake of salt and sugar, which may be harmful to them in other ways. Most disorders of the sense of smell involve temporary conditions that keep the stimulus from reaching the receptors. The best thing to do is wait for the cold or allergy to clear up, or to treat the allergy. Damage to the cerebellum is permanent, and no treatment is available at the present time.

Sensory Absence

Blindness caused by damage to the retina or to the nervous system is permanent, and the best treatment is to help the person accept the disorder and learn to get along in the world. Many aids are available for the blind, ranging from "talking" calculators to seeing-eye dogs. Most blind people can learn to use the input from other senses to get around well. Deafness is more difficult to treat. We must be quick to pick up the nature of this disorder and work to help the person learn a language. Help is available for the deaf, and there is even a college for the deaf. Most states have special schools for the deaf, schools to which deaf individuals can be referred.

Somatoform Disorders

Up to this point, we have been able to talk about an appropriate treatment for each disorder. However, we have now reached the point where there is no particular treatment. Nearly all types of psychotherapy are used to treat these disorders, but none with remarkable success. In this instance, psychology is long on diagnosis, but short on cure. Rather than seeing these somatoform disorders as sensory disorders, most psychologists believe that the individual is experiencing psychological stress as a physical symptom, usually as a way to escape the stressful situation. Let us consider some methods of treatment for these disorders.

The symptoms of conversion disorders can be removed through hypnosis or narcosis interviews. The psychologist can then attempt to remove the stressful conditions that seem to be responsible for the disorder. He or she should then discourage the person from coping with stress by getting sick again. Finally, he or she should teach the person more appropriate methods for dealing with stress, methods that include greater reliance on God. Although conversion reactions are dramatic and were widely discussed during the last century, they are relatively rare today in better-educated individuals.

Psychological treatment of psychogenic pain disorders has not been very successful. People with these disorders believe their pains are physically based and will not accept a psychological interpretation. Since many doctors make no distinction between psychogenic pain and organic pain, they treat all pain the same. Therefore, many of these people have medical complications, such as addiction to pain-killing drugs. In recent years, behavior modification has been increasingly used to treat "pain behavior." We need to reduce or eliminate the rewards these people get for being sick and treat them much as we treat those with conversion disorders.

Hypochondriacs are quite resistant to treatment. If they are told that nothing is organically wrong with them, they look for a new physician or psychotherapist. However, they are usually willing to continue treatment as long as the physician or psychotherapist is willing to listen to their many complaints. They can be treated as one would treat those who have the other somatoform disorders.

From our perspective of seeing the somatoform disorders as sensory disorders, we need to develop an appropriate treatment. As a matter of fact, no type of psychotherapy has been developed emphasizing sensation. The closest thing would be behavior modification, in which the sensation would be viewed as the stimulus in a stimulus-response model. Behavior modification will be discussed in chapter 8.

Conclusion

In this chapter we have added another part of general psychology, that of sensation, to our Christian perspective. It is important that Christian counselors know the structure of the receptors and the neural pathways to the brain so that they can determine what is wrong with their counselees, whether it is organic or psychological. They also need to know what, if anything, can be done about the disorders so that they can make appropriate referrals. They also need to develop adequate treatments for the somatoform disorders.

Suggested Readings

The "Sensation" chapters in general psychology textbooks are recommended reading. A number of books are available on "Sensation" or "Sensation and Perception," but they all tend to be too technical and detailed. Chapters on "The Senses" in physiological psychology texts are usually good, as are chapters on the "Somatoform Disorders" in abnormal psychology textbooks. Bootzin and Acocella (1980), Brown and Wallace (1980), Coleman, Butcher, and Carson (1980), Koteskey (1980), and Leukel (1976) expand on material discussed in this chapter.

PERCEPTION

The sensations we talked about in chapter 5 do not enter a blank nervous system. The central nervous system is not simply a passive receiver of stimulation, but reacts in an integrated manner to these inputs. Current sensations interact with memories of past experiences. Motivations, emotions, and expectations all contribute to the interpretation of the sensations. The organization and elaboration of these sensations into meaningful wholes is the process of perception. The sensations essentially provide the "raw data" for the perceptions, but these raw data are then combined with the mental processes to create the world we experience. It is not likely that any of us can experience a "pure sensation," because any sensation we have is automatically elaborated upon.

In lower animals, the patterns of reaction to sensations seem to be innate. In higher organisms, especially humans, these reactions are organized and altered by learning and thinking. When talking about sensation, we said that humans were quite animal-like, but now that we are talking about perception, we are talking about the more God-like aspects of humans, as shown in the lower central part of Figure 6:1 (Awareness—Perception). This is not to say that animals do not also organize their world, but to say that human beings do it in a more meaningful, cognitive way than animals. We are made in God's image, and this has an influence on how we perceive the world around us.

Figure 6:1 Perception and perceptual disorders from a Christian perspective.

HUMANS

Created..............in the..............Image of God
Like Animals .... Like God
Overt Behavior.........Definition............ Mental Processes
Understand................Goals............. Make People
Creation ....Like God
Psychoanalysis............Systems................Humanistic Psychology
Behaviorism

(DISORDER)..............Experimental..............Methods..............Descriptive..............(DISORDER)
Organic Disorders.............Physiological..............Structure..............Spiritual..............Spiritual Disorders—Sin
(Organic Mental Disorders) ....(Personality Disorders)

Physical Disorders.............Immaturity..............Development.............Maturity.............Spiritual Immaturity
(Disorders Appearing in Childhood or Adolescence) ....(No DSM-III Category)

Sensory Disorders.............Sensation..............AWARENESS...... PERCEPTION......PERCEPTUAL DISORDERS
(Somatoform Disorders) ....(PARANOID DISORDERS)

Perception enables us to organize the many incoming impulses into some stable form or figure. We do not perceive the world around us as bits of color, brightness, loudness, or pitch; we perceive *things* around us. We see houses, trees, and people. We hear trains, animals, and words. The most fundamental perceptual process is the capacity to form figures and see (or hear) them on a background. Certain stimuli are seen as belonging together to form an object (figure) that stands out from the background, which seems to be relatively formless and extends continuously behind the figure. The figure seen or heard often depends on the past experiences of the observer and what he or she is expecting to see. Furthermore, through selective attention, our brains select only certain stimuli to which they will attend. We need to realize that different people perceive the world differently, depending on what they are expecting to see. Counselors and counselees may perceive their counseling relationship quite differently from each other. Christian counselors will find the same thing when counseling families. Husbands and wives or parents and children may view the same situation quite differently. It is extremely important to find out how different people involved view the problem.

Although the retinal size, shape, brightness, and color of objects constantly change, we do not perceive the world around us as full of such kaleidoscopic changes. Instead, we perceive it as stable. This stability of the world as we experience it, even though our retinal images of objects are changing greatly, is called perceptual constancy. If we analyzed the pressure variations reaching our ears during a normal conversation, we would conclude that it is a miracle that we understand each other at all. It may be that some people have trouble forming a stable, constant world, but live in a kaleidoscope of changes. We must remember that not everyone is able to put speech sounds together to form a language or a tune. Although they can hear all the sounds, they cannot organize them into a meaningful perception. Both the art and the thinking of disturbed individuals seem to indicate severe perceptual problems.

Spiritual Perception

We have already seen how perception is intimately related to sensation, and thus to all the topics listed above sensation in Figure 6:1. Let us now consider how perception is related to the areas above itself in Figure 6:1. As was pointed out in chapter 3, we are spiritual beings, and thus we are capable of spiritual perception. Things are not always as they appear to be. When the King of Syria sent a great number of horses and chariots that surrounded the city where Elisha was, Elisha's servant was very frightened. Then Elisha asked God to open the servant's eyes so that he could see that those with him were more than those against him. The servant then saw that the mountain was full of horses and chariots of fire around Elisha.

The best examples of spiritual perception are summarized in the "faith" chapter, Hebrews 11. Faith is defined as perceiving as real fact that which is not revealed to the senses (Amplified). It is by faith that we can understand that the world we see is framed by the Word of God: the things we see were made out of things not visible. Noah was warned by God about things not yet seen and he responded to this warning by building an ark, which saved him and his family. Moses left Egypt because he endured as one who saw him who is invisible, God. Many more individuals could be cited from this chapter who saw through the eyes of faith. We need to develop our spiritual perception, and our counselees', because we read that without such faith it is impossible to please God. Since faith may be a special form of perception and since perception depends on past experiences, faith too, depends on past experience. Just as perception is modified by experience, faith is changed by experience.

Our ordinary perceptions are initiated by sensory stimuli. Many people believe that humans can perceive objects without making use of the usual stimuli of light, sounds, temperature, pressure, chemicals, and so forth. This capacity to perceive without making use of these known sensory inputs is called extrasensory perception. Although many Christians have rejected extrasensory perception as a part of occult mysticism, from our perspective, we see at least some of ESP as an aspect of the image of God in humans, a type of spiritual perception. Since humans are made in God's image, they can communicate with him in an extrasensory manner.

Developmental Changes in Perception

Perception develops with maturation, but even infants are able to perceive things, as shown by their changes in attention. For example, Fantz (1961) found that infants in the first six months of life spent twice as much time looking at a bulls-eye or print as at brightly colored, but unpatterned, discs. Furthermore, they would spend three to four times as much time looking at a pattern of a human face.

Children (ages 2-7) have an egocentric viewpoint—they cannot take the point of view of another person. For example, you can take children to the front of the house with you and have them look at the house. Then send them over to the side of the house and ask them to describe what the house looks like from where you are standing. They will be unable to describe it in any way different from what it looks like from where they are at the moment. At this age, children do not seem even to realize that things may look different from a different perspective. As Christian counselors, we must not expect people to see things above their developmental level, but we should urge and aid their development.

Disorders

Perceptual disorders can cause marked changes in behavior and mental processes. These perceptual disorders fit into our Christian perspective as shown in Figure 6:1. These can range from deficits whose cause is obvious to disorders whose cause we do not know. A person with one eye or one ear may have problems with spatial perception. A person with two eyes has all the cues available to a person with one eye, plus the extremely important cues of retinal disparity. In this, the two eyes get slightly different images of a three-dimensional world and the brain then integrates the differences to enable us to see depth. However, even people with one eye can learn to use certain cues to make very accurate judgments of depth.

Our capacity for selective attention may lead to problems in other parts of our lives. People attending to one thing may be unaware of other important events around them and not respond appropriately. For example, students may be daydreaming about some anticipated event and not hear the teacher call on them. A husband may be concentrating on a television football game so intently that he does not even hear what his wife says, even though he says, "uh-huh." People walking down the sidewalk may be lost in thought so that they do not even see their friends. Their friends may conclude that they have been snubbed, when they were never even perceived. A major part of treatment, then, becomes checking out perceptions against reality.

Brain Damage

Some perceptual disorders are known to be caused by brain damage. These are truly perceptual disorders, because the people are receiving all the sensations, but just cannot put all of these sensations together into a meaningful whole.

Agnosia. Agnosias are disturbances in the perception of the significance of sensory stimuli. Individuals with agnosias receive sensations, but do not understand the information presented to them. For example, they may have normal touch sensitivity but be unable to recognize objects or forms by touch. They can tell you that they are touching something, but not be able to say whether it is a ball or a block. When they reach into their pocket, they cannot tell whether they have grasped their comb or their pencil. This condition is called astereognosis. People may also have auditory agnosia, in which they have a deafness for noises and music deafness, even though their hearing of simple tones is normal.

Visual agnosias also occur. Some people may have visual object agnosia, meaning they are unable to recognize familiar objects. There is no blindness or even loss of visual acuity, but these people cannot combine the parts of an object to recognize it. A person looking at a picture of a pair of eyeglasses may note that it has two circles with a bar connecting them and conclude that it is a bicycle. Color agnosias also occur, in which the victims are not color blind, but they have difficulty in understanding color as the quality of an object. Other people have a spatial agnosia, in which they have difficulty in getting around in the world. They do not recognize even familiar landmarks in their environment. They make frequent wrong turns, and even become lost in their own homes. Some people have prosopagnosia, in which they have difficulty recognizing human faces. They may not even recognize themselves in the mirror.

Sensory Aphasia. Aphasia refers to disorders of language resulting from brain damage. People with sensory aphasia have difficulty understanding language, even though their eyes and ears are functioning normally and they do not have any agnosias. Victims of auditory aphasia (word deafness) have difficulty understanding the meaning of language as heard. These people may have normal hearing levels, express themselves normally in both speaking and writing, and read normally, but they cannot understand the spoken language. This happens when certain pathways to the auditory cortex are damaged.

Other individuals may have a visual aphasia (word blindness, alexia) in which the perception of written language is difficult. Although these individuals have normal vision, express themselves normally in both speaking and writing, and can carry on a normal conversation, they cannot read anything. In fact, they may be able to write but be unable to read what they have just written. Such disorders are caused by damage to some parts of the brain.

Hallucinations

Hallucinations are perceptions of objects or events without any appropriate sensory stimuli. That is, people "perceive" things that are not really there. These hallucinations are perceptions (not sensations) because they are organized, integrated experiences, rather than flashes of light, bits of sound, or tactile sensations. These disorders fit into our Christian perspective on the God-like side because they are basically disorders in perception.

Hallucinations are one of the major symptoms of psychotic disorders. They indicate a major break with reality because people perceive things that are not there. Hallucinations may be caused by a variety of things, such as extreme fatigue, drugs, high fever, brain pathology, demonic forces, and sensory deprivation. They can also occur in nearly any of the senses, although the visual and the auditory hallucinations are the most common.

Auditory hallucinations involve hearing. People with such hallucinations may hear voices telling them what to do, criticizing their actions, warning them of punishment, or saying socially unacceptable things. These voices may come from "friends" commenting favorably on their actions, from "enemies" persecuting them, or from "God" giving them a major assignment to help humanity. Sometimes they do not know who is talking. The voices may come from any object in the room, from a nonexistent telephone held to the ear, or even from all directions.

Although auditory hallucinations are the most common, other senses may be involved. People with visual hallucinations may see angels or the devil, heaven or hell, or just clouds floating around the room. They may see other people or animals attacking them, or even pornographic pictures. People with olfactory hallucinations smell things that are not there, such as poison gasses being pumped into their room to kill them. Individuals with gustatory hallucinations taste nonexistent things, such as poison that has been put in their food to kill them. Finally, those with tactile hallucinations feel nonexistant things, such as roaches or snakes crawling all over their skin.

Normal people are able to have vivid images in the different sensory modalities in about the same proportions as psychotics can. People with eidetic imagery (photographic memory) are able to look at a page in a book, then close the book and read the page from their image of it. About half of the normal population can experience vivid auditory images, just about the same proportion as reported by some categories of psychotics. Mintz and Alpert (1972) have proposed that such psychotics do not differ from normal people in terms of having imagined perceptions, but in their inability to distinguish between these and experiences due to external stimuli. Normal people can tell the difference between imagined and real experiences, while psychotics cannot make this distinction.

Paranoid Disorders

A look at DSM-III for disorders in which the main problem seems to be one of perception leads us to look at the paranoid disorders. We can place these in our Christian perspective, as shown in Figure 6:1. The key features of the paranoid behaviors are a pervading suspicion and distrust of others, along with the conviction that the intentions and behaviors of other people are hostile. Thus, the basic problem of those with paranoid disorders is that their perception of the world is distorted. If you accept their basic perception of the world, their behavior makes a great deal of sense. In fact, many people with paranoid disorders make a relatively good adjustment to life, even while living with the belief that they are being persecuted.

Paranoia. Paranoia involves an intricate, logical, highly

organized delusional system. It is relatively rare in mental hospitals, but may occur more frequently in the general population. Except for this disordered perception, such people seem quite normal and can function in society. They are often jealous, persecuted, or exploited—at least they perceive themselves in this way. They feel mistreated, taken advantage of, spied on, ignored, stolen from, and so forth. They usually blame other people for their problems. They may become dangerous if they decide to take action against those they believe are persecuting them.

People with paranoia are able to marshal a great deal of evidence to justify their way of interpreting the world. Although the evidence is tenuous, inconclusive, and circumstantial, the paranoid will not accept another way of interpreting it. In fact, when the counselor questions the interpretation, that only convinces paranoids that the counselor is against them too. This, of course, makes sense if one accepts their perception of the world. Although hallucinations play no prominent role in paranoia, it may well be that these delusions bring order and meaningfulness to an otherwise disordered series of sensations. Paranoia is still a perceptual disorder, an erroneous interpretation of the perceptual world.

Other Paranoid Disorders. The acute paranoid disorder has transient, changing delusions. This is often related to some stress in people's lives and tends to disappear when stress is removed. Acute paranoid disorders develop more rapidly than paranoia, and their victims do not have the highly logical, systematized view of the world.

A shared paranoid disorder is one in which two (or more) people share the same paranoid thoughts. These are usually two people who are very close emotionally, and who gradually develop a mutual way of interpreting the world. Shared paranoia may even develop in larger, isolated, highly interdependent groups who believe they are being persecuted by other groups.

Paranoid schizophrenia is similar to the acute paranoid

disorder. It is, however, dominated by absurd, illogical, and changeable delusions. Such persons may believe they are being watched, followed, poisoned, or influenced by thought waves sent by enemies. This schizophrenic is not as withdrawn as other schizophrenics and may be able to live in society.

Paranoid states are often involved in other disorders. For example, one of the personality disorders (Axis II) is the paranoia characterized by suspicion, rigidity, argumentativeness, envy, and a tendency to blame others for problems. Such individuals are aware of power and rank, envying those in such positions and disliking those who seem soft or weak. They are always expecting to be tricked and are quick to interpret things that way.

We must take into account how our counselees perceive the world and try to determine the causes of perceptual disorders so that we can give appropriate treatments if available.

Treatment

After we have determined that the problem is a perceptual disorder, we can treat it as such. Sometimes the treatment is obvious. If the counselees have lost sight in one eye so that their depth perception is permanently affected, the treatment may be to teach them to use the monocular cues. Making them conscious of such cues and giving them practice using the cues can improve their depth perception.

Treatment for Brain Damage

If the disorder is due to brain damage, such as in agnosia or sensory aphasia, nothing can be done to repair the brain itself. As we learned in chapter 2, damage to neurons in the central nervous system is permanent. Although the neurons themselves are permanently damaged, some recovery of function may occur as other neurons apparently take over for the damaged ones. If counselees are suspected of having brain damage, they should be referred to a physician.

Psychotherapy

The most widely used treatment for hallucinations and the delusions which are a part of the paranoid disorders is the use of drugs. Drugs will usually remove these symptoms, but they do not bring about a lasting change. When the drugs are stopped, the symptoms return. We must look for a treatment that has longer lasting effects with fewer side effects. Since these are disorders in perception, we need to treat them as such, with an emphasis on restoring correct perception. Various psychotherapies are used to deal with hallucinations and with paranoid disorders, even though most of them do not emphasize changes in perception. Therefore, I have chosen to discuss therapies that emphasize such changes.

Although most psychotherapies do not view themselves as modifying perception, from our Christian perspective, we can interpret them in this way. The types of therapies that are most likely to emphasize a change in perception are those in the "third force." These humanistic-existential therapies work within a phenomenological framework. The premise is that we know "reality" only through our personal and subjective experience. In spite of the obvious importance of this phenomenological experience, psychology has tended to ignore it in attempting to be scientific.

Client-centered therapy. Rogers (1951b) has treated this subject specifically in his chapter, "Perceptual Reorganization in Client-Centered Therapy." He looks at both clinical and objective evidence of reorganization of visual perception, perception of others, and self-perceptions. Rogers' approach was first known as nondirective therapy, reflecting his concern with the techniques by which therapy was conducted. However, with the publication of *Client-Centered Therapy* in 1951, his approach changed and came to be known by this label. More recently he has expressed a preference for the term "person-centered," but it has not been generally adopted. Rogers kept the nondirective techniques, but began emphasizing the importance of his clients' perceptions, of entering his clients' world of subjective experience and focusing on their perceptions of themselves and others.

Rogers (1951b) discusses the process of therapy and its perceptual changes. Normal individuals have organized patterns of perceptions of themselves and themselves as related to others and the environment. Some of these perceptions may be incorrect with regard to objective reality, but as long as the individuals do not realize this, they serve adequately. As long as the self is firmly organized and no contradictory material is perceived, it is seen as worthy and acceptable. However, when the self is no longer able to meet the needs of reality and discrepancies are perceived, these people may deny or distort this inability. If they enter therapy in which they feel freed from threat, they begin to explore their phenomenal field to discover the faulty generalizations. They can then actually perceive the denied experience, reconstruct the self, and reperceive the self, including its new experiential element.

The direction this perceptual reorganization will take depends on the self-ideal, the self the person wants to be. Rogers (1951b) measured changes in self-perception. He measured the self and the self-ideal before, during, and after therapy. Before therapy the self and the self-ideal were quite dissimilar. After therapy, clients had become much more like the people they wanted to to be. Although therapy brought minor changes in what clients wanted to be, it brought great changes in the self. Thus, client-centered therapy is basically a process for changing perceptions. According to Rogers, therapists must be accepting, permissive, and nonjudgmental, so that they and their clients can explore the client's subjective world. Therapists are to accept, reflect, and clarify the meaning of the patient's feelings, playing a relatively passive role.

Gestalt Therapy. Although the term Gestalt was, perhaps, chosen too casually and prematurely to describe what Fritz Perls did, it is a widely used term. Perls had been trained in psychoanalysis, but came more into existential psychology through Goldstein. Although there are great differences between classical Gestalt psychology and Perls' Gestalt therapy, there are also some similarities.

Gestalt psychology was concerned with how people perceived their existence. Although he was not a Gestalt psychologist, Perls began urging his patients to alter their perspective or awareness as a means of changing their behavior. Thus, changing the current Gestalt meant the initiation of new behavior. For growth to occur there must be an increasing awareness of the here and now, and a greater readiness to accept the responsibility for one's actions.

Although Christian counselors cannot accept all of the assumptions or practices of client-centered therapy or Gestalt therapy, they must be aware that these therapies are doing something about altering the perceptions of individuals. From our perspective, it is crucial to correct the perceptions of our counselees so that they will have a more accurate view of themselves and their environment. "Reframing" is a popular technique used by counselors to change perceptions. Christ's parables were means of reframing, as was Nathan's parable to King David about the rich man killing the poor man and stealing his one sheep.

Defense Mechanisms

Students of general psychology often study long lists of defense mechanisms that are said to be good as protection from anxiety. They are told that everyone uses these mechanisms and that their use is acceptable as long as it is not carried to extremes. However, we must be very careful in advocating the use of defense mechanisms. Although they may enable us to go on with life by avoiding what we cannot face, we must not forget that they involve self-deception. The defense mechanisms do not alter objective reality, only the way we perceive or think about that reality. They may so distort our view of reality that they keep us from working to change that reality. Cameron (1951) noted that some of the defense mechanisms are really techniques of perceptual reorganization. Let us now consider some of the defense mechanisms that involve perception.

Projection. When using projection, we see others as responsible for our own shortcomings and as having our own unacceptable impulses. We blame the teacher for our failing the test or our parents for our wrong choices. If we have lustful thoughts, we perceive such thoughts in other people. Notice that this does not change us, it merely removes the responsibility for our failures or wrong desires from us and keeps us from dealing effectively with them. It changes our perception of ourselves without changing us.

Fantasy. By imagining that we have reached a goal, we can overcome our frustration of not having achieved it. In the conquering hero fantasy, we imagine that we are a renowned figure who performs an incredible feat. In the suffering hero fantasy we do not need to admit inferiority because we have tried in spite of suffering from some terrible disease or handicap. Although our performance has not been great, everyone realizes the courage it took to even try. Students in the frustration of exams and papers often fantasize about being a great surgeon, teacher, preacher, or politician. Again, the fantasy does nothing to change the reality; it only changes our perception of reality by removing us from it for a while.

Denial. Simple denial of reality by refusing to acknowledge it is probably the most primitive defense mechanism. We turn from unpleasant sights, refuse to discuss certain topics, deny criticisms, or get so immersed in our work that we cannot deal with our personal problems. People with life-threatening illnesses may deny that they fear death, or even the possibility that they may die soon. Denial, like other defense mechanisms, does not change reality, it just keeps us from working on our problem.

Rationalization. Rationalization involves giving "logical," socially approved reasons for behavior. Sometimes we use a "sour grapes" rationalization when we give a reason for not doing something we wish we could. The boy who has been turned down when asking for a date decides the girl was too fat anyway. Students doing poorly in school say they do not want to get caught in the rat race. Sometimes we use a "sweet lemon" rationalization as a reason for making a poor decision look good. Our "new" used car burns a quart of oil every one hundred miles so we talk about all its other good points, how nice it looks, how well it rides, and so forth. Again, our rationalizations do not change reality, only our perception of it.

As Christian counselors we must encourage our counselees to face reality rather than just changing their perceptions of it. We must point out the strategies they are using to deceive themselves and help them work on their real problems.

Conclusion

We have seen that perception fits into our Christian perspective as a God-like attribute of humans. Perception enables us to organize our sensations into a stable, coherent view of the world. We also have spiritual perceptions because we are spiritual beings and we communicate with God in an extrasensory manner. Perceptual disorders may arise because of damage to the brain. Hallucinations can be seen as perceptual problems in that they are perceptions in the absence of sensory stimuli. The paranoid disorders are basically perceptual disorders in which wrong interpretations are made of common events. No adequate treatment exists for perceptual disorders due to brain damage. Some types of psychotherapy can be seen as emphasizing perceptual change. Client-centered therapy and Gestalt therapy are examples. Finally, the defense mechanisms, often presented as normal methods of adjustment are not that, but are disorders of perception because they involve self-deception.

Suggested Readings

The "Perception" chapters in general psychology textbooks are recommended reading. Bartley (1969) is a good introduction to perception. Chapters on "Paranoid Disorders", and "Humanistic-Existential Therapies" in abnormal psychology textbooks are recommended. Agranowitz and McKeown (1964), Blake and Ramasey (1951), Brown (1972), Coleman, Butcher, and Carson (1980), Corsini (1973), Korchin (1976), Koteskey (1980), Rogers (1951a), and Stephenson (1975) expand on material presented in this chapter.

STATES OF CONSCIOUSNESS

Up to this point we have been talking about sensation and perception when the individual is awake and in a normal state of awareness. Psychologists have traditionally spent most of their time studying sensation and perception under these conditions, but in recent years many have turned to the study of sensation and perception under altered states of consciousness. As more people voluntarily altered their states of awareness by taking drugs and using different meditation techniques, psychologists became interested in sensation and perception under these conditions.

Although the study of consciousness was the initial subject matter of psychology, such study all but disappeared when behaviorism dominated psychology. Since Watson (1913/1968) knew of no objective way to study consciousness, he concluded that it must be discarded as a part of the subject matter of psychology. Although psychoanalysts did include consciousness as a component of the mind, it was a very small part and not nearly as important in determining behavior as the much larger unconscious. However, during the 1960s, many young people began experimenting with drugs and Eastern religions that altered consciousness. With these questions being raised about altered states of consciousness, psychologists began to turn their attention to these states and found some changes that could be studied by the methods of science.

From our Christian perspective we welcome this change, because consciousness is a God-like attribute of humans, as shown in the lower central part of Figure 7:1 (States of Consciousness). Of course, psychologists never eliminated the study of consciousness from psychology, because the study of sensation and perception is really the study of consciousness, but it is good to see it being recognized again. The organization of this chapter is slightly different from that of previous chapters. We will consider three altered states of consciousness, and each will be a mini-chapter in itself, with basic facts, disorders, and treatment.

Sleep and Dreaming

Sleep is not a state of total unconsciousness, because we all have dreams during the night and can carry out simple plans while asleep. Although many people say they consider sleeping a waste of time, they spend many hours sleeping when given the chance. We can lose a few hours of sleep one night, or even a whole night's sleep, and function normally the next day. However, if we try to miss several nights' sleep in a row, dramatic effects begin to occur. When one remains awake between 50 and 100 hours, one reaches a turning point where changes become severe, with the appearance of hallucinations.

Since we know that we do need some sleep, the next question is how much. There is no simple answer, although research has found some general facts. In general, the older you get, the less sleep you need. Infants may spend sixteen hours of each day in sleep, but this declines to about ten hours per day by ten years of age. The decline continues throughout life, so that most college students need about eight hours of sleep, but retired people function well on seven hours a night. However, individuals vary widely, so there is no point in trying to be average. If you need ten hours of sleep, including a nap, that is your particular need and you should get it. If you only need seven, there is no point to lying in bed the extra

Figure 7:1 States of consciousness and substance use disorders from a Christian perspective.

HUMANS

Created..................in the..................Image of God
Like Animals   Like God
Overt Behavior........Definition..........Mental Processes
Understand..............Goals..........Make People
Creation   Like God
Psychoanalysis..........Systems..............Humanistic
Behaviorism   Psychology

(DISORDER)   (DISORDER)
Experimental............Methods..............Descriptive
Organic Disorders............Physiological..............Structure..............Spiritual..............Spiritual Disorders—Sin
(Organic Mental Disorders)   (Personality Disorders)

Physical Disorders............Immaturity..............Development..............Maturity..............Spiritual Immaturity
(Disorders Appearing in   (No DSM-III Category)
Childhood or Adolescence)

Sensory Disorders............Sensation..............Awareness..............Perception..............Perceptual Disorders
(Somatoform Disorders)   (STATES OF CONSCIOUSNESS—   (Paranoid Disorders)
                                  SUBSTANCE USE DISORDERS)

hour. Trying to get eight hours is like trying to wear size ten or size seven shoes on size eight feet. We should tell our counselees to get the sleep they need, not some "average" amount.

During the study of sleep, psychologists noted that the eyes of a sleeping subject begin to make rapid movements periodically during the night. The two most basic stages of sleep now appear to be REM (rapid-eye-movement) sleep, and NREM (non-rapid-eye-movement) sleep, and we need both to function normally. At first, psychologists thought that dreaming took place only during REM sleep, but we have now found that dreaming takes place during both. Many people have asked what, if anything, dreams mean. Some think that dreams are simply confused, crude thinking like that done by senile people or people under the influence of some drug, such as alcohol. Others have argued that the contents of our dreams are influenced by the events we have experienced or are anticipating. The major theory for the interpretation of dreams is that of Sigmund Freud, the psychoanalyst. Freud believed that dream analysis was one of the major ways of investigating the contents of the unconscious.

DeBecker (1965/1968) reviews the role of dreams in Christianity as well as in other religions. He notes that there are about fifteen dreams recorded in the Old Testament, most of them coming at the beginning of vital stages in Israel's history. In the New Testament, dreams are again essential to the beginning of the Christian faith. Dreams are referred to as frightening things in some instances. In others, writers portray God speaking through dreams. In the prophecy of God's pouring his spirit on humanity, Joel noted that some would dream dreams and others would see visions. Since dreams are a way God has spoken to humans in the past, we should take a closer look at them. Rather than abandoning the interpretation of dreams to psychoanalysis, we need to examine the content of dreams from a Christian point of view. We must have a more positive view of dreaming; i.e., that it is a potential means of communication from God to humans. We must develop criteria for distinguishing between dreams from God and other types.

Disorders

Estimates indicate that as many as twenty-five percent of the population has problems sleeping. Treatment costs many millions of dollars a year. Sleeping problems often accompany other mental disorders, but frequently, the only complaint is the sleeping problem. Women report sleep disturbances more often than men, and older people report them more often than younger people.

Insomnia. Insomnia is the chronic inability to sleep that disturbs the person's daily functioning. Some people have great difficulty falling asleep when they go to bed. Others fall asleep rapidly, but awaken repeatedly throughout the night. Still others fall asleep rapidly and sleep well, but awaken very early and cannot fall asleep again. These sleep disturbances begin to worry the insomniacs, so they develop an anticipatory anxiety. When they go to bed, they begin to worry about whether or not they will get to sleep, whether or not they will sleep well, and so forth. The worry itself is enough to cause sleeping problems. Some people with insomnia wake up many times during the night because they cannot breathe. This occurs when the diaphragm does not contract properly, and when this happens frequently during the night, it can result in a very disturbed sleep, called central sleep apnea.

Narcolepsy. Other people have the opposite problem. Rather than having difficulty falling asleep or staying asleep, they have recurrent brief episodes of sleep during the day with a sudden loss of muscle tone without a clouding of consciousness. They have brief times of hallucinations while falling asleep, accompanied by a brief time of being unable to perform voluntary movements.

Enuresis. Enuresis is a lack of bladder control past the age when it should be achieved. Although daytime wetting does occur, it is quite rare. Bedwetting is more common. There is disagreement about how old children must be and how frequently the wetting must occur before it should be considered a problem. However, parents getting tired of changing wet pants, pajamas, and sheets, may react with anger or rejection and create problems if they do not already exist.

Sleepwalking. Sleepwalking afflicts from one to six percent of the general population and is much more common in children than adults. Sleepwalkers go to sleep normally and get out of bed an hour or two later without waking up. Their eyes are open, and they avoid obstacles, respond to commands, and perform quite complex actions. They may make a sandwich, rearrange books, or even get dressed and leave the house.

Sleep terrors. Sleep terrors are very bad dreams occurring during childhood. Children experiencing these may thrash about in their beds, give piercing screams, talk incoherently, and breathe rapidly. When awakened they may go on yelling and are confused, disoriented, and difficult to calm. Anxiety dreams, the common nightmares found in adults and children, are quite different. Reactions are much milder than in sleep terrors, and when awakened, the dreamers can remember much more of the dream. Of course, these dreams, if occurring frequently, can lead to insomnia, as can enuresis. The person may be afraid to go back to sleep for fear that the dream (or the wetting) may recur.

The sleep disorders are relatively common. Most people have an occasional night when sleep eludes them or they have an anxiety dream. This is little cause for concern, because the major problem with a lost night's sleep is sleepiness the next day. Counselees should not worry about occasional lost sleep. However, some treatments are available for those with chronic problems.

Treatment

Two difficulties can arise when a counselor is trying to treat sleep disorders. The first is in trying to treat a problem that does not exist. People may come to a counselor complaining that they are only able to sleep six hours a night, and then must lie there tossing and turning for two hours, waiting until it is time to get up. The only problem is that they think there is a problem; they believe that everyone should get eight hours of sleep a night. The second problem is that the cure may be worse than the disorder, if the cure includes the use of drugs. The fact is that most sleep-inducing drugs currently used are ineffective for long-term use, and they may be unsafe and habit-forming as well.

Insomnia. Many people believe they have insomnia when they do not. A few years ago, most people who complained about insomnia were given prescriptions for sedatives that were supposed to help them sleep. Unfortunately, this "cure" resulted in a new disorder, drug-dependent insomnia. As such individuals become more tolerant of the sleep-inducing effects of the drugs, they increase the dosage to get sleep, and most of the drugs are addictive. As the dosages increase, the people spend less and less time in REM sleep. When they try to withdraw from the sedatives, the REM sleep increases so that they have nightmares and disturbed sleep. Then, to get better sleep they take more pills.

If insomnia is caused by some other disorder, such as an anxiety disorder, we should treat the other disorder and let the insomnia take care of itself. If the problem is overarousal, so that the person has difficulty falling asleep, relaxation training, biofeedback, and procedures for strengthening the response of falling asleep may be helpful. Physical exercise early in the evening and good ventilation of the bedroom may help. Sometimes, telling the person to stay awake all night will result in sleep. Of course, insomnia is the side effect of many drugs, even nonprescription drugs. Drug-dependent insomnia is extremely difficult to treat because patients believe they have insomnia and need the drug. Several drugs may be used on inconsistent schedules with addiction resulting. Furthermore, sudden withdrawal of the drug can result in convulsions, and even after withdrawal is over, sleep disorders may continue for weeks or months. Unfortunately, in our search for sleep, we have produced many middle-aged drug addicts. No good treatment is available for central sleep apnea. People with this disorder particularly should not take sedatives of any kind. Since sedatives are a respiratory depressant, a combination of central sleep apnea and the drugs could prove fatal.

Narcolepsy. There is no good treatment available for this disorder. Amphetamines are often tried, but individuals quickly develop a tolerance for the drug and keep increasing the dosage to dangerous levels, often becoming addicted.

Enuresis. Enuresis may result from organic conditions, so patients should be examined by a physician first. If no organic problem exists, parents may consider some effective conditioning procedure. Battery-powered bedwetting alarms are available (Sears, Roebuck and Co.), which sound an alarm to wake the child when the first few drops of urine wet a sheet separating two foil pads. Awakening causes the children to inhibit urination then, and the bladder pressure soon becomes a conditioned stimulus to the response of awakening. This technique will not help organic problems and should not be used for ordinary toilet training.

Sleepwalking. Very little attention has been given to treating sleepwalking in terms of stopping it. However, a number of misconceptions about it exist. Sleepwalkers may be injured by falling downstairs or walking into the street. It is not dangerous to waken sleepwalkers. Although they are difficult to awaken and may be confused, they are not "crazy" or violent. The best thing is to wake them gently and get them back to bed.

Sleep Terrors. This type of bad dream is almost exclusively confined to childhood, so we need to help children through each episode and wait for maturity. Simply wake them, try to calm them down, and walk them around the room. Eventually they will go back to sleep and the next morning they will not even remember what happened. Anxiety dreams are common in adults and children and are a necessary part of sleep. Once

131

the dreamers are awakened, they become calm and rational and can tell that their dream was just a dream.

As Christian counselors, we must get at the source of the problem and treat it there. First, we must determine whether or not a problem really exists, then treat its source. We need to tell our counselees how much sleep is needed, help them stop worrying about getting less than "normal," and be honest in cases for which no treatment is available.

Drugs

Since ancient times, people have been smoking, sniffing, swallowing, and (during the last century) injecting chemical substances to relieve pain, relax, sleep, produce alertness, produce calmness, reduce anxiety, achieve insight, produce excitement, and briefly escape a harsh reality. During this time, societies have been trying to limit the use of these drugs by restricting their availability. Sometimes the legal sanctions seem quite arbitrary, because one drug is widely and legally available but quite dangerous, while other, less dangerous drugs are not available at all. Much of the questionable legality of drugs is the result of how many people use the drug before its effects are determined. For example, alcohol, caffeine, and tobacco are still legal drugs taken by millions of people, while cocaine and heroin are restricted and illegal.

Since we are interested in the effects of these drugs on states of consciousness, we will classify them with respect to their effects on the central nervous system. Since the central nervous system has a high rate of metabolism, it is more sensitive to drugs than are other cells of the body. Some drugs stimulate the activity of the central nervous system and are called *stimulants*. Others depress or slow down the system's activity and are called *depressants*. Still others disorganize the system's activity, bringing about a distortion of perception and thinking, and are called *hallucinogenic* or *psychotomimetic* (generating hallucinations or mimicking a psychosis) drugs.

Stimulants. Stimulants are substances that increase the

metabolic rate of neurons in the central nervous system and increase their excitability. Some stimulants have a generally exciting effect on the whole central nervous system, while others act selectively on certain parts. These stimulants often prevent sleep when affecting the brain. Following are some common stimulants and their effects.

Caffeine is an example of a mildly addicting cortical stimulant which is present in coffee, tea, cocoa, and many soft drinks. It increases the metabolic rate by ten to fifteen percent, gives a lift, increases heart rate, and increases blood pressure. Tobacco smoke acts as a stimulant, leading to increased activity in the sympathetic nervous system. It causes an increased heart rate, release of blood sugar from the liver, and so forth. Many smokers report that the act of smoking itself feels good, reducing tension and anxiety.

Amphetamines are synthetic drugs that mimic some of the effects of the arousal of the sympathetic nervous system. They are also a cerebral stimulant that combats sensations of drowsiness, and may lead to feelings of euphoria in larger doses. Cocaine is a central nervous system stimulant that causes mood swings from euphoria to depression and may even cause hallucinations.

Depressants. Depressants are drugs that depress activity in the central nervous system, resulting in drowsiness, unconsciousness, or coma. After taking depressants, one may feel an initial sensation of euphoria as the central nervous system combats their effects with overexcitation, but the effect of increased dosages is unconsciousness. Taking enough of any depressant will result in a loss of coordination and disordered thinking, because depressants usually affect the higher centers of the brain first. Following are some commonly used depressants.

Alcohol is a depressant used by the majority of American adults. The most notable effects of alcohol are the changes in behavior as a result of its action on the brain. Alcohol first depresses the frontal lobes of the brain, which inhibit aggressiveness and excessive activity. Thus some people think of alcohol as a stimulant when it is really a depressant. At higher levels of concentration in the blood, greater depression of the brain occurs, resulting in incoordination, confusion, disorientation, stupor, coma, or even death. Barbiturates are sedatives that produce a general depression of activity in the brain. They are available by prescription to calm patients or to induce sleep. In small doses such drugs have an effect similar to alcohol's, but large doses can cause coma or even death.

Codeine, morphine, and heroin all come from the opium poppy. They all can be used to kill pain, but are addictive. Heroin does not cause great changes in consciousness related to thinking or sensations, but primarily changes one's emotions. Immediately after injecting it intravenously, the user feels a "rush" or thrill that is intensely pleasurable. This is followed by a longer-lasting effect, which is best described as a general sense of well-being. There are no great changes in conscious experience, but anxiety is reduced. Users feel at peace and may alternate between wakefulness and sleep.

Hallucinogens. Some drugs disorganize the activity of the central nervous system so that they cause distorted perceptions or hallucinations. The most widely used minor hallucinogenic drug is marijuana, which produces a feeling of well-being and a dreamy, carefree state of relaxation at the usual low doses. The user also has altered perceptions, which include an expansion of space and time, along with a more vivid sense of touch, sight, smell, taste, and sound. LSD's hallucinogenic potential was discovered accidentally in 1943. Its discoverer reported feeling restless and dizzy, sinking into a delirium marked by extreme fantasy. He closed his eyes and saw brilliant visions. Others have reported that ordinary objects seem suddenly to have great beauty, with music taking on great emotional power. Visions of beautiful colors, patterns, and forms occur.

Disorders

Many disorders in DSM-III are associated with the use of drugs. In fact, one major category of organic mental disorders is called "substance-induced" disorders and includes everything from hallucinogens, to barbiturates and amphetamines, to alcohol, tobacco, and caffeine. In addition, an entirely separate category exists called "substance use" disorders, including most of the same drugs. Although consciousness is a God-like attribute of humans, since we are altering it by physiological means, we will place these substance use disorders between the God-like and the animal-like as shown in the lower central part of Figure 7:1 (Substance Use Disorders).

The effect of a given drug depends to some extent on the users of the drug and their past experience with it. Users of many drugs develop a tolerance to them so they must keep increasing the dosage to get the same effect. The steady use of some drugs can alter the functioning of the central nervous system so that it cannot function normally without the drugs. This is called addiction. Once such dependence is established, the users of the drug must continue to take it even to feel normal. They experience the painful process of withdrawal when they stop taking the drug, as the central nervous system adapts to functioning without it.

Stimulants. People who take too much of any stimulant may have a variety of symptoms, which get worse as they develop a tolerance for it. Caffeine is a legal drug that has been incorporated into our culture in such a way as to minimize its hazards, but even 7-10 cups of coffee a day can produce sleeplessness, restlessness, and tension. People habitually drinking that much coffee are likely to show withdrawal symptoms of depression, restlessness, and lethargy when coffee is withheld. Cigarette smoking is an addictive behavior. As tolerance to nicotine increases, so does the smoking of cigarettes, until the person is smoking several packs a day. When deprived of their cigarettes, smokers become drowsy, nervous, lightheaded, anxious, fatigued, and have headaches.

The habitual user of amphetamines must take ever-increasing doses as tolerance develops. Unfortunately, amphetamines do not supply energy, but only speed the expenditure of the body's resources. Repeatedly over-extending one's body in this way can lead to many serious physical symptoms, from ulcers to cerebral hemorrhage. The after-effects of an amphetamine high can be uncomfortable and dangerous, including fatigue, nightmares, confusion, depression, irritability, and aggression.

Of course, the question arises as to whether or not Christians should use stimulants or other drugs to alter states of consciousness. Since the Bible has nothing to say directly about the use of stimulants, Christians draw the line at many different places. As Christian counselors, we must make sure that our counselees (and we ourselves) can function normally without stimulants. If not, Christians should stop taking their stimulants until their central nervous system can function without them. Some individuals become dependent on coffee and have to "kick the habit" like any other addicted individual. Individuals need to be able to do more than *say* that they can do without their stimulant—they need actually to go without it for a few days to see if they can still function.

Depressants. Drinkers find that they must consume ever-increasing amounts of alcohol to produce the effects obtained with the original amount. Withdrawal symptoms may be moderate, such as weakness, tremors, anxiety, perspiration, and a craving for alcohol. They may also be serious, including nausea, vomiting, fever, convulsions, hallucinations, and delirium. Barbiturates are particularly dangerous when used with alcohol, because the effects of the two drugs are multiplied by a drug interaction in which the alcohol enhances the effect of the barbiturates. Overdoses of barbiturates often occur when the first dose is followed by a second and a third as the user becomes forgetful or uninhibited. Unconsciousness comes first, then the barbiturates so depress activity in brain centers controlling heart rate and respiration that death results. Addiction to heroin results within about three weeks, but there do not seem to be any major physiological changes other than the need for heroin itself. If people cannot get the drug after becoming addicted, they go through severe withdrawal symptoms including vomiting, repeated yawning, sweating, and even collapse.

As with stimulants, Christians disagree about the use of depressants. Although the Bible does not discuss most drugs, it does discuss the use of alcohol, pointing out that alcohol is a deceiver and drunkenness is a sin. Following our general principle of not allowing anything to control us, we would avoid the use of addicting drugs in quantities which would lead to tolerance and dependence. The National Institute of Mental Health (1968) says that the only absolute insurance against alcoholism or problem drinking is lifelong abstinence. Of course, there are other reasons for not drinking. From our Christian perspective there is little reason to drink alcohol. Rather than becoming more like God, people who have taken alcohol become less inhibited, less rational, less able to control their movements, and so forth. Many people oppose drinking on the basis of its social consequences. We need to help our counselees deal with their problems in some way other than by taking depressants.

Hallucinogens. Although inexperienced users of marijuana may experience little change in consciousness, there are still dangers in its use. Although there is no evidence that it is addicting in the physiological sense, many users become psychologically dependent on the drug rather than finding other ways to deal with their problems. Furthermore, the heavy use of marijuana is at least as damaging to the throat and lungs as cigarette smoking, and there is some evidence that it, too, may cause cancer. Although some LSD experiences are reported as being good, users may have a "bad trip" in which they experience anxiety and panic. Of course, such individuals want to leave the drug state as soon as possible, but they must simply wait until the drug is eliminated from the body. Although people under the influence of LSD report having dramatic insights into certain problems, such insights, when written down and reviewed when not on a trip, usually seem ridiculous even to the individual who had them.

From the perspective taken here, our goal is always to

become more like God. There seems to be little evidence that hallucinogens make us more like him. God is love, but people under the influence of drugs may be less aware of those around them, less merciful and compassionate. God is a rational being who invites us to reason with him, but people under the influence of drugs may become irrational and lose touch with reality. Rather than being a way in which people become more like God, drugs seem to be a form of escapism. Unable to face themselves and the world around them, people turn to such drugs.

Legal Drugs. Although we usually think of a drug abuser as someone who obtains drugs illegally on the street, an even larger problem is the abuse of prescribed drugs. It is amazing that the most widely prescribed drug (Valium) is not prescribed to combat infection or any physical disorder, but to calm individuals who cannot face their lives without some chemical help. The typical barbiturate addict is a middle-aged housewife or marginally-employed man who began taking them to relieve insomnia. Within two weeks the usual dose no longer gives a good sleep, so the dose is increased, and the vicious circle begins.

Since nearly everyone becomes depressed, anxious, or has trouble sleeping from time to time, the antidepressants, mild tranquilizers, and depressants are in wide use. These drugs are commonly prescribed by physicians whenever their patients request them. Of course, there may be times when we temporarily need such medication, but problems arise when we become even psychologically dependent on them. When we are tired, we take a pill to pep us up. When agitated, we take a pill to calm us down. The world does not seem to be such a threatening place after we have settled down with our tranquilizers. We must learn to face life with God at our side, rather than with a bottle of pills in our pocket.

Treatment

In spite of some reports to the contrary, the track record in treating drug abuse is not good. Although it is relatively easy to get people off their drugs, it is extremely difficult to keep them off. The withdrawal symptoms are over within a few days or a few weeks, but the rate of readdiction within the first year or two is very high. As is so often the case, the best treatment is prevention.

From our perspective, since the disorder was brought on by physical changes, the treatment would involve removing the substances that caused the physical changes. We also need to deal with the psychological or spiritual problems that led to the drug use; problems such as depression, stress, sin, loss of self-esteem, and so forth. Getting the alcohol out of the persons' systems and helping them through their withdrawal symptoms is called *detoxification*. This usually takes a week or less and is done in a hospital, using tranquilizers, vitamins, and anticonvulsants, if needed. Withdrawal from heroin addiction takes from three to five days and is not as devastating as novels and movies have depicted it, although it is probably worse than any discomfort the average person has experienced. Withdrawal symptoms from large doses of barbiturates may last for as long as a month but are usually over in a week or so. Withdrawal from barbiturates may be extremely dangerous, with convulsions and psychosis. Withdrawal from any drug should not be attempted without medical supervision. Although withdrawal from heroin rarely results in death, withdrawal from alcohol or barbiturates may do so.

Getting through the withdrawal symptoms is the easy part. Mark Twain said he could stop smoking with ease, and he had done so hundreds of times. In general, treatment programs show this same pattern. Although nearly twenty percent of the total annual cost of hospital care for adults is spent for alcoholics, even the most successful programs have a success rate of about forty percent in terms of a permanent cessation of drinking. Success rates may run as high as eighty percent when alcoholism is detected early, to near zero with hard-core alcoholics.

The high readdiction rate to heroin after the physical dependence is gone is well known. Such people seem to have an overpowering craving for the drug even though not physically dependent on it. Readdiction to barbiturates is not as severe a problem because this craving does not seem to be present. Although physical dependence may not occur with some drugs, such as amphetamines, there is a strong psychological dependence. Withdrawal from amphetamines is painless, but the person goes into a depression peaking 48-72 hours after the last dose. The depression eases after a few days, but mild feelings of depression may last weeks or months following the last dose, leaving the person ripe for beginning again.

Many different types of treatment have been tried, including psychotherapies of all kinds, behavior therapy, occupational therapy, relaxation training, group therapy, family therapy, and so forth. In some cases "treatment" of addiction consists of substituting one drug for another, such as methadone for heroin. The most successful programs involve lifetime follow-up. The most successful program for alcoholics is Alcoholics Anonymous (AA) which assumes that once people are alcoholics, they are always alcoholics, and that they cannot stop drinking alone. Alcoholics are seen as having a lifelong problem, so they must abstain from drinking and rely on AA for help through regular meetings and the buddy system. Residential treatment centers modeled after AA have been founded for treatment of the abuse of other drugs as well.

We must be aware that drug abuse programs meet with limited success. Although programs such as AA have a strong spiritual basis, they are not Christian forms of treatment in themselves. We need to take some of these principles and apply them in the church as the body of Christ. A commitment to God with an intensive, life-long follow-up in an intensive, warm, caring Christian fellowship can work. Perhaps even AA-type groups can be started in larger churches.

Other States of Consciousness

Although sleep, dreams, and drugs are the major current altered states of consciousness, many people are trying others. We will briefly consider a few here.

Transcendental Meditation

The leader of the Transcendental Meditation movement is Maharishi Mahesh Yogi, who left India in 1958 to begin a tour of the West. Within fifteen years he had inspired about a half million meditators. During a brief training, meditators are given a secret "mantra" (meaningless sound) to be repeated during meditation whenever their minds wander to concrete thoughts. The goal of meditators is unity with the impersonal god, and they reach this by the repetition of the secret mantra for twenty minutes each morning and evening. This leads to a state of consciousness without any specific objects or subjects, a state of unity with the impersonal god. According to the Maharishi's philosophy, the observable world is neither real nor unreal, but it is always changing. Meditators wish to go beyond all thought to a state of pure awareness.

Many people report only a sense of calmness when meditating, a state of being relaxed and relieved of the tensions of everyday life. However, some report more dramatic changes in consciousness. For example, subjects who meditated on a blue vase several times a week for three weeks came to see the vase as more vivid, or saw changes in the apparent size and shape of the vase. Some experienced a sense of merging with the vase. Others said that the vase seemed to take on a life of its own. They also reported tingling sensations or other unusual bodily sensations.

Disorders. Since meditators report pleasant states of relaxation and freedom from stress, should we as Christian counselors recommend it to our counselees? Maharishi Mahesh Yogi has founded Mahirishi International University (MIU) where he says higher consciousness is the goal of

141

higher education. In the fall of 1979, he began a new program where one could take a "junior year at MIU for growth towards enlightment" in the study of "Consciousness: the field of all possibilities."

Before we send our young people to MIU for a year of study, we should realize that Transcendental Meditation (the Science of Creative Intelligence) is really a form of Hinduism. Many people begin Transcendental Meditation without understanding the Hindu philosophy of religion behind it. The ultimate goal of meditators is to lose their individuality in pure Being, mere abstract Being. Transcendental Meditation is a version of the Hindu religion, and advanced meditators find themselves adopting Mahirishi Mahesh Yogi's Hindu philosophy.

Treatment. The first part of treatment, as usual, is prevention. Many Christians do not realize that Transcendental Meditation is a form of a different religion and simply see it as a good way to relax and reduce tension. Our first task is one of education so that they will realize what it is.

This does not mean that Christians should not meditate. The Bible contains many passages calling us to meditation. God told Joshua to meditate on his Word "day and night" so that he would act according to what was in it. The apostle Paul urged Timothy to meditate on the things of God and to give himself completely to them. Not only are we told to meditate on God's law day and night, but when we are in a right relationship to him, we find that this is a delight. As Christians, we certainly are to meditate, but not to strive to go beyond all thought to a state of pure awareness. Christian meditation is centered on God himself. Our mind is guided by the Scripture under the guidance of the Holy Spirit.

We need to encourage our counselees to do a study of what the Bible says about meditation and encourage them to practice Christian meditation. In our rushed age, twenty minutes morning and night meditating on God and his Word will bring relaxation and peace.

Visions

Related to the altered states of consciousness are the visions that make up a part of our Christian faith. God frequently communicated with humans through visions, but we must be careful to distinguish between visions from God and the hallucinations of the mentally ill.

God Speaking Through Visions. God seemed to use visions at major turning points in the history of his people, just as he used dreams. God appeared to Abram in a vision to promise him a son when he thought he would have none. He spoke to Jacob in a vision to tell him to not be afraid to go down into Egypt. In New Testament times, God used a vision to send Ananias to see Saul, who had just experienced a vision of Jesus. When God was trying to convince the apostles that the Gentiles were included in Christianity, he used a vision to persuade Cornelius to send for Peter and a vision to enlighten Peter concerning the Gentiles. On his second missionary journey, it was a vision that made Paul decide to change his route and go over into Macedonia.

There were also visions of God and things that were simply not describable in human language. When Isaiah saw the Lord, he described seraphims having six wings, crying "Holy, Holy, Holy," and the house filled with smoke. When Ezekiel saw the Lord, he saw a whirlwind, a cloud, a fire, wheels, and rings, and heard loud noises. The apostle John had a vision while on the island of Patmos. In it he heard a loud voice behind him and he saw Christ with hair white like wool or snow, eyes like fire, and feet like brass. The Bible also records numerous prophetic visions, such as those of Ezekiel and Daniel. When Peter, James, and John went with Jesus into a high mountain and saw him transfigured, they had difficulty describing Jesus. The apostle Paul wrote about his vision of paradise which he called the "third heaven." He was not sure whether he was in or out of the body and said that while there he heard unspeakable words.

Visions and Hallucinations. In some circles it is no longer quite "respectable" for Christians to have visions. Some Christians believe that visions ended with the Book of Acts and that anyone who has them now is somewhat suspect. They are prone to call such things hallucinations and try to explain them away. However, God did communicate with humans in visions and he can still do so. As Christian psychologists, we need to develop criteria for distinguishing between visions and hallucinations. Secular psychologists are not going to develop these, so it is our responsibility. God can communicate with us through visions, and we must not dismiss his communication as a mere hallucination.

Let us consider an example. In May, 1979, a man was convicted in federal court for lying on his tax forms. He told the jury that "The Lord told me not to pay income taxes and get out from under it the best I could." He said that he had claimed forty exemptions when only entitled to three "because the Lord told me to." When asked whether or not he had filed a tax return for the current year, he would not reply, saying, "That's between me and God, and he's dealing with me." One might question whether or not God actually told him to do this.

There are probably at least two criteria for judging whether an experience is a vision from God or an hallucination. First, is the vision consistent with Scripture? As much as we all hate to pay taxes, we need to see what the Bible has to say about paying taxes to see whether or not this man's experience was from God. We also need to see what the Bible has to say about lying, claiming 40 exemptions when entitled to only three. A second criterion for distinguishing between visions and hallucinations is found in looking at the other behaviors of the individuals having the "visions." A walk through the wards of most mental hospitals will reveal many people who claim to have visons from God, but other aspects of their lives reveal behavior out of touch with reality. They also claim to be Napoleon or Jesus Christ returned at his second coming. Although you say one could really be Jesus returned to earth, what do you do when three men on the same ward make the same claim? They cannot all be Jesus. At least two of them have to be wrong!

Conclusion

In this chapter we concentrated on sleep, dreaming, and the use of drugs to alter consciousness. We discussed a variety of sleep and dreaming disorders. We must be careful in treating sleep disorders because the cure may be worse than the disorder, if one even exists. We also discussed stimulants, depressants, and hallucinations, noting that treatments for drug abuse usually meet with limited success. We noted that Transcendental Meditation is primarily Hinduism. We attempted to distinguish between visions and hallucinations.

Suggested Readings

Chapters on "States of Awareness" or "States of Consciousness" in general psychology textbooks are recommended to elaborate on material presented in this chapter. Also recommended are chapters on "Addictive Disorders" or "Substance Use Disorders" in abnormal psychology textbooks and "Sleep" in physiological psychology textbooks. Bootzin and Acocella (1980), Brecher (1972), Brown and Wallace (1980), Coleman, Butcher, and Carson (1980), Forrest (1975), Koteskey (1980), Lewis (1975), Luce and Segal (1966, 1969), and Mendelson and Mello (1979) expand on material presented in this chapter.

LEARNING

The last three chapters have been concerned with how humans become aware of the world around them. With this chapter we begin a new topic area of general psychology, one dealing with the intellectual processes. The next three chapters will be devoted to the areas of learning, cognitive processes, and memory. Although there is some debate whether or not any human behavior is instinctive, everyone agrees that learning and higher mental processes influence human behavior. Even innate responses, such as eating, elimination, and crying, are modified by learning.

Psychologists usually define learning as a relatively permanent change in behavior as a result of experience. This excludes changes in behavior due to maturation, fatigue, drugs, injury, and so forth. We usually consider learning to be a much simpler process than other intellectual processes. The study of learning can be placed in our Christian perspective as shown in the lower central part of Figure 8:1 (Learning—Intellect). That is, humans are very similar to animals in the way they learn many simple responses. In fact, much of the study of learning has been the study of the way animals learn, with the concepts generalized to humans. Of course, we must not forget that humans are also like God, and that this will influence even the way they learn simple responses.

Let us briefly consider the relationship of learning to the topics above it in Figure 8:1. Learning is obviously related to

Figure 8:1 Learning and learning disorders from a Christian perspective.

HUMANS

Created......in the......Image of God
Like Animals   Like God

Overt Behavior......Definition......Mental Processes

Understand......Goals......Make People
Creation   Like God

Psychoanalysis......Systems......Humanistic
Behaviorism   Psychology

(DISORDER) ......Experimental......Methods......Descriptive......(DISORDER)

Organic Disorders......Physiological......Structure......Spiritual......Spiritual Disorders—Sin
(Organic Mental Disorders)   (Personality Disorders)

Physical Disorders......Immaturity......Development......Maturity......Spiritual Immaturity
(Disorders Appearing in   (No DSM-III Category)
Childhood or Adolescence)

Sensory Disorders......Sensation......Awareness......Perception......Perceptual Disorders
(Somatoform Disorders)   (States of Consciousness—Substance Use Disorders)   (Paranoid Disorders)

LEARNING......LEARNING......INTELLECT......
DISORDERS

physiological psychology. We have seen that endocrine imbalances or changes in the nervous system can make learning more difficult, and even lead to mental retardation. Changes in learning take place over the life-span of an individual. Classical conditioning is possible even in the womb, and throughout much of the life of the person. However, the capacity to learn such responses apparently decreases with age, because little conditioning is found in old adults as compared to children and young adults. Sensation is obviously related to the stimulus-response kind of learning discussed in this chapter. The stimulus is a sensation of some kind, and this sensation is then paired with a response. If there is no sensation, there is no stimulus, and no learning.

Learning has contributed more to treatment than any other part of general psychology, so we will spend much more time discussing the basic facts about it here. Learning is usually divided into two major areas, those of classical and operant (or instrumental) conditioning. These two areas differ at least in the procedures used to bring them about, but they may both have the same underlying processes. We will begin with the study of classical conditioning, then turn our attention to operant.

Classical Conditioning

Classical conditioning is practically synonymous with the work Ivan Pavlov did with dogs. While Pavlov (1927/1960) was studying the physiology of digestion in dogs, he noticed that the dogs began to salivate at the sight and sound of the experimenter. He first called these "psychic" secretions, but soon found that they were produced by any stimuli that regularly preceded food. Pavlov then studied this secretion of saliva under carefully controlled conditions and discovered much of what we know about this type of learning.

Although the salivation of dogs might seem to be far removed from the counseling room, much of what Pavlov discovered is directly related to counseling. Classical conditioning occurs in many species, including humans. Classical conditioning of humans has been most often studied using the kneejerk and the eyeblink responses, but classical conditioning is involved far beyond these simple responses.

Classical conditioning of emotions often occurs in humans. Sometimes we meet someone we immediately do not like. If the new acquaintance looks or acts like someone we dislike, the dislike generalizes to the new person. The most well-known early work on classical conditioning in humans was the conditioning of fear of rats in children by John Watson and his associates. Children who initially showed no fear of the rats showed a conditioned fear response after the presence of the rat was paired several times with a loud noise. Fears in our counselees may simply be conditioned responses and not indicate anything other than a conditioning history. As we noted in chapter 3, guilt feelings may also become conditioned responses. Such guilt feelings do not indicate the presence of guilt, but are classically conditioned responses.

Some word meanings are classically conditioned responses. Parents who use physical punishment know that if they say "No" followed by a slap on the child's hand several times, soon the "No" will bring the same response as the slap did earlier. The "No" is the conditioned stimulus and the slap on the hand is the unconditioned stimulus. Crying which originally occurred only to the slap now occurs to the word "No." Meanings can then be transferred from word to word by the principles of conditioning. Our counselees may be experiencing conditioned emotional responses to words that are neutral to us, and we must be aware of such conditioned meanings.

Operant Conditioning

Although B. F. Skinner did most of his experiments on animals, he has promoted operant conditioning as one of the primary ways humans learn. The most common apparatus used to study this kind of learning is the operant chamber, commonly called the "Skinner box." This is simply a box that contains a lever or disc and a food or water dispenser, so that whenever the lever is pressed, a pellet of food or drink of water is given to the rat or pigeon. Rather than making a new stimulus-response connection, operant conditioning takes a response which the subject is already making and strengthens it with reinforcement.

Reinforcement is anything that increases the probability that the response will be given. Although there has been much controversy over whether or not reinforcement is necessary for learning to take place, everyone agrees that reinforcement is necessary to bring about changes in performance. Let us now look at positive and negative reinforcement.

A positive reinforcement is any stimulus that increases the probability of response when the stimulus is presented following that response. If the subject is hungry, food is a positive reinforcer. If the subject is thirsty, water is a positive reinforcer. If the person has been ignored, attention is a positive reinforcer. If the individual is lonely, social interaction is a positive reinforcer. Since most people view reinforcement as one of the most efficient ways to bring about changes in behavior, parents, teachers, and psychologists make extensive use of it.

Although psychologists often present reinforcement as a means of bringing about permanent changes in behavior, Bufford (1981) has shown that the changes produced by reinforcement are no more lasting than those produced by punishment. When the punishment is discontinued, the punished behavior reappears. In the same way, when reinforcement is discontinued, the behavior of "not responding" reappears, only we call it extinction. This view of reinforcement may force us toward a redefinition of learning, because we now see that we are unable to bring about lasting changes in behavior through either reinforcement or punishment. From the perspective taken here, we would say that in our animal-likeness in learning, we respond only to the reinforcing or punishing events in the world around us, but in our God-like cognitive processes, we are able to evaluate rationally the world around us, make a decision, and permanently change our behavior, regardless of conditions around us.

Although secular psychologists are interested in changing behavior and see reinforcement as the most efficient means of bringing about the change, Christians see reward in terms of justice as well as behavioral change. That is, reward is given because the person deserves it for having made the response. We do not give it only to manipulate the person into doing what we want. Although reinforcement increases the probability of response, correct responses are not enough for the Christian! We can use reinforcement to bring about behavior change, but we should not give reinforcement when it has not been "earned."

A negative reinforcement is a stimulus that, when removed, strengthens a response. Negative reinforcers are noxious stimuli, such as electric shock, which we try to escape or avoid. Humans, like animals, learn responses that remove noxious stimuli and responses that prevent noxious stimuli from being presented. Note that even though noxious stimuli are used, we call this reinforcement.

Noxious stimuli are sometimes involved in the reinforcement of religious behavior. For example, most people consider guilt feelings to be noxious stimuli, so they make responses to escape or avoid such feelings. People may witness, pray, attend church, and tithe to avoid the guilt feelings they know will come if they do not do these things a Christian "should" do. If they already have the guilt feelings, one popular escape route is through confession and tears. The people vent their misery through crying and confessing some misdeeds. This leads to a temporary reduction in guilt feelings without doing anything about the actual guilt itself. This leads to a series of "weeping in confession responses," usually during a time of spiritual emphasis. Actual guilt cannot be removed without repentance and forgiveness from God. As

Christian counselors, we are interested in dealing with actual guilt as well as guilt feelings. Let us now consider several types of operant conditioning.

Reward. The most widely studied form of operant conditioning is reward learning, in which a reinforcement is given whenever the appropriate response is made. This occurs naturally when someone picks out a response we make and starts reinforcing it so that we begin repeating it. When they stop reinforcing the response, we stop making it. If our counselees are not making a response they should be making, we should check to see that they are being reinforced for making it. For example, if children are not reinforced for making sounds, they do not learn to speak a language. On the other hand, if a response is being made and we want to stop it, we must remove the reinforcement. For example, children may cry for attention every time they are put to bed, so the parents pick the child up to stop the crying—thereby rewarding the child for crying. The parents must stop picking up the child.

Psychologists do not wait for complex responses to be made so they can be reinforced. Techniques have been developed for shaping or molding behavior as one would mold a piece of clay. The basic idea is to reinforce any responses that begin to approximate the desired one. The old children's game of "hide the thimble" is an example of shaping behavior. Telling children looking for the thimble that they are getting hotter and hotter is the reinforcement, and in a few seconds, the children can find the thimble. These same principles of shaping behavior can be applied to programmed learning. The idea is to take the learner in very small steps, with reinforcement for more nearly correct responses at each step.

Escape. Escape learning is similar to reward learning, except that a different kind of reinforcement is used. In escape learning, the subject learns to escape from a noxious stimulus that is turned on and then not turned off until the appropriate response is made. For example, children use escape learning to teach their parents to pick them up. The children turn on the crying (a noxious stimulus to most parents) and do not turn it off until the parents pick them up. Children can cry for a long time, longer than the resistance of most parents. When the parents pick up the children, they stop crying. Our counselees need to be aware of the role of escape learning in their lives.

Avoidance. Avoidance learning is another type of instrumental learning similar to escape learning except that it involves turning on a signal before the noxious stimulus is presented. At first, the subjects do not realize what response must be made and only escape from the noxious stimulus when it is presented. However, they soon learn that if they make the correct response after the signal comes on, but before the noxious stimulus comes on, the noxious stimulus is not presented. Avoidance learning may be involved in our counselees' lives when they avoid doing things that they know they should be doing. For example, if another person bores or irritates them, they may avoid contact. A man whose wife or children irritate him (are a noxious stimulus) may simply stay away from them. One important characteristic of avoidance learning is that it is very resistant to extinction, so that long after the noxious element is turned off, the person will still stay away. Even after the wife stops nagging, the husband stays away.

Punishment. A noxious stimulus is also used in the punishment situation, but it is not presented unless the given response is made. This type of learning is widely used by parents and society. Nothing happens until the children or the criminals make the forbidden response, then the noxious stimulus occurs. Although punishment can be very effective when used in combination with reward learning, we must be aware of several facts about its use. First, it is often accompanied by emotional side effects so that, although the response is made, the person is angry, fearful, or resentful. Second, punishment only temporarily suppresses the inappropriate response. Parents who use only punishment usually have model children when they are present, but the children may be very bad when away from their parents. Finally, punishment suppresses the response that occurred immediately before it is given, and sometimes we inadvertently punish the wrong response. For example, if a child comes in the house confessing that he or she just broke a window and you spank him or her, you are not likely to stop window breaking, but you are likely to suppress the confessing behavior. The next time the child breaks something, he or she is less likely to confess his or her part in it.

Some people in the parent-effectiveness-training movement have advocated the use of particular types of punishment; natural and logical consequences. Natural consequences are the noxious stimuli that arise naturally from misbehavior and are allowed to occur if they will not permanently harm the person. If children do not wash the dishes, they are not fed, because there are no clean dishes for the food. Logical consequences are noxious stimuli closely related to the behaviors. If children do not clean their rooms, they are not allowed to have friends over, because their sloppiness would be a bad example.

As Christians we see punishment in terms of justice also. C. S. Lewis (1949/1970) takes this position in his indictment of the humanitarian theory of punishment so prevalent today. This theory views criminals as psychologically sick and in need of psychotherapy to cure them. There is no idea that people should be punished because they deserve it. Although this sounds good, this theory is based on a very low view of humanity, because it puts adult human beings on the level of infants and animals. To be punished because we deserve it is to be treated as responsible human beings made in the image of God. Although efforts at rehabilitation are right and good, they must never replace just discipline. Christian counseling is appropriate only when done in the context of justice and moral responsibility. Humans are responsible beings created in God's image, and we must recognize that only regeneration can provide a lasting answer to humanity's basic spiritual problem.

Disorders

Disorders associated with learning are shown in our Christian perspective in Figure 8:1. These disorders could be called learned disorders, meaning that the person has learned an inappropriate behavior, and this is typified by the phobic disorders in DSM-III. Their reinforcement history has resulted in the learning of a response that society does not accept as normal. Nearly any such response can be learned, but in this section we will consider the phobic disorders that have been most widely studied.

Phobic Disorders

A phobia is an intense fear of some object or situation that presents no actual danger to the person, or if it does present a danger, the fear is out of all proportion to the actual danger. Although the symptoms involve motivation and emotion, I am placing the phobic disorders here (with Learning Disorders) because many of the phobias are learned responses. Although other causes may exist as well, we do know that these fears can be learned. Such fears can be of open spaces, closed spaces, heights, water, guns, snakes, certain animals, animals in general, blood, storms, being in a crowd, being alone, and so forth.

Phobic individuals will go to great lengths to avoid the feared stimulus, even if it means becoming a recluse and generally withdrawing from life. If they come near the feared stimulus, they experience a full-blown anxiety reaction with increased heart rate, sweating, and perhaps even a panic attack. Normal people may feel some uneasiness in the same situation, but their life will not be disrupted.

I saw a phobia develop in one of my children at about eighteen months of age. He was frightened by two different "friendly" dogs within a one-month period. The dogs knocked him down and stood over him, licking his face. Although the dogs were trying to be friendly, the specter of these huge animals standing over him was intensely fear arousing. He learned to fear the sight of dogs; any dogs. This fear of dogs was learned in only two trials and then generalized to the sight of any dog and even to some other animals. The sight of a dog would literally send the child climbing up the clothing of the nearest adult.

Treatment

The treatments most directly involving learning principles are those usually called *behavior therapy* or *behavior modification*. Although many different names have been given to minor modifications of these techniques, all are based on basic learning principles. Let us now consider the various techniques in the context of learning.

Behavior Therapy Techniques
Involving Classical Conditioning

The techniques using classical conditioning are usually aimed at changing a person's emotional responses (likes, dislikes, fears) in order to change overt behaviors. The basic idea is that inappropriate responses to certain stimuli have been learned and that the person must be reconditioned. This reconditioning can take two primary forms: that of extinction of the inappropriate response, or that of conditioning an incompatible response.

Extinction. The basic idea in extinction is to present the conditioned stimulus but not follow it with the unconditioned one. When this is done repeatedly, the conditioned response gradually drops out, as when Pavlov sounded the bell but did not follow it with the meat. Soon salivation to the bell alone stopped. This extinction can be attempted gradually or rapidly, and verbally or in real life, as shown in Figure 8:2. Since counselors cannot control the environment twenty-four hours a day, extinction may be difficult. Family and friends may reinforce responses counselors are trying to extinguish.

Figure 8:2 Classification of therapies based on classical conditioning.

	Verbal Techniques	Real Life
Gradual Extinction	Systematic Desensitization	
Rapid Extinction	Implosive Therapy	Flooding
Counter-conditioning	Covert Sensitization	Aversion Therapy

If extinction is attempted gradually and verbally, it is called *systematic desensitization* and involves three steps. First, patients are trained in relaxation, usually some form of progressive, systematic muscle relaxation. Second, patients and therapists construct a list of fear-arousing situations in a hierarchy of fearfulness. For example, people with a fear of dogs may have little fear of a playful puppy, more of a cocker spaniel, and a terror of a snarling Doberman pinscher. Third, the patients relax and imagine themselves experiencing the situations in their hierarchies, beginning with the lowest and gradually moving to more fearful ones. When fear replaces the relaxation, they drop back in the hierarchy for a while. The basic idea is to extinguish the fear gradually.

Extinction may be attempted gradually and in real life, but the principle is the same. This was the technique we used when our son developed his phobia of dogs. We actually got a small puppy, which elicited only a minimal amount of fear. Soon he was able to play with the puppy without fear, but was still afraid of larger dogs. It was simply a matter of time until the puppy grew into a dog, and the boy's fear of dogs gradually extinguished as the puppy grew. Fears of heights can be extinguished gradually by standing in higher and higher places, fear of closed spaces by being in smaller and smaller rooms, fear of crowds by being around more and more people, and so forth.

If extinction is attempted rapidly and verbally, it is called *implosive therapy*. The idea here is to arouse as much fear as possible, an inward explosion (implosion) of fear. This is done repeatedly in the safe setting of the therapist's office and the fear soon extinguishes. The therapists find out from the clients what are the most feared stimuli, then ask the clients to imagine these feared things over and over, embellished with the most fear-producing things the therapists can imagine. At first great fear is aroused, but over several sessions the fear subsides until it is gone.

If extinction is attempted in real life, the process is called *flooding*. Rather than imagining the most terrifying situations, patients are actually placed in them repeatedly. For example, if patients are afraid of heights, they are actually taken to the top of the tallest building and required to look down. This obviously brings a "flood" of fear, but when nothing bad happens, the fear extinguishes. If the patients have a fear of crowds, they are actually taken into the largest crowds that can be found so that the fear can be extinguished. As Christian counselors, we can make use of these techniques, which work so well on the phobias. Although they were developed from working with animals, we can use them because humans are like animals in many ways.

Counterconditioning. Extinction works by removing the unconditioned stimulus. Counterconditioning works by pairing the conditioned stimulus with a new, aversive, unconditioned stimulus. This presentation of the unpleasant and unconditioned can be done either in real life or verbally, as shown in Figure 8:2.

If the stimulus is actually paired with the aversive stimulus in real life, the process is called *aversion therapy.* The basic idea is to pair an aversive stimulus with the stimulus that ordinarily produces the maladaptive response. In this way that original stimulus itself becomes aversive through classical conditioning, and the response is not made. For example, electric shocks may be paired with the sight, smell, or taste of alcohol so that an alcoholic will withdraw from it rather than drink it. Another example would be to pair electric shocks with nude pictures of people of the same sex to decrease homosexual activity. The people would then make a negative response rather than a sexual response. Note that this is classical conditioning, not punishment. The alcoholic is not punished for drinking, nor is homosexual behavior punished. Rather, stimuli ordinarily eliciting such behavior are paired with aversive ones so that they also take on aversive value.

If the stimulus is paired with the aversive stimulus only verbally, it is called *covert sensitization.* Rather than actually receiving the stimuli, the patients only imagine them. They imagine both the behavior they are trying to eliminate and an extremely revolting, painful stimulus at the same time. For example, problem drinkers may imagine they are taking a drink at a party, then immediately imagine that they have become very ill and vomited all over themselves and their friend's living room. Then they imagine taking another drink and some other revolting situation. Again the idea is to pair stimuli eliciting the maladaptive behavior with aversive stimuli, until they no longer elicit the behavior.

We can use these techniques of classical conditioning where they are appropriate. If the cause of the problem is a learned inappropriate response, we can use the principles of learning to get rid of the response. The use of the "healing of memories" or "inner healing" (to be discussed in chapter 10), so popular recently in Christian circles, is really a combination of these extinction and counterconditioning techniques with the work of the Holy Spirit. Although many who practice healing of memories do not realize it, they are using techniques originating in animal learning.

Behavior Modification Techniques
Involving Operant Conditioning

The techniques involving operant conditioning are usually aimed at directly changing individuals' overt behaviors. The basic idea here is that inappropriate responses have been reinforced, and the task of psychologists is to change the reinforcement so that this will no longer happen. As with classical conditioning, this involves either extinction or counterconditioning. It may also involve punishment.

Extinction. Behaviors that have been learned by being reinforced will soon disappear if the reinforcement is discontinued. The task of the psychologist in this case is to find the reinforcer and, if possible, discontinue it. For example, children may become real problems in the classroom because they are deprived of attention. Their disruptive behavior is then reinforced by attention from teachers and other students. The problem is solved by extinguishing the disruptive behavior by turning off the attention. Another example is children who cry when left in the church nursery or when put to bed at home. When they cry, the parents pick them up, reinforcing their crying. (Of course, we must realize that the children are using negative reinforcement to reinforce their parents' picking them up. When they turn off the noxious stimulus—stop crying—this makes it more likely that their parents will pick them up.) The way to stop the crying is to stop reinforcing it, to stop picking the children up.

Simple extinction is difficult to use, because when it is first begun, the unwanted behavior occurs in much greater amounts. Ignoring the disruptive child in the classroom will result in a great increase in such behavior temporarily, but it must still be ignored. Ignoring a crying child may result in two or more hours of crying, but the crying must be ignored. Another problem is that everyone involved must consistently ignore the behavior. If the teacher ignores it, but other students give their attention, the misbehavior will continue. If parents ignore the crying child, but a visiting grandparent picks the child up, the crying will continue.

Reinforcement. Positive reinforcement is currently the most widely used form of behavior modification. Many different specific techniques of reinforcement are used, but they all involve using reinforcement to increase the probability of a given response. Let us now consider some of the most common techniques.

People in institutions are often made members of *token economies.* That is, tokens (poker chips, slips of paper, points on a chart) are given them when they make the desired response. The tokens can then be exchanged for candy, games, books, a better room, television time, or a weekend pass. The tokens are conditioned reinforcers because they have gained their reinforcement values from association with primary reinforcers, such as food or recreation. The psychologists have specified the desirable behaviors for each patient, and the patient must perform those behaviors to get the tokens, which can be exchanged. This procedure is also called *contingency management* or *contingency contracting,* depending on how specific the requirements are for the responses.

Positive reinforcement is often used in *shaping behavior,* as was mentioned earlier. People are reinforced for making responses that successively approximate the desired one. For example, you do not wait for withdrawn patients who have not spoken for weeks to utter a complete sentence before you reinforce them. At first, you may give candy or gum for a grunt, then for a word, then for a phrase, and finally for a complete sentence. Again, you pick the desired response and reinforce closer and closer approximations of it. We must be careful not to reinforce behavior that occurs naturally, because (as we will see in chapter 11) externalizing motivation may result in a decrease in desired behavior when we cease reinforcement.

Modeling may be used when the psychologist does not wish to take the time involved in shaping behavior. In modeling, patients first come to emit the behavior by watching someone else do it. It is the old principle of monkey-see-monkey-do. Children with a fear of dogs may watch another child play with a dog, then go pet the dog themselves. Then the petting of the dog is immediately reinforced by praise, candy, or some other reinforcer. Giving the reinforcement makes this a type of operant learning, but the modeling is used to get the response made in the first place. Of course, this is a major part of our talking about being Christ-like or God-like, from our Christian perspective.

Other types of reinforcement may be used; sometimes in combination with cognitive processes, sometimes in combination with punishment. However, the main idea of reinforcement is to get the person to make the response, then reinforce it. Christian counselors should use this very powerful way to change behavior. Humans are animal-like in some ways, and there is nothing wrong with using what we know about these animal-likenesses.

Punishment. Punishment may be used to lower the rate of responding. This is particularly effective when used with positive reinforcement. One use of punishment is quite similar to aversion therapy, in which classical conditioning is used. However, in punishment the aversive stimulus is not given until the response is made. For example, problem drinkers may be given a drug called Antabuse. This is a chemical that produces a very unpleasant reaction if the individual drinks alcohol. Drinking is punished even if no one is present. When these people drink, they flush, their heart rate increases, they become very nauseated, and they feel very ill. Antabuse stops impulsive drinking, because the drinkers must stop taking

Antabuse at least two days before they can drink comfortably. Electric shock or other punishments can be used. However, many people frown on the use of these types of punishment.

One type of punishment that is more commonly used is *time-out from positive reinforcement.* This is much like the old practice of making children stand in the corner. When the patients make an undesirable response, they are removed to a place where they stop receiving reinforcement. Several important conditions must be met for this to work. First, the place they go must contain no reinforcers. Sending children to their rooms does little good, since they can play there. Second, there must be clear rules to start the time-out and to stop it. For example, a temper tantrum starts it and they must stay there until they calm down. Finally, time-out must be imposed dispassionately, so that the patients do not have the reinforcement of knowing they have angered their parents or the therapist. Christian counselors can make use of any of these techniques of behavior modification using operant conditioning.

Conclusion

Christian counselors need to be familiar with the psychology of learning. Classical and operant conditioning and the phenomena related to them have a profound impact on our behavior, since most of our behavior is learned. We also considered learned disorders, such as the phobias, where the undesirable responses were learned ones. Treatments emphasizing learning are primarily behavior therapy techniques involving both operant and classical conditioning.

Again, it must be emphasized that we choose a treatment or treatments appropriate to the disorder. For example, when I talked about my child who had a phobia of dogs to a therapist who emphasizes spiritual treatment, he said that my child had a spiritual problem. He then quoted the line, "perfect love casts out fear," saying that anyone with a fear has a spiritual problem. Even my protest that I had seen the dogs standing over the child and licking his face, and the fact that the child was too young to talk, could not convince this psychologist that it was not a spiritual problem. Such attempts to make everything a spiritual problem are just as narrow-minded as trying to see everything only as a behavioral or physiological problem.

Suggested Readings

Chapters on "Learning" or "Conditioning" in general psychology books are recommended. Also recommended are the chapters or sections of chapters on "Phobias" and "Behavior Therapy" in abnormal psychology textbooks. Bootzin and Acocella (1980), Coleman, Butcher, and Carson (1980), Erwin (1978), Garfield and Bergin (1978), Kanfer and Phillips (1970), Kazdin (1978), and Koteskey (1980) expand on material presented in this chapter.

COGNITION

Although learning is very important, it is among the animal-like parts of our intellectual processes, as we saw in the last chapter. Humans also have a God-like aspect of their intellectual processes, which we call *cognition*—shown in the lower central part of Figure 9:1 (Intellect—Cognition). Cognition refers to the symbolic or mental processes of human beings engaged in thinking, reasoning, creating, and solving problems. It refers to the active role we play in these activities by organizing, reorganizing, and using strategies to learn. This, of course, is the direct study of the mental processes, part of the definition of psychology. Let us begin by looking at each area above cognition in Figure 9:1.

Spiritual Cognition

Although some people try to place faith and reason in opposition to each other, they are intimately related. God is onmiscient. His understanding is infinite. Human beings made in his image have the capacity to understand and know. God repeatedly encourages us to seek knowledge and understanding, especially in the book of Proverbs, whose third chapter has an extended passage promising life, safety, and happiness coming with wisdom and understanding. Immediately following a passage about our being partakers of the divine nature, Peter says that we must add a variety of

165

Figure 9:1 Cognition and thinking disorders from a Christian perspective.

HUMANS

Created	...in the...	Image of God
Like Animals		Like God
Overt Behavior	Definition	Mental Processes
Understand Creation	Goals	Make People Like God
Psychoanalysis Behaviorism	Systems	Humanistic Psychology

Experimental	Methods	Descriptive
Physiological	Structure	Spiritual
(DISORDER)		(DISORDER)
Organic Disorders		Spiritual Disorders—Sin
(Organic Mental Disorders)		(Personality Disorders)

Immaturity	Development	Maturity
Physical Disorders		Spiritual Immaturity
(Disorders Appearing in Childhood or Adolescence)		(No DSM-III Category)

Sensation	Awareness	Perception
Sensory Disorders	(States of Consciousness—Substance Use Disorders)	Perceptual Disorders
(Somatoform Disorders)		(Paranoid Disorders)

Learning	INTELLECT	COGNITION ... THINKING DISORDERS
Learning Disorders		
(Phobic Disorders)		(SCHIZOPHRENIC DISORDERS)

things to our faith, including knowledge. If knowledge is not added to our faith, we will be spiritually shortsighted and forget that we are cleansed from our sins.

God chose to make his special revelation to us through language, a capacity animals do not have. Thus, we must rely on our mental processes to understand God himself. In the first chapter of Isaiah, God told us to come and reason with him, and the reasoning was about our sin and what could be done about it. Regardless of how close we are to our dogs or cats, we do not reason together with them. We may "talk to" them but not "reason together" with them because they are a different order of creation. God can reason with us about our sins because we are cognitive beings made in his image.

Developmental-Maturity

We already saw in the chapter on developmental psychology that cognition changes as we mature. Piaget showed that we begin life thinking much like animals in the sensorimotor stage, then develop toward a more God-like abstract thought as we mature. Although Piaget did not study it, we commonly think of wisdom's coming as people grow older, ask God for wisdom, and face more of life's problems. Such wisdom is a God-like attribute.

We commonly talk about an "age of accountability," meaning that cognitive processes have developed to the point that people can tell the difference between right and wrong and can be held responsible for doing the right. This age varies from culture to culture, but many cultures recognize that there comes such a time.

Perception

Perception and cognition are intimately related. We often see what we expect to see. That is, we organize our sensations into perceptions based on what our cognitions expect. Then we use those perceptions to decide whether or not our hypothesis was correct. If we are not careful, this can lead to circular reasoning and incorrect conclusions. Some psychologists maintain that the world we perceive is determined largely by the categories given to us by our language. People who speak different languages may perceive the world quite differently.

Probably the clearest effect of the influence of perception on cognition is found in the deaf. Deaf people are unable to hear language, so their cognitive development is very different from that of a person who can hear. Their thinking develops at a slower rate and usually to a lower level than that of a person who can hear normally. Of course, the person who is both blind and deaf has an even more deficient cognition. Helen Keller was very much the exception rather than the rule.

Disorders

Cognition is obviously involved in the disorders counselors work with. All through this book, we have been talking about DSM-III, a manual for classifying "mental disorders." We talk about the "mentally ill" being in "mental hospitals." These disturbances in the mental processes mentioned in the definition of psychology are repeatedly referred to as being problems with which we must deal. Let us now consider some of the thinking disorders that may be placed in our Christian perspective as shown in Figure 9:1.

Delusions

The major symptoms of thinking disorders are delusions, firm beliefs that have no basis in reality but are maintained in spite of evidence to the contrary. Delusions are as varied as the human imagination, and it may be very difficult for the counselor to distinguish between what is real and what is delusional in the counselee's thinking.

Although delusions vary widely, some common categories

exist. Some people have delusions of persecution. They believe that they are being plotted against, spied on, threatened, and so forth, often by several persons or groups in a conspiracy. Others have delusions of control, or influence. These people believe that someone or something else is controlling their thoughts and feelings. They may believe that their thoughts are being broadcast to the whole world, that someone is inserting thoughts into their head, or that someone is removing thoughts.

Others have delusions of reference, in which they see unrelated events as referring to themselves; such as believing that their lives are being depicted in a television program. Some have delusions of sin and guilt; believing they have committed some great sin, perhaps "the unpardonable sin." Others have hypochondriacal delusions, in which they think they have some terrible physical disease, such as their brains becoming moldy or their liver being carried away by termites. Some have nihilistic delusions; they believe that they have ceased to exist. Others have delusions of grandeur, in which they believe they are some important person, such as Napoleon or Jesus Christ.

Schizophrenic Disorders

Schizophrenic disorders can be seen as being primarily disturbances in thought, as shown in Figure 9:1. *Schizophrenic* is the label used to describe people who have severe disorders in their thinking along with disorders in perception and emotion. Schizophrenia is not a single disorder, but a group of disorders, and sometimes serves as a "wastebasket" category people can be tossed into if they do not clearly fit other categories. Schizophrenia is a very common disorder, as demonstrated by the fact that about half of the patients in U.S. mental hospitals are diagnosed as schizophrenic.

Although psychologists generally agree on the major symptoms of schizophrenia, they disagree on which ones are most basic. In this chapter we are emphasizing disturbances in thought. The most striking thought disorder is the delusions found in schizophrenia. About three-fourths of those diagnosed as schizophrenic have such delusions. In addition, schizophrenics have a loosening of associations or a "cognitive slippage": their speech is rambling, disjointed. Normal people follow a single train of thought with ideas logically connected, but the schizophrenic jumps from thought to unrelated thought. Speech may even become incoherent. Even though it sounds reasonable at first, reflection reveals that the schizophrenic has said nothing rational. Schizophrenics also have difficulty in conceptualization, so that they cannot think in abstract terms. They also use neologisms (literally "new words") in their speech. Sometimes they make up new words, and at other times they use common words in a unique way. Sometimes they use words that have no relationship to each other except that they rhyme (called clanging). Finally, their communication may become so bad that it is called "word salad," in which there seems to be no relationship between words at all. Words seem to be coming only in a random order.

In addition to these thinking disorders, schizophrenics may have disorders in perception. They may have hallucinations or report other differences in perception. They typically report heightened perception, although actual tests show that they do poorly on perceptual tasks. Schizophrenics may also show disorders of emotion. Some show little or no emotion. Others give an emotional response that is inappropriate for what has happened. For example, they might laugh when told their child has just died. They sometimes become overactive, inactive, or have bizarre, repetitive behaviors. They may also show signs of social withdrawal, disturbances of their sense of self, and a lack of volition.

DSM-III lists five subtypes of schizophrenia, and most of these show disorders in cognition. Disorganized schizophrenics have an incoherenct speech, such as neologisms, clanging, and word salad. Catatonic schizoprenics may go into a stupor in which they remain completely motionless and usually do not speak. The paranoid schizophrenic is characterized by delusions of persecution and grandeur, often accompanied by related hallucinations. Undifferentiated schizophrenics have thought disorders, are perplexed, depressed, fearful, confused, have delusions, and do not clearly fit into one of the other subtypes. The residual category is for people who have recovered from schizophrenia, but still have some of the symptoms.

Psychotic Disorders Not Elsewhere Classified

In DSM-III several new categories have been created, categories that are very much like schizophrenia except for the duration of the disorder. In fact, these would formerly have been classified as types of schizophrenia. The brief reactive psychosis, formerly called an "acute schizophrenic episode," is characterized by a known stressful event that leads to a rapid onset of the disorder followed by a rapid recovery in less than two weeks. During the brief episode, however, the person may have any of the various schizophrenic symptoms. If the disorder lasts for more than two weeks but less than six months, it is called schizophreniform disorder. At present, all new cases showing schizophrenic symptoms would be given this diagnosis. Then if the symptoms last longer than six months, the patient would be rediagnosed. As one might expect from the name, the schizoaffective disorder is characterized by a combination of symptoms of schizophrenia and the affective disorders.

Obsessive Compulsive Disorder

Obsessions are thoughts that recur even though the individuals do not want to think about them. Such people realize that these thoughts are irrational, but seem powerless to control them. The obsessions recur day after day and torture those who have them. Obsessions often include thoughts of violence to loved ones and are accompanied by guilt and anxiety. These thoughts may be obsessions with bodily functions, attempting suicide, committing immoral acts, or even thinking repeatedly about some problem. Although these thoughts are not usually carried out, they torment the obsessed person.

Aphasia

Any disorder of language that results from brain damage is called *aphasia*. Sensory aphasia, already discussed in the chapter on perception, results in disturbances in hearing or reading a language, while motor aphasia results in a difficulty in expressing things in language. One type is agraphia (manual aphasia), whose victims have difficulty writing. They can read, hear, and speak the language, but are unable to write it.

Another type is word muteness (speech aphasia), whose victims have an inability to express language vocally or to think in terms of a language. This may involve a verbal aphasia, in which they have difficulty forming the words themselves either for thinking or for expressing themselves orally. It may also be a syntactical aphasia, in which they lack the balance and rhythm necessary to make sounds easily comprehensible. Although they can make all the sounds, they cannot make them with the right timing to be understood easily by others. People may have a nominal aphasia, and be unable to use words as names. Although they can think of the objects, they cannot think of the words to use to refer to them. Finally, they may have semantic aphasia, in which there is a disturbance in the connected sequence of words. They may have the right words, but get them in the wrong order so that the words do not make any sense.

Christian counselors are likely to encounter at least two of the disorders found in this chapter. Since schizophrenia is such a common disorder, we are likely to see someone with it; if not in the active phase, at least in the residual phase. People who suffer strokes are likely to have one of the aphasias, so we are likely to encounter this frustrating condition of being unable to express oneself to others adequately.

Treatment

Although treatment involving cognition was relatively ignored for many years because of the dominance of the Freudian psychoanalytic theory of personality, several forms of it have been proposed more recently. These approaches to therapy were not developed to treat the thinking disorders we have discussed, but they do emphasize the thinking aspects of humans. Rogers' client-centered therapy and Kelly's fixed-role therapy both put some emphasis on cognition aspects since they consider the human being as basically conscious and rational. However, Ellis and Beck have placed an even greater emphasis on cognition, so we will consider them in more detail here.

Rational-Emotive Therapy

During the 1950s, Albert Ellis developed a method of therapy which has come to be called rational-emotive therapy. Although emotion is mentioned, the emphasis is on the rational. Ellis (1958) first called it "rational psychotherapy," founded the Institute for Rational Living, the Institute for Advanced Study in Rational Psychotherapy, and the journal, *Rational Living*.

Ellis' idea is that emotional disturbances are not the result of objective events in people's lives, but the result of irrational beliefs used in interpreting these events. For example, when people fail a task, it is not failure itself that causes them to be depressed and depreciate themselves. Rather, disturbances occur when people interpret that failure through the belief that they should be competent, adequate, intelligent, and successful in all possible respects. Thus, it is not the failure that causes depression, but the person's belief that one should never fail. The real causes of the disorders are the beliefs of the people themselves, not what happens to them.

Ellis (1973a) believes that humans are born with a potential to be rational, but that they are pushed toward the irrational by their culture, especially their family. They think, feel, and behave simultaneously, so we need to treat all these areas in therapy. Therapists should have good rapport with their clients, but may use a variety of impersonal methods, including bibliotherapy, behavior modification, audio-visual aids, and activity-oriented homework assignments. The goal is not just symptom reduction, but a change in the underlying thinking that produces the symptoms. Insight into the cause of the symptoms is not enough. The individual must eliminate the irrational thinking, and this takes hard work and practice.

Practitioners of rational-emotive therapy do not just use understanding and acceptance. They may bluntly point out the irrationality of the counselees' thinking. For example, they may say, "So what if your father doesn't love you. That's his problem!" They use firm, hard-headed methods to convince the clients that they must resort to more self-discipline.

Christian counselors may reject this method when they read some of the "irrational beliefs" Ellis wants to eradicate. For example: "one needs something stronger or more powerful than oneself to rely on," or "certain acts are awful or wicked, and people who perform them should be severely punished." Although we may disagree with his calling these particular beliefs irrational, many other beliefs are simply untenable, and people need to change them. For example, certain ideas—that we should be loved by everyone for everything we do; that we should be thoroughly competent, intelligent, and achieving in all respects; that we must have certain and perfect self-control at all times; or that we have virtually no control over our emotions and cannot help having certain feelings— are simply not true.

We can filter these beliefs through our Christian value system and use Ellis' basic approach if our counselee's problem is one of irrational thinking. Such directive techniques seem odd to many Christian counselors who have been trained in psychoanalytic or client-centered approaches, but there is nothing unbiblical about being directive. Jesus himself was quite directive with many of the people he encountered.

Cognitive Therapy

Beck (1976) has proposed that psychological problems are not the product of mysterious, uncontrollable forces, but come from faulty learning, drawing incorrect conclusions from too little or wrong information, and not distinguishing adequately between imagination and reality. Disorders can be treated by sharpening discriminations, correcting misconceptions, and learning more adaptive attitudes—a process he calls cognitive therapy. This approach brings treatment much closer to everyday experience, to common sense.

Cognitive therapy consists of all the approaches to treatment that aim at correcting faulty conceptions and self-signals. This emphasis on thinking does not mean that emotion is ignored, only that one gets to emotions through cognition. Many methods may be used to help patients make more realistic appraisals of themselves and their world. The "intellectual" approach consists of identifying misconceptions, testing their validity, and substituting appropriate concepts. The "experiential" approach gives the patient experiences that are powerful enough to change misconceptions. The "behavioral" approach helps the patients develop specific behaviors that change the way they view themselves and the world.

Beck (1976) notes that some people make direct, tangible distortions of reality. These distortions may be obviously delusional, or may be less obvious (e.g., "I have lost my ability to drive") when the person has simply not tried to do something recently. Other people have not distorted reality, but have illogical thinking. Their system of making inferences or drawing conclusions from their observations is faulty. They may overgeneralize and think the whole house is falling apart because a faucet leaks and a light switch is broken. They may magnify the importance of minor undesirable events, selectively perceive bad events and ignore good ones, and engage in "all-or-none" thinking.

In cognitive therapy, the therapist is seen as a collaborator, rather than playing an omnipotent and omniscient God-like role. The patient-therapist relationship becomes a joint effort. Both work together to reach a consensus on the nature of the problem, the goal of therapy, and a plan to reach the goal. They agree on the nature and the duration of the therapy. The patients gather information about themselves through experiments that allow them to refute their false beliefs. Together, therapist and patient discuss the patient's assumptions, beliefs, and expectations. Then they design behavioral-disconfirmation experiments in which the patient has a series of successful experiences. They may even schedule the patient's activities on an hour-by-hour basis.

Individuals are also encouraged to examine their maladaptive thoughts, which produce unnecessary discomfort or suffering, or lead to self-defeating behavior. These are automatic thoughts, which the person needs help in identifying. These thoughts take place between the stimulus and response and must be identified. The thought that comes between the sight of a dog and a phobic response may be "It is going to bite me." These thoughts need to be recognized and dealt with, as do many attitudes similar to the ones we discussed in Ellis' rational-emotive therapy, such as: "To be happy I must be accepted by all people at all times," "If I make a mistake, it means that I'm inept," "I should never feel hurt but always be happy and serene," or "I should always be spontaneous and I should always control my feelings."

Behavioral Contracting

Sometimes the connection between cognition and behavior is made even more explicit, as in behavioral contracting. In this form of treatment, two parties draw up an agreement, often put it in writing, and even sign it. The therapist and client, or parent and teenager, or husband and wife, agree on what behaviors need to be changed and specify the responsibilities and rewards involved for both parties. The emphasis is on behavior, but it is agreed to cognitively. Treatment is a joint enterprise in which both parties have some responsibility.

This agreement is good in several ways. The structure of the treatment relationship is explicitly stated, so that all parties involved know exactly what is expected of them. A system of rewards for changed behavior is built in. The limitations of treatment—such as duration, topics to be discussed, and so forth—are specified. Behaviors not listed in the contract are not of concern during treatment. Goals and criteria for reaching them are written into the contract.

Faulty "Christian" Thinking

Christian counselors can use many of the techniques and insights of the treatments emphasizing the cognitive dimension of humans. Although we cannot accept all parts of these therapies, humans are cognitive beings made in God's image, so disorders in their thinking may have a great effect on their behavior. In addition to insights from these secular psychologists, we must correct faulty concepts that Christians may have about the Christian faith.

About God. Many Christians have incorrect concepts of God. These lead to a poor relationship with him. Some come from distortions of his attributes, while others are a matter of thinking about God as people think about their parents. Frequently these individuals can give all the correct definitions or verbalizations about God, but their thinking behind these verbalizations needs to be discerned and clarified by the Christian counselor. A major part of Christian counseling is correcting the thinking of those one counsels.

Some people think of God as a hostile God. They think of

177

him as someone keeping a record of all of their wrong actions, just waiting to punish them. This punishment may come in the form of accidents, financial failure, disease, and so forth. When people have this concept of God, they ask, "Why is God doing this to me?" or "What sin have I committed?" when something bad happens. Although God does know about our sins, it is incorrect to think of him as hiding behind a cloud spying on us and ready to "zap" us with a bolt of lightning as soon as we make a wrong move. Although he knows all of our sins, he loves us and has taken the initial steps toward reconciliation.

Other people think of God as unpredictable. Such individuals may have grown up in a home where their parents were loving at one moment and hostile the next. This may not always be obvious. For example, many young people worry about finding God's will for their lives, afraid that they will miss his will and be punished for not doing it. They need to be asked about the God they worship. Is he a God who reveals his will to some, but not to others, and then punishes those who do not even know what he wants them to do? Their God is a capricious God who apparently will not tell them what he wants, then punishes them when they cannot guess it.

Still others think of God as a God of love who could never punish anyone. Overemphasizing love and mercy, these people believe that they can do whatever they want and God will forgive and save them anyway. They become universalists, believing that God is going to work out some way to save everyone. They forget that God is also a God of justice.

Others focus on the infinite aspects of God and depersonalize him to make him only some kind of "force," or the "absolute," or "energy." This depersonalization makes him less than he is. In their attempts to keep from anthropomorphizing, these individuals have not made God more than a person, but less.

This is not a complete list of the wrong concepts of God, but it is enough to illustrate the point. We should be aware of the literature on concept formation so that we can focus on changing the concept of God in those we are counseling. Without an adequate concept of God, people cannot have a correct concept of themselves. We must remember that individuals are made in God's image, and if we have a wrong image (concept) of God, we will have a wrong concept of what we are and what we can be. Although I want to be like God, I do not want to be like some people's concept of God.

About People. Our counselees often have wrong concepts about people, including themselves. Let us begin by discussing concepts about unregenerate people. Christians tend to look down on the unsaved, but we must remember that they are also made in God's likeness. That is why we are not to murder other humans. James reminds us that we cannot bless God on the one hand and curse humans on the other, because those humans are made in God's image. During the 1960s, when overpopulation and pollution were first of great concern, the term "people pollution" came into use, meaning that the earth was becoming polluted with people (who made more pollution of other types). This was saying that beings made in God's likeness were pollution. Rather than thinking of people as pollution, God thought they were important enough to send his son to die for them.

Our counselees are even more likely to have wrong concepts about Christians. We seem to expect absolute perfection out of other members of the church. We have the concept that we should have arrived at some final state, although Scripture does not indicate this. The apostle Paul addressed his first letter to the Corinthian church to those who were sanctified in Christ Jesus and called to to be saints. Even a quick reading of that letter will reveal that that church had a lot of room for growth and improvement. We must look for improvement and not absolute perfection in the church.

Finally, many Christians have the wrong concept of themselves. Many books have been written about the self-concept. Personality theories have centered around it. Ellison (1976) edited a book approaching the topic of self-esteem from a Christian perspective. As Christians, we must not center on our sinful past or our present shortcomings, but rather upon ourselves as new creatures in Christ with the potential of becoming increasingly like him. Furthermore, we are children of God, not merely slaves or servants.

Will Power

Around the turn of the century, most psychology textbooks contained a chapter, or even several chapters, on *will* or *volition*. In fact, such chapters usually came at the end of the book because they were seen as the major integrating factor between thought and action. However, the concept of *will* came into disrepute in psychology. By mid-century one could hardly find the word *will* in the index of most general psychology textbooks. That is still the case. This section on volition should probably be a separate chapter. Since psychology ignores it today, we will place it here because it involves thinking and choosing.

The reason for the abandonment of the term *will* was a philosophical one. As we saw in chapter 1, both of the major forces in psychology (behaviorism and psychoanalysis) during the first half of the century made strongly deterministic assumptions. People were seen as "being controlled by" rather than as "controlling." Behaviorists saw humans as being controlled by their environments, while psychoanalysts saw humans as being controlled by unconscious forces. In neither system did psychologists see humans as having the capacity to make real choices. Choice was only illusory. Furthermore, since we could not make choices, we could not be held responsible for what we did.

In his book, *Love and Will,* Rollo May (1969) finally broke the silence on will when Part II of his book was simply titled "Will." I would have liked to have called this section "will therapy," but that term has already been used by Rank (1931/1936), and I have something quite different in mind here.

We must reaffirm the fact that human beings can actually

make choices and are held responsible for the choices they make. God tells us to choose whom we will serve, and Jesus said that he came that we might be free. There is no indication that these choices or this freedom are not real. As beings made in God's image, we actually have the capacity to choose. Of course, this does not mean that we have absolute freedom to make any choice, but within limits we can make real choices.

The most important choice is for or against God. When we respond to God's call, we have more freedom, "freedom from" sin and "freedom to" become more like God. As we counsel individuals, we must consider the freedom they have and its limits. Non-Christians may have less freedom to stop doing certain actions because they are slaves to sin. The compulsion to do wrong may be much stronger. Christians are freed from the compulsion to sin and free to mature in him.

As Christians counseling other Christians, we do not have to accept the philosophical assumptions of the behaviorists and psychoanalysts who say that people *cannot* stop their inappropriate actions. We say that they *will* not stop them. For example, consider compulsive eaters who do not stop eating. It is not that they cannot stop, but that they will not stop. This is not to say that it will be easy to stop, but that people have the ability to do so if they develop the will to stop.

The apostle Paul gives us specific commands concerning "willing" what we should think about. In chapter three of Colossians, he tells us to set our minds on things above, not on earthly things. Then he elaborates on kinds of behavior we should "put on" and "put off." In chapter four of Philippians, he goes into considerable detail about the types of things we should think about, things that are true, noble, right, pure, lovely, admirable, excellent, and praiseworthy. We are commanded to think about such things. As Christians we do have the capacity to direct our thoughts, to think about certain things and not about others.

We must consider this as a possible component of therapy when we attempt to help people. We must get a commitment of the will, rather than rely on such things as reinforcement in behavior therapy. As we saw in the last chapter, behavior therapy is effective, but only as long as the reinforcement is continued. From the perspective taken here, we would say that cognition, specifically a willing commitment, is necessary for a permanent change in behavior. Since psychologists have de-emphasized the will during this century, many people will not be familiar with making such commitments, but they do have this God-like capacity, and we must capitalize on it.

Conclusion

We have seen that humans are like God with respect to their cognitions, and this is related to their spiritual nature, maturity, and perception. One of the major symptoms of psychosis—delusions—is based on disorders of thinking. Schizophrenia, obsessions, and aphasias involve primarily our cognitions. Cognition has been involved in a number of recently developed therapies. Rational-emotive therapy, cognitive therapy, and behavioral contracting all involve cognition. We must also consider the fact that people have the power of choice as we are counseling them.

Suggested Readings

Chapters on "Thinking" or "Cognition" in general psychology textbooks and chapters on "Schizophrenia" in abnormal psychology textbooks are recommended reading. Although there are several books on the cognitive processes, they are too technical to be of much use to counselors. Agranowitz and McKeown (1964), Beck (1976), Bernheim and Lewine (1979), Bootzin and Acocella (1980), Brown (1972), Coleman, Butcher, and Carson (1980), Corsini (1973), Ellis (1973b), Koteskey (1980), O'Brien (1978), and Walen, DiGiuseppe, and Wessler (1980) expand on material discussed in this chapter.

MEMORY

An intellectual process closely associated with both learning and cognition is memory. What is learned must be remembered. Some things may be remembered when they are simply learned by rote memory. Others are better remembered when the learning involves cognition. In one sense, all learning and thinking involves memory. If someone cannot remember material, we do not think he or she has learned it. Thinking itself involves manipulating cognitions remembered about the past. Let us begin by considering areas of psychology, above "memory" in Figure 10:1, as they are related to memory.

Structure

For many years psychologists looked for the memory trace, assuming that learning made some kind of change in the nervous system. Psychologists thought that this trace could be kept active through use, but that it faded or became distorted when it was not practiced. After a lifetime of research on the physiological basis of learning and memory, Karl Lashley (1950) was unable to find any such trace and said that he was tempted to conclude that learning was impossible.

We know that learning and memory do occur, but what happens in the nervous system remains a mystery. Some psychologists have thought that DNA may be involved, and

Figure 10:1 Memory and memory disorders from a Christian perspective.

HUMANS

Created............in the............Image of God
Like Animals............Like God
Overt Behavior............Definition............Mental Processes
Understand............Goals............Make People
Creation............Like God
Psychoanalysis............Systems............Humanistic
Behaviorism............Psychology

(DISORDER)............Experimental............Methods............Descriptive............(DISORDER)
Organic Disorders............Physiological............Structure............Spiritual............Spiritual Disorders—Sin
(Organic Mental Disorders)............(Personality Disorders)

Physical Disorders............Immaturity............Development............Maturity............Spiritual Immaturity
(Disorders Appearing in............(No DSM-III Category)
Childhood or Adolescence)

Sensory Disorders............Sensation............Awareness............Perception............Perceptual Disorders
(Somatoform Disorders)............(States of Consciousness—Substance Use Disorders)............(Paranoid Disorders)

Learning Disorders............Learning............Intellect............Cognition............Thinking Disorders
(Phobic Disorders)............(MEMORY—DISSOCIATIVE DISORDERS)............(Schizophrenic Disorders)

others have tried to implicate RNA. The most popular current theories hold that changes in protein molecules in the brain cells or changes in the anatomical structures, primarily at the synapses, underlie memory. Since animals, as well as humans, can remember, it would seem reasonable to assume that some anatomical and physiological changes take place in learning so that what is learned can be remembered.

Although the word "memory" is seldom used in the Bible, the word "remember" occurs frequently. We are exhorted to remember God, his people, and his word. The capacity to remember is a God-like attribute, as shown by frequent prayers, especially in the psalms, wherein God is asked to remember (or remember not) something that happened previously.

Development

Although we do not usually associate memory with developmental psychology, memory makes our development toward God-likeness possible. Without memory, experiences would be forgotten as soon as they became a part of the past. Every experience would be completely new, so that we could not use past experiences to modify our present behavior to make it more effective. Furthermore, we would have to learn the same information over and over. Memory, even of bad experiences, makes it possible for us to act more effectively in the present.

Awareness

Both sensation and perception affect what gets into our memory. We are unable to recall some things because they never got into our memory. We direct our attention toward what we consider more important information at a given time. This selective attention to one kind of input while turning down other kinds is called *sensory gating*. This allows us to keep our attention focused in one place, but does so without eliminating all information from the other senses. When there is an unexpected change in the other senses, our attention will shift to them. We can even select information within a single sensory channel through selective attention. The "cocktail party phenomenon" refers to our ability to pick out and listen to one conversation even when several conversations are going on at the same time.

The first part of memory is called sensory storage or sensory memory. This is the very short persistence of sensory information after the stimulus has ceased. For example, if people are shown three rows of four letters and numbers each, they can recall only about four or five. However, if a signal is quickly flashed telling them to give the letters of a particular line, they can usually do so. Thus, the subjects had a brief impression of the entire set of letters and numbers. However, this impression fades rapidly, in a fraction of a second. In fact, it seems to be completely gone in only one second.

Intellect

Learning and cognitive processes become involved in what is usually called storage, beyond the sensory storage already discussed. Much of what we call verbal learning and cognitive processes seems to be the processing of information so that it can be permanently stored and not forgotten. As we said, information can be kept in the sensory store only about a second, then whatever is not transferred to the short-term memory is forgotten.

The short-term memory has two basic features. First, it can retain information only 15 or 20 seconds unless something is done to keep it there. In fact, it seems that much of the forgetting we do from short-term memory is intentional. Since we no longer need that information, we throw it out, as in the case of adding a column of two digit numbers when we need only the final sum, not each sum along the way. If we want to retain information for more than a few seconds, we must rehearse or repeat it. The second characteristic of short-term memory is that it can hold only a limited amount of information, usually only about five to nine items. Most people can dial a strange seven-digit telephone number without looking at it halfway through the dialing—unless someone interrupts them so they cannot keep rehearsing it. However, most people have trouble doing the same thing with a long distance (ten digit) telephone number including the area code. We can keep more information in the short-term memory if we code it in some way.

We should put information we want to remember for a long time into our long-term memory. Unlike the short-term memory, the long-term memory seems to be permanent. Once the information gets into the long-term storage it may remain there in some form throughout a person's life. Furthermore, the capacity of the long-term store seems to be limitless. It apparently never gets full, so that we never reach the place where we cannot learn and remember more. Of course, the crucial thing is to get information into this memory. Although we do not know in detail how information gets in, we do know that the more we associate with the information, imagine it, and relate it to other things, the more likely it is to get into long-term memory. The crucial thing is to organize the material in some way and relate it to things already in the long-term memory.

Retrieval

Even after we have paid attention, gotten the information through the sensory buffer, through the short-term memory, and into the long-term memory, we have not completed the task. Finally, we must retrieve it from that long-term memory. Many times we find that we cannot remember something we know that we have learned. Nearly all students have had the experience of being unable to recall something for a test, and recalling it perfectly as soon as they walk out the door after handing in the paper.

Many things can interfere with such retrieval. One major

problem is that of interference. Material learned later may interfere with it. Some memory is state-dependent. That is, material one learns while under the influence of a drug may not be easily retrievable when one is not under the influence of that drug. In fact, rats can be trained to make one response while under the influence of a barbiturate and the opposite response when given no drugs, and the responses do not even interfere with each other.

Disorders

Memory disorders range from simply having a poor memory to having a total loss of memory. These disorders can be placed in our Christian perspective as shown in the lower center of Figure 10:1 (Dissociative Disorders). The memory disorders are placed between learning and cognition because both of these are so much involved in memory, and memory is an intellectual function of humans. Let us now consider some of the memory disorders.

Too Little Memory

Most people think that this is the only memory disorder, because it is the one we hear about most often. We often forget material we want to remember. This being unable to remember may have organic causes, or it may occur even when nothing is organically wrong.

Poor memory. Some individuals have a poor memory because they have never learned how to go about memorizing. There is nothing wrong with their nervous system, and they have no psychological stress, but they simply have trouble remembering. They meet a person, hear the person's name, and fifteen seconds later they have forgotten it. They go over and over lists of words that they know are going to appear on a test, but cannot remember the lists. These individuals have a poor memory because they have never learned how to get things into long-term memory or how to retrieve material from it.

Organic Disorders. As we would expect, changes in the nervous system bring about changes in the person's ability to remember. Currently most of these changes are brought about by physical damage to the brain or by altering its functioning through the use of drugs.

Brain damage may occur suddenly or slowly in a variety of ways. The most familiar sudden damage is that caused by strokes. The sudden blocking or rupture of a blood vessel in the brain may lead to confusion and loss of memory. A sudden loss of memory may also occur through a blow to the head or through some object actually penetrating the cranium.

Some types of amnesia may be caused by damage to the brain during surgery. Some epileptics undergo brain surgery to prevent seizures. Although they have relief from their epilepsy, they may be left with anterograde amnesia, in which they can no longer retain new experiences. That is, although their memory for events occurring before brain surgery is unaffected, they can no longer transfer information from short-term to long-term memory. A similar kind of loss of memory occurs with Korsakoff's Psychosis. Although old information is available, no new information is transferred to permanent storage.

Retrograde amnesia may occur following head injuries. Memory for new events since the accident is normal. The memory deficit is only for events occurring before the injury. Electroconvulsive shock therapy and carbon monoxide poisoning may also produce this effect. Apparently the consolidation of the memory is not completed, so recent memories are more fragile than older ones. The person may be able to remember events of the distant past, and events until a few days or hours before the injury, but there is a period of time between this and the accident for which memory is gone.

Memory impairment may come on more gradually when

the damage to the brain is more gradual. For example, one of the most frequent early signs of a brain tumor is memory impairment or confusion. In general paresis, memory defects are noticeable in the early phases, but become even more obvious later. As people get older, memory defects, especially for recent events, become more obvious. The same is true for individuals with cerebral arteriosclerosis, in which an insufficient supply of blood to the brain gradually develops.

Memory disorders may also occur with the use of drugs. Those associated with alcohol are the most widely known. We have already mentioned that associated with Korsakoff's Psychosis, but even problem drinkers experience "black-outs." At first these lapses of memory occur only at high alcohol levels, but in heavy drinkers they may occur even with moderate levels of alcohol. During these blackouts, individuals may carry on conversations and other complex activities, but remember nothing about them the next day. Pathological intoxication may occur in people whose tolerance to alcohol is lessened by exhaustion or stress. Such people may become confused and violent after only moderate amounts of alcohol, then fall into a deep sleep and remember nothing about it. Both stimulants and depressants may produce memory impairments. Excessive use of barbiturates leads to impaired comprehension and memory. Where brain damage has occurred from the use of amphetamines, residual effects may include an impaired memory.

Dissociative Disorders. As the name suggests, these disorders involve a dissociation, or splitting, of parts of the personality that are normally together. They also involve a lack of memory for some parts of the personality. These disorders seem to be a way of avoiding stress and responsibility while gratifying needs by simply escaping or dissociating from parts of the personality.

We saw that amnesia may be caused by organic damage, but *psychogenic amnesia* appears with no underlying organic cause. It tends to appear suddenly, usually following some severe psychological stress, and the forgetting is selective so that only the trauma or some unacceptable behavior is forgotten. These amnesiacs are typically not too distressed by their disorder, and the forgotten events are not really gone, but can often be recalled under hypnosis. Individuals often cannot remember their names, do not know where they live, and do not recognize close friends and relatives. However, their basic behavior patterns, including the ability to drive, read, talk, and so forth, remain, so that they seem normal except for their amnesia.

Although amnesia is highly dramatic, it is quite rare. Psychologists have identified four types of psychogenic amnesia. First, localized amnesia occurs when all events in a given period of time are blocked out. This frequently happens to events surrounding a trauma, such as a natural disaster. Second, selective amnesia occurs when the person forgets only selected events in that given period of time. Many events may be remembered during the period, but the most stressful are forgotten. Third, generalized amnesia occurs when the people forget their entire past life. Although this is common in novels and movies, it is rare in real life. Finally, continuous amnesia occurs when amnesiacs forget everything that happens after their amnesia began. If it began two weeks ago, they cannot remember what they did last week.

Closely related to amnesia is *psychogenic fugue*. In this state, patients go one step beyond amnesia in that they not only forget the past, but they actually leave home and assume a new identity. Amnesiacs may wander about aimlessly, but fugue patients are purposeful in their movements because they have made a new identity for themselves. Usually such people will go no further than to a nearby town, spend the day there, check into a hotel, and recover by morning. However, some travel far away, make up a past history, and live a totally new life for months or even years. During the fugue, such people will appear normal to others. When they suddenly recover, they will not remember anything that has happened during the fugue.

The most dramatic, and rarest, dissociative disorder is the

multiple personality, in which an individual alternates between several distinct, integrated, well-developed personalities. Although this disorder is widely known, it is extremely rare, with only about a hundred reported cases in all the psychological literature. The relationships between the personalities follow many different patterns, increasing as the number of personalities increases. The personalities may alternate or be conscious at the same time. It is unlikely that any given counselor will encounter such a person.

The most common of the dissociative disorders is the *depersonalization disorder.* This occurs most frequently in adolescents and young adults. Suddenly they feel different, like they have become someone else or that their body has drastically changed. They may report an "out of body experience" in which they feel like they have left their body and are floating around without it. Between such episodes they are able to function normally, but with a fear of losing control again. Christian counselors are more likely to encounter this type of person than someone with psychogenic amnesia, psychogenic fugue, or multiple personality.

Too Much Memory

Although we do not usually recognize it, the capacity to forget is a great blessing. Not being able to forget is a disorder even though it is not given a psychiatric classification. We saw this when we discussed anterograde amnesia in which a person's memory before the brain damage is unaffected, but it can never be changed. When such individuals move to a new house they can never learn their new address, so they keep returning to the old one. Imagine the problems you would have if memory were permanent. You could never learn a new telephone number, address, name (when someone married), and so forth.

Luria (1968) studied an individual who had difficulty forgetting. This person had learned to code words by making them into images and looking for them mentally. He would use what we call the "method of loci" and place these images at various points along a mental walk down a well-known street so that he could recall them forward or backward by taking such a mental walk down the street. When he turned professional and had to memorize long lists of words day after day, his mental streets became very cluttered; and if he was not careful, he found himself recalling the wrong list of words. This inability to forget became a source of great confusion to him in his career as a professional mnemonist.

Experiments using electrical stimulation of various parts of the brain indicate that perhaps all memories are permanent. Neurosurgeon Wilder Penfield found that by stimulating certain parts of the cerebral cortex he could activate vivid "reruns" of past events. It was not that the persons just remembered having the experience, but they felt as if they were actually reliving the experience. One woman heard a song so clearly that she thought a record was actually being played in the operating room. Many psychologists believe that all our memories are permanent, that we never actually forget anything. When we say that we have forgotten, it does not mean that the material is no longer there, just that we are no longer able to retrieve it.

Sometimes the emotional content associated with these memories can result in problems. If we have been hurt by others or have hurt others, the emotions connected with these memories may plague us for years. The woman who hates her father because of the memories associated with his rejection of her may find herself rejecting others in the same way, or even becoming physically ill. Rather than just trying to suppress these memories, something must be done to remove their emotional content. Christian counselors are likely to meet many such individuals and need to know how to deal with such problems.

Treatment

As we have repeatedly stated in this book, we must determine the cause (or causes) of the disorder and then give appropriate treatments if available, or help the persons live with their disorders if no treatment is available. Let us now consider the disorders mentioned in the previous section.

Too Little Memory

We can easily help some people with too little memory; and some others recover on their own, and some are never able to recover their memories. Although there are no magic formulas, those with poor memories can do some things to improve memory. They should learn material well originally. Such material is more resistant to forgetting than material barely learned. They can make material meaningful by using coding techniques, such as some of the mnemonic devices described below. Learning under the conditions where you will have to recall the material is most effective. When learning, try to provide yourself with retrieval cues so that you will be able to retrieve the information when you need it. Actually practice the material. After reading a section in a book, stop and recall it, or after you are introduced to someone, use his or her name several times in the conversation. Do not learn while under the influence of drugs. You may get state-dependent learning and not be able to recall unless you take the same drugs again.

Mnemonic Devices. In addition to the above suggestions, many persons can improve their memories by using mnemonic devices. These memory aids all serve to organize information and use information already stored in memory. Some of the most common mnemonic devices are discussed here.

The *method of loci* involves the use of a series of places already in memory, a series of locations that can always be recalled in order. Each place then becomes a place associated with a thing you are trying to recall. If you imagine a walk down your street, you may imagine the first object being on your mailbox, the next one in your neighbor's tree, the next one on the roof of the next house, and so forth. When you need to recall them, imagine the same walk down the street and visualize the objects in their respective places. Using this technique, almost anyone can memorize a list of fifteen words by going through them only one time, and be able to recall them a week later.

The *peg system* involves having a list of "memory pegs" already known to you on which you can "hang" the objects to be memorized. For example, one is a bun, two is a shoe, three is a tree, four is a door, five is a hive, six is sticks, and so forth. Then make an association between "bun" and the first word on the list, "shoe" and the second word, "tree" and the third word, and so forth. The list—bun, shoe, tree, door—can be recalled easily because each sounds like a number. Then the corresponding objects can be recalled easily.

Acronyms can be created using the first letter of each word in a series. I still recall the colors of the spectrum by remembering "ROY G. BIV," an acronym I learned in elementary school, representing red, orange, yellow, green, blue, indigo, and violet. A similar technique is known as *narrative chaining,* in which you make up a story centered on the words you need to recall. Making a *rhyme* helps us remember facts about given things, such as "I before E except after C" or "Thirty days hath September, April, June, and November. . . ." We know the letters and the months, but if we get the wrong ones the rhyme will not work. *Coding numbers to letters* can be used to remember a series of numbers. Each digit is assigned a consonant and you memorize the code. For example, $O = B$, $1 = C$, $2 = D$, $3 = F$, $4 = G$, $5 = H$, $6 = J$, $7 = K$, $8 = L$, $9 = M$. Then my office telephone extension (224) becomes DDG or D. DOG. If you think of me as D. Dog, remove the vowels and decode the consonants to get my extension. Most phone numbers, addresses, and zip codes can be coded in this way.

Organic Disorders. Recovery from organic disorders depends on the amount of damage done, and how successfully one can remove the cause of the memory loss. Damage done during brain surgery may be permanent. Some epileptic patients who have surgery to prevent seizures cannot form new memories even several years later. However, people who have Korsakoff's psychosis may regain much of their capacity to form memories when given a diet rich in vitamins and minerals.

People who have retrograde amnesia due to brain injuries often recover some of their memories simply with the passage of time. The memory return is usually gradual, with memories from the more distant past returning first. They may never recover the memories of events immediately preceding the injury. Damage due to senility and arteriosclerosis is permanent, but there may be some recovery. Memory loss due to drugs is likewise permanent, although in state-dependent learning the person may recover some of the memory when in the drugged state again.

Dissociative Disorders. Treatment of the dissociative disorders does not involve concentration on the dramatic symptoms. Although the symptoms may be removed by hypnosis, they usually disappear spontaneously. Some people with amnesia or fugue live that way for the rest of their lives, but most remit suddenly by themselves any time from the next day to several years later. People with psychogenic fugue may not even know where they are or what has happened to them during the fugue. Multiple personality is so rare that no standard treatment exists. People who have depersonalization disorders function between episodes. The major treatment for the dissociative disorders is to work on coping with the stress or conflict that brought on the disorder in the first place.

Too Much Memory

As previously mentioned, it is likely that we actually store all of our experiences, and then become unable to retrieve many of the things that are nonessential. The person Luria (1968) studied had the problem of being unable to forget those nonessentials. Since he was a professional mnemonist, this was serious because he had to memorize long lists of words day after day, and previous lists interfered with the ones he was currently learning as a part of his act.

Although we are unlikely to work with people who have too good a memory for facts, we are very likely to counsel someone who has not been able to forget the emotional content associated with some memories. Such individuals continue to have problems with these memories even though they have tried to forget and have prayed about it. The treatment of this condition has come to be called "healing of memories" or "inner healing."

Linn and Linn (1974) point out that these people must make a choice in the healing of memories. They must decide whether they will let past hurts control them (keep them acting in self-centered ways), or let the peace and love of the Holy Spirit take control. Such individuals need to go back over their memories one by one and turn them over to the Spirit. Although God can heal instantly, Linn and Linn note that he generally works through the people, calling them to go through a series of about six steps.

The first step is to thank God for the gifts he gives. Rather than rushing into healing, we need to know ourselves so that we can see ourselves as created in God's image and thank him for making us. Such concentration on our blessings is not an ego trip. We do it not to boast of ourselves, but boast of God. We must see ourselves as a whole and see how that memory fits into our whole person.

The second step is to ask God what he wants to heal in us. Many times we want to be healed just to experience fewer tensions or to live up to what someone else expects of us. Our motivation must be to become more like Christ, and we must be sure that we really want to be healed, regardless of what other people think.

The third step is to share with Christ a painful memory that keeps us from being healed. We must go back to the memory of the original event causing our problem. Rather than focusing on the immediate problem of depression, mistrust, impatience, and so forth, we must go back to the experience where it started. If we are aware of the memory, we can go back to it. If not, we must allow the Holy Spirit to bring the memory to consciousness.

The fourth step is to replace the hurt with love. We have a part in this by forgiving those involved in the painful memory as God would forgive them. Even though the people causing the hurt may no longer be alive, we must forgive them unconditionally. Our forgiveness, like God's, must not depend on the other person's changing and becoming worthy. We focus not on the hurt, but on change and growth.

The fifth step is to continue to replace the hurt with love by becoming thankful for that painful memory. Since we believe that all things work together for good, let us look for that good. For example, Joseph in Egypt did not let his painful memories fester, but forgave his brothers and told them later that even though they meant their deed for evil, God had used it for good. Another example would be when we find it difficult to speak because other children laughed at us when we gave the wrong answer. This painful incident may have led to new methods of communication, such as writing or painting. It may have also made us more compassionate toward others.

Finally, we thank God for healing and imagine ourselves acting in his healed way. We must be aware that the healing is of God, not just a matter of extinction, and we need to thank him for it. All or some of these steps need to be repeated as the Spirit points out other memories that need healing.

Conclusion

We have seen how memory is related to the other aspects of the person in our Christian perspective. Disorders of memory can include remembering either too little or too much. If memory loss is due to organic damage, some recovery may be possible, but total recovery is not likely. Psychogenic amnesia and fugue usually end in spontaneous recovery. If people are bothered by emotions tied to memories, this may be treated by the healing of memories.

Suggested Readings

Chapters on "Memory" or "Forgetting" in general psychology textbooks and chapters on "Dissociative Disorders" in abnormal psychology textbooks are recommended. Baddeley (1976), Bootzin and Acocella (1980), Coleman, Butcher, and Carson (1980), Linn and Linn (1974), and Seamon (1980) expand on material presented in this chapter.

BIOLOGICAL MOTIVATION

The previous three chapters have been concerned with the intellectual processes of humans. This chapter begins a new area of general psychology, one dealing with motivation. Motives arouse and direct behavior. They get you going and direct you toward a particular goal. For example, the thirstier you get, the more likely you are to get up (arousal) and get a drink of water (direction). Psychologists usually divide motivation into two sections that go by different terms, such as primary and secondary, innate and acquired, biological and cognitive, or physiological and psychological. In this chapter we will consider the first type, which we will call biological motivation.

Biological motivation fits into our Christian perspective as shown in the lower central part of Figure 11:1 (Biological— Motivation). Animals as well as humans have these biological motives, and humans are quite animal-like in many of these motives. In fact, much of what we know about them comes from the study of animals. Although there are many biological motives, psychologists have concentrated on the study of hunger, thirst, and sex. As we look at each of these three major motives, let us relate them to the areas of psychology listed above them in Figure 11:1.

Hunger

In order to stay alive we must eat enough so that our energy use does not exceed our caloric intake. Daily variations in the

Figure 11:1 Biological motivation and biological motivational disorders from a Christian perspective.

HUMANS

Created.................. in the.................Image of God		
Like Animals	Like God	
Overt Behavior........Definition......Mental Processes		
Understand.............Goals............Make People		
Creation		Like God
Psychoanalysis.........Systems..........Humanistic		
Behaviorism		Psychology

(DISORDER)		(DISORDER)
	Experimental........Methods........Descriptive	
Organic Disorders........Physiological......Structure.......Spiritual..........Spiritual Disorders—Sin
(Organic Mental Disorders)		(Personality Disorders)
Physical Disorders........Immaturity.........Development.......Maturity.........Spiritual Immaturity
(Disorders Appearing in		(No DSM-III Category)
Childhood or Adolescence)		

Sensory Disorders..........Sensation.........Awareness........Perception.......Perceptual Disorders
(Somatoform Disorders)   (States of Consciousness—Substance Use Disorders)   (Paranoid Disorders)
Learning Disorders........Learning.........Intellect........Cognition.........Thinking Disorders
(Phobic Disorders)   (Memory—Dissociative Disorders)   (Schizophrenic Disorders)

MOTIVATIONAL.........BIOLOGICAL.........MOTIVATION......
DISORDERS   MOTIVATION
(PSYCHOSEXUAL
DISORDERS)

amount we eat may not cause many ill effects, but in the long run there must be a balance between intake and expenditure. If there is not, the person becomes obese or starves. Many different factors influence what and how much we eat. Let us consider those factors in the areas above motivation in Figure 11:1.

Physiological. Anatomical and physiological factors play a prominent role in biological motivations. Early theories emphasized that hunger was due to sensations coming from the body, particularly from contractions of the stomach. However, psychologists found that cutting nerves between the stomach and the brain did not decrease food intake. In fact, removing the stomach entirely did not decrease intake. Theories emphasizing events in the central nervous system then began to dominate psychology. One part of the brain, the hypothalamus, seemed to play an important role. Destruction of one part of it resulted in animals or people who overate and gained weight rapidly, then maintained the new higher weight. Destruction of another part resulted in animals who refused to eat at all and died unless kept alive by tube feeding. Although they then recovered, they never became completely normal. More recently psychologists have shifted emphasis from the hypothalamus itself to pathways passing through it. Furthermore, psychologists once again see peripheral factors as playing a role. The liver apparently monitors the body's fuel supply and sends information to the brain.

Developmental. It is quite obvious that hunger is a major motive even early in life. Infants seem to engage in two major activities, sleeping and eating. Maslow (1954) pointed out that the biological motives (including hunger) are the most basic ones, and that higher motives do not appear until these are satisfied.

Sensory. Taste and smell obviously affect our eating. The odor or first taste of good food increases the flow of saliva, the secretion of insulin and the movement of muscles in the digestive tract. When someone makes food taste better, we increase our intake, and when they make it taste worse, we decrease our intake. When someone changes the texture to make it more or less pleasant, we will increase or decrease our intake in response. These sensory factors controlling food intake seem obvious, but even the sight of food will start people eating. This is especially true in obese people who are not hungry. They eat less than normal persons when food is not in sight, but more when larger quantities of food are set before them.

Learning. Our food preferences are greatly influenced by learning. Fried grasshoppers or live termites do not sound very appetizing to most Americans. However, if they think in technical terms about what they actually eat, their food does not sound much better. A slice of buttered toast is really ground embryos (of plants) that have been heated very hot (baked), cut up and burned again (toasted). Then the secretions of the mammary glands of the bovine ruminant (milk from cows) are allowed to separate, one part is stirred until it hardens (butter), and it is spread on the burned embryos. Of course, we have to learn to like many of the things we eat. Unfortunately, we learn to like foods that are not very good for us—coffee, chocolate, foods high in sugar, and so forth.

Thirst

In order to stay alive we must also drink enough so that our water loss does not exceed our water intake. Water is lost through urination, defecation, perspiration, and breathing. Day-to-day variations in water intake can occur without ill effects, but a certain minimum amount of water is necessary for life. We can go without food for weeks, but we cannot live without water for more than a few days.

Physiological. Several anatomical and physiological mechanisms regulate the water balance of the body. One mechanism is composed of cells located in or near the hypothalamus, which become deformed or shriveled from loss of water through osmosis. Neural activity is then triggered, resulting in water's being reabsorbed by the kidneys and in the person's drinking. Another mechanism is composed of receptors that respond to decreased blood volume, resulting in the constriction of the blood vessels and more drinking.

Developmental. Drinking is associated with eating at the beginning of life, as it is all through life. Immediately after birth all nourishment is taken by means of drinking. The infant responds to the nipple in its mouth with the sucking reflex and then swallows the milk.

Sensation. The sensation most often associated with thirst is dryness of the mouth. Although we usually drink before our mouth becomes dry, we are acutely aware of the dryness when it does occur. Dryness of the mouth is one of the factors associated with the beginning of drinking, but we drink long after water has moistened these tissues. Even if our salivary glands were tied off so that our mouth would always be dry, we would drink no more than usual. We would drink more often, but less each time.

Learning. The kind of drinking we have been talking about up to this point is called primary drinking, drinking related to loss of water from within the cells or around the cells. Most of our drinking is secondary drinking, drinking done in anticipation of our need for water rather than in response to water actually lost. When shifted to a high protein diet that requires more water, animals first drink extra water after the meal (primary drinking), but within a few days they drink the extra water during the meal (secondary drinking).

Sex

Nearly everyone discussing biological motivation includes the sexual drive, but hastens to add that it is different from the other biological drives. It is not vital to the survival of the individual, it uses energy rather than restores it, and there are many restrictions (when, where, and with whom) on its satisfaction. These are not only cultural restrictions, but have moral implications as well.

BIOLOGICAL MOTIVATION

Physiological. Two physiological factors have been implicated in sexual motivation: hormonal and neural. Hormonal factors are extremely important in determining sexual motivation in animals, but they play a relatively minor role in adult humans. Although some studies have found a small positive correlation between the level of estrogen in the bloodstream and likelihood of intercourse in women, other studies have found a negative correlation. Although castration before puberty may prevent copulation in males, most studies show little decrease in sexual motivation in adult males following castration—unless they think it will have an effect. Surprisingly, the one hormone that does affect sexual motivation in both men and women is testosterone (secreted by the adrenals as well as the testes). As long as there is a minimal level in the bloodstream, sexual motivation will be normal. These hormones do not elicit particular sexual behaviors, but produce a readiness to respond to sexual stimuli.

Neural factors are very important for sexual behavior in both men and women, although we do not have the same experimental data we have for hormones. In general, the more similar animals are to humans, the more important are neural mechanisms and the less important are the hormones. Both the hypothalamus and the cortex are important in human sexual behavior. Chemicals at the synapses are also involved, but their role is far from clear at the moment. For example, women who use amphetamines (which produce dopamine) frequently are likely to show sexual dysfunction. However, men who take L-dopa (which increases dopamine) for Parkinson's disease have reported an increase in sexual desire.

Developmental. Although we typically think of sexual motivation as characteristic of adults, children also engage in sexual behavior. Boys are capable of erections and orgasms long before they are capable of ejaculation, and girls are capable of orgasms long before their first menstrual period. Although Freud overemphasized childhood sexuality, most people underemphasize it.

Sensation. Sensation is obviously related to sexual motivation. As was noted previously, hormones produce a state of readiness to respond to sexual stimuli. Of course, almost any stimulus can be sexually arousing, depending on the experiences of the individual. However, visual stimuli have traditionally been the most sexually arousing to the male. This is the reason for the popularity of books, magazines, and movies capitalizing on presenting the nude female body or people in various sexual postures. Recently, more women are reporting being sexually aroused by visual stimuli. Traditionally, touch has been the most erotic stimulus for women. This is the reason for the popularity of petting, in which the male manually stimulates the various erogenous zones of the female, leading to her sexual arousal.

Learning. Learning plays a very important role in sexual behavior. Although orgasmic responses are reflexively controlled, other sexual behaviors must be learned. This is the reason for the popularity of marriage manuals and books about sexual techniques. People do not innately know the sexual behaviors expected of them. These behaviors are different in different cultures. Each culture has its own set of stimuli which are considered to be erotic, and members of that culture learn sexual responses to them. For example, in some cultures the sight of a woman's breast is considered highly erotic, while in others it is not. In some cultures the smell of perspiration is considered highly erotic, while in others it may be considered offensive, so members of that culture do all they can to remove it.

Disorders

Just as there can be disorders in other areas, so can there be disorders in biological motivation, as shown in Figure 11:1. Psychosexual disorders are shown in Figure 11:1 because they are the largest category of motivational disorders in DSM-III. There are other disorders as well, and these are discussed in this section. Again, it is crucial that we determine the source of the problem so that we can use an appropriate treatment. We must also remember that the primary problem may create secondary ones that also need treatment.

Eating Disorders

Eating disorders can be in the form of eating too much, too little, the wrong foods, or some combination of the three. Some people, such as alcoholics, eat all they want, but still suffer from malnutrition. Eating the correct foods is crucial during pregnancy and during the early years of life, as we have seen when discussing retardation.

Bulimia. One eating disorder specified in DSM-III is bulimia, excessive overeating or uncontrolled eating binges. This leads to obesity, an excessive amount of fat on the person's body. Obesity not only makes people socially unattractive, but it can lead to a variety of physical disorders. Our society prizes thinness, but obesity is prevalent, and at least a quarter of American adults are overweight.

Of course, we ask why people are overweight, and the simple, obvious answer is that people get fat because they eat more calories than they burn. Then the question becomes, Why do they eat so much? The answer may be a physical cause. Reeves and Plum (1961, as cited in Balagura, 1973) reported the case of a young woman who developed a tumor in the hypothalamus. Within two years her body weight had doubled and her behavior changed markedly. Obesity may also be caused by endocrine imbalance, such as an underactive thyroid.

Only about one in twenty who are overweight have brain damage or a glandular disorder. The rest simply eat too much. Obesity in adulthood may be the result of developmental problems related to the size and number of fat cells in the body. Overfeeding infants causes them to develop more fat cells, predisposing them to obesity. When adults lose weight, the size of the fat cells is reduced, but the number remains the same, providing a basis for the weight to be regained.

Obesity may result when eating comes under the control of external rather than internal cues. Numerous experiments have shown that obese subjects eat more than normal ones when food is in sight, tastes good, and takes little effort to get. Surprisingly, these obese subjects eat less than normal people when food is out of sight, tastes bad, and takes much effort to get. Thus, for them, obesity is a sensory problem—they eat in response to external cues rather than to internal cues.

Obesity may simply be due to habitual overeating. Most people tend to gain weight with advancing age. This may be because, as they get older, they tend to reduce their activity, but continue their former eating habits. Rather than decreasing their food intake, they eat the same amount they learned to eat in early adulthood.

In a society where food is scarce, most people have little trouble with obesity. However, in an affluent society such as ours, many individuals have problems with what the Bible calls "self-control" or "gluttony." We hear very little preaching or teaching on the subject of gluttony today, perhaps because so many preachers and teachers are obese themselves. The apostle Paul talks about being temperate in all things and bringing his body into subjection. Unfortunately, "temperance" has come to be associated only with consumption of alcoholic beverages, even though it has a much broader meaning in Scripture. We must be aware that gluttony is not only a psychological disorder, but a sinful behavior as well.

Anorexia Nervosa. Anorexia nervosa is a disorder in which individuals fail to eat enough over a long period of time; the opposite of bulimia. This disorder is found primarily among adolescent girls and young women. Although the disorder was once quite rare, it seems to be increasing in recent years. Since some anorexics (as many as 25 percent) literally starve themselves to death, some type of therapy is necessary immediately.

The most dramatic physical evidence of anorexia nervosa is weight loss. Anorexics beginning at a normal weight may drop to a weight of only fifty or sixty pounds. This disorder usually begins with a period of dieting, common among adolescent girls in our culture. However, anorexics develop a great fear of becoming obese. Even though they have protruding ribs and claw-like hands, they continue to eat little and exercise vigorously to reduce even more. In the early stages, some have normal appetites and may even become preoccupied with food. They may cook elaborate meals for others and go through periods of bulimia, followed by self-induced vomiting so that they will not get fat. Menstrual periods stop and weight loss begins. As the disorder progresses, appetite for food disappears, sexual desire disapppears, and the breasts and hips shrink to the point where the patient is unrecognizable as a female.

Thirst

Too much food leads to obesity, but too much water simply leads to many trips to the bathroom. Although drinking too much may lead to vitamins and minerals being taken from the body, it is not very serious and not a known disorder to be treated. There are times, however, when the person will have great thirst because of some physiological malfunction, so great thirst and drinking of large quantities of water should indicate that the person needs to see a physician.

Although we typically think of insulin as affecting the use of food, it also affects thirst. If there is insufficient insulin, the glucose cannot get into the body cells, so it accumulates in the blood. To reduce the blood sugar level, the glucose is excreted in the urine and the individual needs to drink an increasing amount of water to filter off the glucose. An untreated diabetic becomes very thirsty.

Psychosexual Disorders

There is a great variety of disorders of the sexual drive. Although there have been great changes recently in what our culture considers normal sexual behavior, the list of sexual disorders in DSM-III remains long. We will consider these in several categories.

Psychosexual Dysfunction. Our society has come increasingly to emphasize sexual technique and sexual gratification, resulting in an increasing emphasis on sexual dysfunction. This refers to disorders in either the desire for sexual gratification or the capacity to enjoy it. Until recently, all such disorders in men were labeled impotence and in women were labeled frigidity. However, Kaplan (1974) devised a new classification system based on the phase of the sexual response cycle in which the disorders occur, and this has been largely incorporated into DSM-III.

If people do not have an interest in sexual activity, they have disorders of the desire phase. This failure to experience such interest is called *inhibited sexual desire.* The second phase is called the *excitement phase,* and in it a number of physiological changes occur. Men experience an erection of the penis as its tissues become engorged with blood. Women experience a similar congestion of tissues in the genital region and a lubricant is secreted by the walls of the vagina. When these responses are weak or absent, the disorder is called *inhibited sexual excitement.* The final phase of the sexual response cycle is the orgasm, in which sexual pleasure peaks and triggers rhythmic contractions of muscles in the genital region. In men, semen is ejaculated from the penis at this time. If the man ejaculates very quickly so that either he or his partner is disappointed, he is said to have premature ejaculation. If he cannot ejaculate, or if ejaculation is delayed for a very long time, he is said to have an inhibited male orgasm. Such a delay in women is called inhibited female orgasm.

Two other dysfunctions are also listed. First, pain during intercourse is called *functional dyspareunia,* when there is no physical reason for the pain. Although this can occur in males, the disorder is usually seen in females. The second disorder is also in females, in which the muscles around the entrance to the vagina contract involuntarily when the male attempts to insert his penis. This is called *functional vaginismus* and makes intercourse either impossible or difficult.

Paraphilias. The paraphilias are usually called sexual deviations and are defined in terms of what is sexually arousing to the person. The disorder here is not in becoming aroused, but that the arousal is caused by something other than what is considered normal. The list of objects that can bring about sexual arousal seems to be nearly endless, so we will consider just a few here.

Fetishism is sexual arousal and gratification through inanimate objects or some particular body part rather than the whole person. Common fetishes are fur, stockings, shoes, gloves, and underwear, but even such objects as well-formed automobile exhaust pipes may be a fetish. Transvestites have a particular fetish; the clothing of the opposite sex. However, they go one step beyond the usual fetishist in that they actually put on the clothing. Zoophilia is sexual arousal by animals. The zoophile may not only be aroused by the animal, but may actually carry out intercourse with the animal if it is large enough, or have an orgasm by rubbing against it if it is small. Paedophilia refers to child molesting, gratification of the adult through sexual contact with children.

The two sex offenses most commonly reported to police are exhibitionism and voyeurism. Exhibitionism is obtaining sexual gratification by showing one's genitals to an involuntary observer. When the observer shows horror, fear, or disgust, this arouses the exhibitionist. Voyeurism refers to getting sexual gratification from secretly watching others in states of undress or in sexual activity. Such "peeping Toms" replace normal sexual activity with looking at others.

Finally, pain is sometimes mixed with sexuality. Sadism is the obtaining of sexual gratification through inflicting pain on others. Masochism refers to obtaining such gratification by having pain inflicted on oneself. The pain may range from biting or scratching, to whipping or cutting, to murder and mutilation.

Gender Identity Disorders. Finally, DSM-III lists gender

identity disorders as psychosexual disorders. Although fetishists may become aroused by clothing of the opposite sex and transvestites will dress in such clothing, transsexuals actually believe that they do belong to the opposite sex. They may dress in clothing of the opposite sex, but they do not feel sexual arousal, only relaxation. In fact, they feel strange in the clothing usually worn by their own sex. It is not the object of sexual arousal, but the person's own gender identity that is different.

Sin. Secular psychologists have no absolute standard of what is acceptable or unacceptable in terms of sexual behavior. If the person is sexually interacting with a consenting adult and the behavior is accepted as normal by most adults, it is considered acceptable. As Christians we have some specific standards set in Scripture about what is acceptable sexual behavior. Some sexual behaviors are prohibited, some are encouraged, and some are not mentioned. In this section we will deal with some of those prohibited in Scripture, but not considered deviant by our society. Leviticus chapter 20 lists numerous sexual sins, but here we will consider only adultery, fornication, and homosexual behavior.

Adultery is prohibited in the Ten Commandments and was serious enough to be punishable by death. Jesus made it plain that adultery was not just a physical act, and adulterers are listed among those who will not inherit the Kingdom of God. Of course, the current term for adultery is extramarital sex, and people are increasingly engaging in it, or at least they are more willing to admit it. *Fornication* is used in scripture to refer to a variety of sexual acts outside of marriage, including (but not limited to) premarital sex. Fornication is forbidden, and fornicators are listed along with adulterers as those who will not inherit the Kingdom of God. Premarital sexual activity is rising in incidence as fast as, or faster than, extramarital sex.

Homosexual behavior is listed among the sins in the first chapter of Romans, and was one of the sins that resulted in the destruction of Sodom and Gomorrah, according to most interpretations of Scripture. Until 1973, homosexuality was listed as a sexual disorder, but since then it has been officially declared a normal form of sexual life. Currently the disorder called "ego-dystonic homosexuality" does not mean ordinary homosexuality, but people who are homosexual in their preferences but wish to change. Thus, the only ones considered disordered are those who want to become heterosexual. Although recently it has been much more widely discussed, apparently the incidence of homosexual behavior has remained relatively constant during the last thirty years.

Many counselees of Christian counselors will have some of these sexual disorders. They will have engaged in sinful sexual activity, and we must deal with that. We must remember that the treatment for sin is God's forgiveness, and we must help them find it. We tend to think that such activity does not occur among Christians, but the surveys of sexual behavior indicate that it happens nearly as frequently among regular church-goers as among those who do not go to church. Of course, not everyone who goes to church is a Christian.

Treatment

Again, we must discover the cause of the disorder to give an appropriate treatment. Unfortunately, the motivational disorders that do not have known physiological causes have proven quite resistant to treatment.

Eating Disorders

Although eating disorders seem relatively straightforward, treatment with lasting effects is difficult. The simple answer to overeating or undereating is to increase or decrease the amount of food eaten, but it is difficult to get people to change.

Overeating. If the cause of being overweight is due to endocrine imbalance, correcting that will result in weight loss if food intake is not increased. However, as we noted, 95 percent of those who are overweight have no physical problem, but simply eat too much with too little exercise.

Americans spend more than eight billion dollars a year on diet aids of one type or another. Unfortunately the success rate of these weight loss programs is very low. The average long-term outcome from diets is a gain of 105 percent of the weight lost. That is, individuals end up weighing more than when they started to diet. Only about 12 of every 100 of those who seek a doctor's help actually lose weight, then 10 of those 12 regain it within two years. Such people typically diet repeatedly. Unfortunately, this losing and gaining of weight may damage the cardiovascular system, so the person would be better off remaining fat.

Some have tried to lose weight by using anorexigenic drugs. Amphetamines and other diet pills seem to suppress the desire for food and have been widely used to try to lose weight. However, the appetite-suppressing qualities of these drugs are short-lived. Furthermore, the pills may be addictive and become a problem themselves. Finally, if any weight is lost while one is on the diet pills, it is difficult to maintain the weight loss.

If eating has come under the control of external stimuli, the logical treatment is to avoid the sight or smell of food. Filling your plate in one room and eating in another, away from the food containers, can result your in eating less food. If eating is simply due to learning to eat too much, behavior modification can be successful. Operant conditioning techniques using positive reinforcement and self-monitoring can produce a weight loss over a period of time. It is more important to change regular eating habits than to lose weight quickly on some exotic diet.

Some of the weight-loss group programs also have moderate success. Overeaters Anonymous (OA), Take Off Pounds Sensibly (TOPS), and Weight Watchers provide group pressure on members to lose weight. They give public praise for loss, and some of them give public disapproval for failure to lose. Studies have shown that the average weight loss for members remaining in these groups is 14 pounds. The problem is that more than two-thirds of those who begin drop out of the programs within two years.

Since gluttony is also a sin, Christians need to be involved in treatment of obesity. Secular psychologists have not been successful in the treatment of obesity. Perhaps Christians can develop something to offer.

Undereating. Anorexia nervosa is much rarer than obesity, but just is as difficult to treat. Hospitalized patients frequently respond to treatment, but relapse when discharged. Long-term studies indicate that about 20 percent of the anorexics starve themselves to death and another 25 percent to 50 percent have recurrent episodes. One problem is that they see themselves as fat and are determined to lose weight. Another problem is that the appetite actually disappears, and then the person becomes too weak to eat.

With both overeating and undereating we must consider the God-like cognitive factors. Learning techniques using reinforcement bring about only temporary changes because the reinforcement must be maintained. If we can bring about cognitive changes, we may be able to bring about lasting changes.

Over-drinking

Since drinking too much is caused by known glandular malfunctions, people who drink great quantities of water should see a physician. If the cause is a lack of insulin, other symptoms may arise if the insulin deficiency becomes great enough.

Psychosexual Disorders

For many years, the major approach to sexual disorders was the psychoanalytic one. Even though there was little more than anecdotal evidence from clinical practice for its effectiveness, psychologists had no major alternatives to use in treating such disorders. However, a revolution has taken place since 1970.

Psychosexual Dysfunction. Masters and Johnson's *Human Sexual Inadequacy* was published in 1970 and Kaplan's *The New Sex Therapy* in 1974. These books have revolutionized the treatment of sexual dysfunction because they propose a new short-term approach. Although their evidence has been questioned recently, Masters and Johnson initially reported an overall cure rate of 80 percent after a five-year follow-up. They believe that the major cause of sexual inadequacy is the fear of sexual inadequacy. People fear that they will not be able to perform adequately, so they assume the "spectator role." Rather than relaxing and enjoying themselves, they watch and judge their performance, which is usually poor because their attitude blunts their responsiveness to sexual stimuli.

Masters and Johnson (1970) assume that sexual dysfunction is not an individual problem, but one of the marital unit. Thus, they begin with extensive interviews and medical examinations (to rule out organic causes) of husband and wife individually, followed by a meeting with both in which information from the individual interviews is discussed openly. They also assume that the couple must be relieved of all performance pressures in order to regain their ability to respond to sexual stimuli. There is no reason why the methods of Masters and Johnson cannot be used by Christians in combination with a presentation of a positive Christian perspective on human sexuality, so Christian counselors should be acquainted with this approach. Although there are several different specific techniques recommended for different dysfunctions, all sexual activity takes place in the privacy of the couple's bedroom. The only exception to this is the case of vaginismus, where a specialist must demonstrate to the couple the automatic nature of the response.

Paraphilias. Unfortunately, treatment of the sexual deviations has not been as successful as treatment of sexual dysfunction. Although many of these cases have been pronounced cured, such people tend to be repeaters. Since many of these sexual deviations are illegal, many of those treated have not come voluntarily for treatment, but have been forced into it by the courts. Thus, their motivation to change is low, and their motivation to lie to the therapist (to be pronounced cured, and released) is high. Psychotherapy, psychoanalysis, group therapy, and aversion therapy are all frequently tried, but long-term results are poor.

Recently therapies combining several approaches have been tried. One may begin with covert sensitization, in which the patient imagines pairing an aversive stimulus with the unwanted behavior. This may temporarily eliminate the undesirable behavior, but sexual arousal by normal stimuli does not automatically occur. Thus arousal reconditioning is used to gradually transfer the sexual excitement from the deviant stimulus to conventional stimuli. Finally, the patients may be given social skills training if unmarried, or sex therapy for the sexual dysfunctions commonly found in their marriages, if they are married. At this time, not enough long-term follow-up studies have been conducted to know what the success rate is.

As Christian counselors, we would want to combine some cognitive factors and Christian teachings with these techniques. We would not expect aversive conditioning or even arousal reconditioning to have lasting effects unless the reinforcement were continued. As we saw in the chapter on learning, when either reinforcement or punishment is discontinued, the behavior also stops. These techniques may be valuable for short-term changes, but not for long-term ones.

Gender Identity Disorders. Transsexuals are likewise very resistant to change. Consequently, in recent years, some transsexuals have tried to solve their gender identity problems by a surgical sex change. Although such operations were done in the 1930s, it was the highly publicized case of Christine Jorgensen in 1953 that made them well-known. Since then, surgeons have received thousands of requests and actually carried out more than 2500 sex-change operations.

The operation is typically preceded by a year of hormone therapy during which the individual takes hormones of the opposite sex. Then all of the sexual anatomy that can be safely removed is surgically removed and replaced by surgically reconstructed anatomy of the opposite sex. Although follow-up studies in the 1960s reported a high degree of satisfaction, more recent ones have not been as satisfactory.

Christian counselors cannot condone this operation. The operation is irreversible and there is no assurance that it will solve the persons' psychological problems. If they have children, there is also a risk to the children who see their parent change sexually. Finally, the whole question of morality has not been dealt with. Can we change the sexuality of a person, or are we only fooling ourselves?

Sin. Since secular psychologists do not see individuals engaging in premarital sex, extramarital sex, and homosexual behavior as having a psychological disorder, such psychologists do not attempt to treat them. Since people with ego-dystonic homosexuality want to change their sexual orientation, psychologists do try to treat them. However, treatments have generally been quite unsuccessful until recently. Masters and Johnson's (1979) *Homosexuality in Perspective* presents the first indication that a significant proportion of such homosexuals may be reoriented. Although their sample is small, not representative, and the five-year follow-up is not completed, they report a success rate of 65 percent, which is far above anything reported previously.

As Christian counselors we must attempt to help people living in sexual sin, even if secular therapists do not attempt to do so. Sexual sin and its results will have an effect on personality even if we try to ignore it. The best way to combat sexual sin is through forgiveness and the development of positive Christian sexual behavior. Christian counselors need to present to their counselees a positive Christian perspective on sexuality. Although many Christians have seemingly condemned most sexual activity, a positive change has taken place. Even the titles of recent books on Christian sexuality reflect this. Tim and Beverly LaHaye (1976) called their Christian marriage manual *The Act of Marriage,* but subtitled it "The Beauty of Sexual Love." Ed and Gaye Wheat (1977) entitled their Christian marriage manual *Intended for Pleasure.* Dwight Small (1974) called his book *Christian: Celebrate Your Sexuality.* Charlie and Martha Shedd (1979) called theirs *Celebration in the Bedroom.* Human sexuality is intrinsic to the image of God in humans. The very first chapter of the Bible notes that maleness and femaleness are part of the image of God in humans.

Conclusion

We have seen that the biological motives fit into our Christian perspective in that we are animal-like with respect to these motives. Physiological, developmental, sensory, and learning factors all play an important role in hunger, thirst and sex. Disorders can occur in motivation, just as in other areas. People can eat too much, too little, or the wrong things. Great thirst may result from physiological disorders. People may have sexual dysfunctions, sexual deviations, or identity disorders. We must remember that sin may be involved in motivation. Eating may become gluttony. Sexual behavior may become adultery or homosexual behavior. Treatments for these motivational disorders have frequently been rather ineffective with respect to long-term results. As is so often the case, the best treatment is prevention.

Suggested Readings

The "Biological Motives," "Biological Drives," or "Physiological Motivation" chapters in general psychology textbooks are recommended reading. Although a number of motivation books are available, most are not relevant to counseling. Chapters on "Sexual Dysfunction," "Sexual

Variation," or "Abnormal Sexual Behavior" in abnormal psychology textbooks are recommended; as are chapters on "Hunger," "Thirst," and "Sexual Behavior" in physiological psychology textbooks. Balagura (1973), Bootzin and Acocella (1980), Brown and Wallace (1980), Bruch (1973), Coleman, Butcher, and Carson (1980), Koteskey (1980), Masters and Johnson (1970), McCary (1978), Minuchin, Rosman, and Baker (1978), and Wheat and Wheat (1977) expand on material presented in this chapter.

COGNITIVE MOTIVATION

Most psychologists talk about two kinds of motivation. Maslow (1968) discusses deficiency motivation and growth motivation. Korman (1974) emphasizes two major traditions, the biological tradition and the cultural tradition. This chapter is about the second type of motivation: cultural, growth, or cognitive motivation, as shown in the lower central part of Figure 12:1 (Motivation—Cognitive). When discussing our similarity to animals, psychologists basically agree on the motives. However, when discussing humans as created in God's image, they tend to disagree about what the basic motives are. Since there is little agreement on the basic cognitive motives, let us begin by looking at the categories in Figure 12:1 above cognitive motivation.

Spiritual Motivation

As we consider humans as spiritual beings in terms of motivation, the major motive that emerges is love, although psychologists have been quite silent about it. When I checked the indexes of 39 general psychology textbooks by different authors, I found that 56 percent of them did not consider the topic of love important enough to include in the index. Twenty percent of the texts treated love by comparing it to love in animals or in terms of sexual love, and another ten percent treated it as an emotion. Love is most frequently discussed in

Figure 12:1 Cognitive motivation and cognitive motivational disorders from a Christian perspective.

HUMANS

Created	in the	Image of God
Like Animals		Like God
Overt Behavior	Definition	Mental Processes
Understand Creation	Goals	Make People Like God
Psychoanalysis Behaviorism	Systems	Humanistic Psychology

(DISORDER)	Descriptive	(DISORDER)
Organic Disorders (Organic Mental Disorders)	Experimental......Methods Physiological......Structure	Spiritual Disorders—Sin (Personality Disorders) Spiritual
Physical Disorders (Disorders Appearing in Childhood or Adolescence)	Immaturity......Development......Maturity	Spiritual Immaturity (No DSM-III Category)
Sensory Disorders (Somatoform Disorders)	Sensation......Awareness......Perception (States of Consciousness—Substance Use Disorders)	Perceptual Disorders (Paranoid Disorders)
Learning Disorders (Phobic Disorders)	Learning......Intellect......Cognition (Memory—Dissociative Disorders)	Thinking Disorders (Schizophrenic Disorders)
Motivational Disorders (Psychosexual Disorders)	Biological......MOTIVATION......COGNITIVE Motivation	SELFISHNESS (NO DSM-III CATEGORY) MOTIVATION

terms of Harlow's (1971) work with love in monkeys. Fifteen percent of the texts dealt with love in terms of Maslow's hierarchy of basic needs, and only two of these six books had a fairly well-rounded discussion of love.

It is only when we get to the humanistic psychologists that we find love studied in any detail. Maslow (1954, 1968) describes two types of love, D-love and B-love. D-love (deficiency love, love need, selfish love) is found when the person feels the absence of others and hungers for affectionate relationships with other people. B-love (love for the Being of another person, unneeding love, unselfish love) is a richer, "higher," more valuable experience than D-love. B-lovers are less jealous or threatened and "create" their partners. Such love is welcomed into consciousness and enjoyed without end.

May (1969) talks about several kinds of love, including *philia* and *agape*. *Philia* is a kind of vestige from the past when people had time for friendship. Today, people are in such a rush that a significant human interaction is the exception rather than the rule. *Agape* is esteem for the other, concern for the other person's welfare beyond any gain for oneself. Rogers (1959) talks about a similar kind of love, which he calls unconditional positive regard.

As Christians, we can say that B-love and *agape* love are descriptions of the image of God in humans. This love is in itself a motivation. It is what motivated God to send his Son into the world to redeem us, and he expects us, created in his image, to show this kind of love toward others. We must help our counselees develop this kind of motivation in their lives. Our love is to be like God's love, not only in loving our friends, but our enemies as well.

Maturity

Maslow (1968) suggests that there are two types of motivation; deficiency motivation and growth motivation. A deficiency motive is inactive in the healthy person, is preferred over other satisfactions, brings illness when not satisfied, cures illness when restored, and prevents illness when present. These needs are organized in a hierarchy so that as each need is met, a new, higher need emerges. At the lowest level are the physiological needs (discussed in chapter 11). When they are met, the safety needs emerge, and individuals seek an orderly, predictable, organized world. When these are met, the belongingness and love needs emerge, then the esteem needs, and finally the need for self-actualization.

When the deficiency needs are met, growth motivation emerges, and people are ready to move on toward psychological health. These people are now motivated primarily by moving toward self-actualization, toward realizing their potential, fulfilling their mission in life, knowing and accepting themselves, and becoming more unified. Maslow (1968) found these mature people to have a superior perception of reality; increased acceptance of self, others, and nature; more spontaneity; problem-centering; desire for privacy; autonomy; freshness of appreciation; creativeness; peak experiences; improved interpersonal relations; identification with humanity; and a more democratic character structure.

Maslow (1968) drew up a list of the attributes of these people, which he called B-values (being values, growth needs, or metaneeds). Even he, as an atheist, notes that these are the attributes assigned to most conceptions of a god, and that the person is godlike. As Christians, we agree that these are the attributes of God, but God is the original and humans are the copies. It is amazing that an atheist studying the finest human beings he could find would come up with such a complete list of the attributes of God. Of course, this is the reverse of the process we used in chapter 3, where we looked at the attributes of God to see which of them we could see in humans.

Not only is Maslow's list a list of the basic attributes of God, but Christians are commanded to be like God in many of these ways. B-values Maslow listed included wholeness, perfection, completion, justice, aliveness, richness, simplicity, beauty, goodness, uniqueness, effortlessness, playfulness, truth, honesty, reality, and self-sufficiency. Although most of these are obviously attributes of God, two of them need further elaboration. By "playfulness," Maslow does not mean frivolousness, but having a sense of humor or joy, and God certainly has that. The one attribute Maslow found that is not to be characteristic of us is self-sufficiency. God is self-sufficient, but we as finite beings cannot become so. Our sufficiency is of God, so our attempts at self-justification and self-righteousness always fail. Of course, this does not mean we are not to take care of ourselves, or that we are not responsible for our behavior.

We must encourage our counselees to be motivated to develop the God-like attributes Maslow found. He said he found an inner nature that was good (perhaps neutral, but certainly not evil), but was not a strong and overpowering force. Even though it was denied and suppressed, it persisted and forever pressed for actualization. We can see this as the image of God remaining in us and wanting to be realized. We must encourage this growth motivation in our counselees, and not just be content with solving their most pressing problems.

Perception

Although psychologists have investigated the influence of motivation on perception, they have done little regarding the influence of perception on motivation. Maslow did speak of an aesthetic need outside his basic hierarchy of motives. He said that we had an independent need to appreciate the beauty around us. He commented that we can see beauty in nature or in the things we make, and that everyone appreciates beauty in some form.

Cognition

Cognition is obviously related to cognitive motivation. Maslow (1968) pointed out that we have both the need to know and the fear of knowing. This need to know is also outside his hierarchy of needs, and often most obvious in children. We are both curious and afraid of finding out about ourselves, afraid of any knowledge that would make us feel inferior, weak, worthless, or evil. Adam and Eve wanted to know, but the Tree of Knowledge was not to be touched.

Not so widely known is that during the decade of the 1950's at least half a dozen people began independently to study and theorize about what has come to be called *cognitive consistency*. Although they used different terms, all these theories contained the idea that people behave in such a way as to have the greatest consistency in their thinking and to avoid anything that would result in inconsistency.

The most popular of these theories is Festinger's (1957) theory of cognitive dissonance. People have cognitions (thoughts) about the world and themselves. If these cognitions are dissonant (nonfitting, illogical), pressures arise to reduce the dissonance and to avoid increases in it. This may result in changes in behavior or changes in thinking. We must remember that the theory is talking about psychological inconsistencies, not logical ones. Humans are rationalizing beings who attempt to appear rational to themselves and others.

All of the consistency theories assume that there is a basic drive or motive for people to maintain a state of consistency within their thinking. Although none of the theorists say why humans should be motivated to maintain this state of consistency, as Christians we can see that humans are made in the image of an orderly, consistent God. As such, we strive to be consistent, to be God-like. As we counsel people, we must remember that they are striving to maintain consistency in their thinking, that it seems consistent to them even though it may not seem so to us.

Disorders

There seems to be no DSM-III category for disorders in cognitive motivation. This does not mean that there are no disorders, only that the psychiatric community does not recognize them. Although they are not fully socially acceptable, these disorders are not classified as mental disorders.

Most of these disorders center around some variation of selfishness, as shown in Figure 12:1. We have just seen that God is love, and that he freely gives to his creatures. Humans tend to be self-centered and taking. Since people are that way, it becomes the norm and is not even recognized as a disorder. That is why we need some absolute standard (God) against which we can judge ourselves. For many years, racial prejudice was the norm in our country, and few laws or social sanctions existed against expressing prejudices in the form of racial discrimination. Now we have made it illegal to discriminate on a racial basis, and such prejudice is frowned upon.

Cognitive motivational disorders are more covert than overt. They are more what we would call the sins of the spirit than the sins of the flesh. They are less likely to be frowned upon, even by Christians, because they are less obvious and more widely practiced. We must remember that the Bible deals not only with stealing, but also with coveting; not only with murder, but also with anger; not only with adultery, but also with lust. Although we feel more comfortable condemning the sins of the flesh, we must also deal with the sins of the spirit.

The best list of these sins is the traditional list of the seven deadly sins. Fairlie (1978) notes that all of them are demonstrations of love that has gone wrong. Although it is natural for humans to love what pleases them, in sin this love is misplaced, weakened, or distorted. Pride, envy, and anger are sins of perverted love, love directed in a false manner toward oneself. Sloth is a defective love because it is not given in a proper measure. Greed, gluttony, and lust are sins of excessive love in that they interrupt one's capacity to love other deserving objects. Let us now consider each of the seven deadly sins as expressed today.

Pride

Pride is not reasonable and justified self-esteem, but an overwhelming opinion of one's own qualities. Near-synonyms include words such as vanity, conceit, haughtiness, egotism, arrogance, boastfulness, selfishness, and self-glorification. Pride, however, may not be expressed in such nasty ways. It may be expressed in our self-righteousness or even in our "humility."

Although most of these sins are not found in DSM-III, pride may be called the narcissistic personality disorder. Narcissistic people have a grandiose sense of self-importance. They are preoccupied with fantasies of unlimited success and have a need for constant admiration. They expect and demand special treatment from others, while disregarding others' rights and feelings. Since they are so preoccupied with how others see them, it is likely that they have great doubts about themselves.

Pride has been made more acceptable in the individualism and achievement orientation of our culture. Rather than emphasizing cooperation and the good of the group, we emphasize competition and the rank of the individual in the group. Pride may be expressed in having things others do not, appearing better than others, or knowing things others do not. Pride may express itself in racism, saying that one's race, and therefore oneself, is better then other races. As we counsel others, we must be alert for signs of pride and deal with it.

Envy

Envy grows out of coveting and being unable to have the desired object. Envy is more than just coveting what another person has. It is not being able to have it because it is under the control of another. No one easily confesses to envy because it seems to be the nastiest and meanest of the sins. Furthermore, it can never bring gratification—no enjoyment, only endless self-torment as its appetite increases.

Envy assumes that everyone should be able to do, experience, and enjoy everything anyone else can do, experience, or enjoy. Not only must we be able to read poetry, we must be able to write it, so we take courses in "creative writing" even though we have no creativity. We take courses in "self-expression" even though we have no artistic talent. Then when we do not do well, we take revenge. We destroy the rules of poetry and call ourselves poets, or we make a noise and call ourselves musicians. Envy is not merely grieving because of another's good, but wanting to pull the other person down. This leads to resentment, backbiting, spite, and accusation. We should develop the talents we have, but not expect to be "all-talented."

Most social scientists have given little emphasis to envy. However, Schoeck (1966/1969) has developed a whole theory of social behavior around the concept of envy. He found envy at the core of human life. It is universal, and occurs as soon as two individuals begin to make mutual comparisons. He looked at envy in language, black magic, psychology, philosophy, religion, politics, and fiction. Even our system of a graduated income tax is seen as a result of envy. Those who have lower incomes pass laws so that those who have higher incomes must pay a larger proportion of that income in taxes. We must watch for signs of envy in those we are counseling.

Anger

Anger arises as a defense of ourselves in the face of loss of esteem. It is the response to humiliation. Our voices rise, eyes blaze, bodies stiffen, fingers point, and feet stamp. In more "primitive" times objects were thrown, but now it is words that are hurled. Unfortunately, words may do more permanent damage than physical objects. Anger leaves a residue of hatred and a desire for revenge in the person who gets hit with it.

Christians have great difficulty in handling anger, because the Bible at times gives it unqualified acceptance and at other times gives it qualified acceptance. Cerling (1974a) concludes that anger is justifiable as a reflection of God's anger at sin and human suffering, but that it is not justifiable if it is a response to personal offense. More often than not, this is the case. Pederson (1974) argues that since God's anger is personal and is aroused by people, humans must have the same quality. When affected by sins of oppression, we become angry in the way that God does. However, Pederson notes that we are not to take vengeance, for that is God's place. Cerling (1974b) disagrees, saying that anger as a result of personal offense finds no justification in Scripture. God is holy, so opposition to his will is sin, but humans are tainted by the Fall, and opposition to their will is not sin.

We must be aware of anger in our counselees. We must remember that anger is not always sin. It may be sinful at one time and not another. We must be very careful with our own anger, and careful about condemning it in others. However, we must be careful that it does not become wrath, vengeance, and violence. Jesus told us that the peacemakers were the ones to receive a blessing, so let us be peacemakers.

Sloth

Slothfulness is very difficult to define because it is the extreme of idleness and laziness. The Latin term *acedia* can be translated "without care." Physical sloth is an indifference to work, with increased laziness, idleness, and indolence. Mental sloth is a lack of feeling, boredom, apathy, and lack of caring. Spiritual sloth is an indifference to our duties to God. It is described by terms such as indifference, apathy, despair, faintheartedness, and desirelessness. The slothful person has no purpose, cares for nothing, enjoys nothing, hates nothing, lives for nothing, believes in nothing, interferes with nothing, and seeks to know nothing.

Unfortunately, slothfulness is difficult to recognize because it has become so much the norm. At one time people took pride in their work, but now one hears such phrases as "minimum work for minimum pay," and society places social sanctions against anyone who produces too much. We now have more leisure time than any other generation, but this has led to boredom rather than growth. In every role and occupation we find people who do not care.

Before DSM-III there was a psychiatric category called *neurasthenia* used to refer to this condition, relatively common among young adults. The neurasthenic complains of chronic physical and mental fatigue, aches and pains, and a general lack of vigor and interest in life. Such individuals spend a great deal of time sleeping, but wake up feeling even more tired than when they went to sleep. However, when doing something that interests them, they have relatively high energy.

We must watch for signs of slothfulness in our counselees. This often shows up in certain phrases, such as: "I couldn't care less," "I mind my own business," "Live and let live," "What's that to me?" "Hang loose," and "Don't get uptight." This whole uncaring, apathetic approach to life must be seen as sinful, and we must deal with it.

Greed

Greed refers to an inordinate desire, an insatiable longing to possess something. We usually think of it in terms of money, in terms of the miser counting his gold, running his hands through the coins and embracing the piles of money. However, greed is the love of possessing anything, and is a sin common in the middle class. Most of the merchandise we find in boutiques and shopping malls no one really needs. We have been affected by advertising so that we come to the point where we just "have to have" some given item. Then, the more we get, the more we want.

The sin of covetousness is mentioned in the Ten Commandments. The apostle Paul called the love of money (greed) the root of all evil. The most insidious thing about greed is that it can never be satisfied. We always need just a little bit more. As our incomes increase, we typically give a smaller and smaller proportion of them to the Lord. We neglect our families for greed, saying we are laboring to get more money for them. Success is usually defined in terms of money.

We need to watch for signs of greed in our counselees, especially in middle-class counselees. They are more likely to come for counseling, and when they do, they engage in a lot of "poor talk." To hear them talk, one would think that they were very poor. They do not get paid enough. Inflation is killing them. They cannot "get ahead." Someone else with the same job makes twice as much. We should see this kind of talk as an indication of greed and make the counselees face it.

Gluttony

Gluttons are those who exhibit an almost insatiable desire and great capacity for engorgement. Gluttony is usually associated with eating, but does not need to be restricted to this alone. We sometimes use the phrases "a glutton for punishment" or "a glutton for work" to describe someone with an insatiable desire for these things. However, here we will concentrate on gluttony in terms of food.

We typically think of gluttons as fat people whose whole life is ordered around food. They cram, gorge, and wolf down their food. They concentrate on stuffing food into their mouths, only occasionally looking up at others at the table. These kinds of gluttons are obvious to society because they quickly become obese, and we discussed them in chapter 11.

However, gluttony can also be found in many other people, if we think of it as an inordinate interest in food. Obsessive dieters may be just as gluttonous as obese persons. Dieters who constantly think about food, gaze at it in the refrigerator, talk of little else, and hurry to the kitchen to eat the carefully measured cottage cheese are also gluttons. The health food addicts may be just as gluttonous if their whole life revolves around food. They may talk of little other than the dangers of food additives or the wholesomeness of sunflower seeds. This consuming interest in food is disproportionate and unnatural, a form of gluttony just as much as overeating.

As we counsel persons, we must think of gluttony not only in terms of overeating, but in terms of an inordinate interest in food. The persons who spend more time reading their cookbooks or their health food books than their Bibles, are placing more of an interest in the creation than in the Creator.

Lust

Lust is an overpowering appetite or craving for something, usually associated with a great yearning for sex. This is, of course, associated with sexual motivation discussed in Chapter 11. As we saw, lust may express itself in actual immoral sexual behavior, and we must deal with that.

However, we must also deal with the lust which is expressed in nothing more than fantasy. For example, a "holy man" came down from his platform and said that he had not looked upon a woman in thirty years. Since that was the first thing he said, it is logical to assume that women were the major topic of his thought life for those thirty years. People may never express the lustful thoughts in overt behavior, but be just as consumed by them as those engaging in adultery, homosexuality, or the paraphilias.

Of the seven deadly sins, lust seems to be the longest recognized, most prevalent, and most well-known. Most Christians know that Jesus equated lust with adultery in the Sermon on the Mount. However, this verse is often misinterpreted to mean that lust means any sexual thought. Thus, if a person sees someone of the opposite sex and has any sexual thought, adultery has already been committed. This is not what the verse says. It says that when a man looks on a woman "to lust after her," or "in order to lust after her" he has committed adultery. Thus, lust is not a passing sexual thought, but it is when the purpose of looking at the other person is to imagine sexual activity with her or him.

We must be aware of the potential for lust in our counselees and make clear to them the difference between temptation and sin. Some of them feel very guilty about passing sexual thoughts (temptation) and should not do so. Others feel little guilt about their lustful thoughts (sin) and they should feel more. Whatever the case, we need to deal with the sin of lust.

Treatment

As in other chapters, we must use our diagnosis of the source of the disorder to lead to appropriate treatment. However, we face a new problem in this chapter, that of even recognizing these cognitive motivational disorders as disorders so that treatments can be found.

Recognition

Psychologists and psychiatrists do not recognize the existence of this class of disorders. Although neurasthenia was previously called a disorder, and was roughly equivalent to sloth, it is no longer recognized as a disorder. Bulimia is considered a disorder, but one more closely related to the biological hunger drive. Society recognizes that something is not quite right about prejudiced individuals, but they are not considered as having a disorder. Since selfishness, as expressed in the sins of the spirit, has often become the norm for society, it is seen as normal and not in need of any kind of treatment.

Christians also put more emphasis on the sins of the flesh than on the sins of the spirit. We would rather condemn killing than anger, and adultery than lust. However, in the Sermon on the Mount, Jesus elaborated on the commandments, saying that we must concern ourselves not only with killing but also with anger because even a person who is angry at another without cause is liable to judgment. He said that when we look at another person in order to lust after that person, we have already committed adultery with them.

There may be several reasons why Christians emphasize the sins of the flesh. One is that sins of the flesh are easier to monitor than sins of the spirit. Sins of the flesh can be observed directly, but sins of the spirit must be inferred. When you kill someone, there is a dead body, but anger may be completely inside a person, only inferred from the way a word is spoken. Another reason Christians may not condemn the sins of the spirit is that these sins are more common among Christians. Other sins are socially unacceptable, so Christians avoid getting involved in them. However, these sins of the spirit are commonplace, so they do not seem as bad, not even as sinful. Jesus had great difficulty getting the Pharisees to acknowledge their sins.

Forgiveness

Like any other sin, the sins of the spirit need forgiveness. Once we have recognized that they are sins, subtle sins, we must seek God's forgiveness just as we do for any other kind. This seeking for forgiveness will include confession, repentance, and belief in Christ.

Fruit of the Spirit

Living for Christ should result in the fruit of the spirit, rather than the sins of the spirit, being found in our lives. Although they do not perfectly correspond, there is a great similarity between the fruit of the spirit listed in Galatians 5, the attributes of God considered in chapter 3 of this book, and the characteristics of self-actualizing people considered earlier in this chapter. From our Christian perspective, we do not actualize ourselves, but God actualizes us as we mature. We become more like him. Furthermore, the fruit of the spirit is, in many cases, the opposite of the sins of the spirit. Let us now consider the fruit of the spirit listed in Galatians 5.

Love. As we have already seen, God is love. He sent his son because he loved us and Christ told us to love each other as he loved us. Maslow and May found B-love and *agape* love in the individuals they studied. They found people becoming more God-like. Love is the opposite of sloth. Although we usually think of slothfulness as laziness, we saw that its essence is in not caring, not caring about anything. Love is the opposite of this. It is unselfish caring for the other person.

Joy. Although we seem to miss this attribute of God, he is a joyful God. Jesus said that he wanted his own joy to be in us that our joy might be full. Maslow found this characteristic in his self-actualizing people in what he called playfulness. In fact, joy was one of the terms he used to define it, along with fun, amusement, gaiety, humor, and exuberance.

Peace. God is a God of peace. Jesus said that he had told us certain things that we might have peace, and that he had given his peace to us. Maslow called this attribute *completion,* which is roughly synonymous with fulfillment, finality, or a feeling of "it is finished." Peace is the opposite of envy. People who want something another person has can never be at peace with themselves.

Patience. All of us have experienced God's patience. Even when we fail him he gives us a second chance, then a third, a fourth, and so forth. We are likewise told to be patient with others and in waiting for Christ's return.

Kindness. God is a God of kindness, for He is merciful to us, kind to us even when we do not deserve it. We are repeatedly told to be kind to others. Although Maslow does not use the term kindness in his list of Being values, he does use "benevolence" in describing goodness. Kindness is the opposite of greed. Greed has its essence in getting for oneself, while kindness is in giving to others.

Goodness. The term *goodness* appears in all three lists. God is described in the Bible as being good. Maslow found goodness in the self-actualizing people he studied. Goodness is the opposite of pride, or the realization of pride. Pride strongly emphasizes self-righteousness, while goodness is righteousness in itself.

Faithfulness. As we saw previously, God is a faithful God.

He keeps his covenants and expects us to keep ours. Maslow found justice in those he studied, and he defined justice in terms of fairness and "oughtness." If lust is defined in terms of adulterous thoughts, faithfulness is its opposite, and we are to be faithful in keeping our agreements.

Gentleness. In Psalm 18, David talks about God's gentleness. God is described as a shepherd who gently leads his people. The apostle Paul talked about the gentleness of Christ. Gentleness is the opposite of anger, at least of the expression of anger.

Self-control. Of course, God has self-control. He cannot lose control. Futhermore, he is in control of everything else. Maslow found something closely related to this when he talked about self-sufficiency, although we would see this as self-control taken too far. Self-control is the opposite of gluttony. Gluttons are controlled by their appetites rather than controlling their appetites.

Before leaving this section on the fruit of the spirit, we need to consider one approach to treatment that essentially says that the deadly sins are inevitable and the fruit of the spirit is impossible. Classical Freudian psychoanalysis places great emphasis on selfishness and says that it is impossible really to become unselfish. That is, the id is the only structure of personality that has its own supply of psychic energy. It is the instinctive, animal-like, unconscious part of personality with two major drives of *eros* and *thanatos* (or libido and mortido, or sex and aggression, or lust and anger).

According to this type of psychoanalysis, actual change at the deepest levels of personality is impossible. The id cannot be changed. Its energy can be rechanneled, but people are doomed to live forever with the conflict between the id and the superego, the moral aspect of personality. Since the id cannot be changed, treatment is aimed at changing the superego so that the patients will not feel so guilty for what they are doing.

Even though the sins of the spirit may be the norm in our society, and psychoanalysis says that real change is impossible, we must not be pessimistic. We must remember that psychoanalysts are trying to cope with sin using psychotherapy rather than God's forgiveness. Psychotherapy is simply not an adequate treatment for sin.

Conclusion

We have seen that cognitive motivation refers to the God-like aspects of motivation and is related especially to humans as spiritual (love), mature (self-actualization), congitive beings. Psychologists do not recognize the disorders of cognitive motivation as mental disorders, but as Christians we see them as sins of the spirit, as opposed to sins of the flesh. Since these are not recognized as disorders, psychologists have not developed methods of treatment, but we would say that these sins need forgiveness, just as any other sins do. Then they can be replaced by the fruit of the spirit.

Suggested Readings

The "Human Motivation" or "Psychological Motivation" chapters in general psychology textbooks are recommended reading. Fairlie (1978), Koteskey (1980), Lyman (1978), Maslow (1968), and May (1969) expand on material presented in this chapter.

EMOTION

Closely related to motivation is emotion. Not only do the words have the same root, but emotions may serve as motives. Emotions probably command our personal attention more than any other area psychology studies, but they are probably the least understood area of general psychology. Psychologists cannot even agree on a definition of emotion, although most agree that we must consider conscious experience, emotional behavior, and physiological responses.

Although psychologists have not studied emotions as thoroughly as some other areas, emotions are important to us. They are the most vivid experiences we have. We must try to understand them and how they affect our behavior and mental processes. There are two major aspects of emotion that fit into our Christian perspective, as shown in the lower central part of Figure 13:1 (Physiological Emotion—Emotion—Cognitive Emotion). We are similar to animals in terms of the physiological aspects of emotion, and we are similar to God in terms of the cognitive aspects. Let us now consider how emotion is related to each subject area above it in Figure 13:1.

Like Animals

Let us begin by considering the animal-like aspects of emotion, the "physiological" aspects. Everyone agrees that

Figure 13:1 Emotion and emotional disorders from a Christian perspective.

HUMANS

Created...............in the..............Image of God
Like Animals..........................Like God
Overt Behavior......Definition...........Mental Processes
Understand..........Goals...............Make People
Creation   Like God
Psychoanalysis.......Systems............Humanistic
Behaviorism   Psychology
Experimental........Methods............Descriptive
(DISORDER)   (DISORDER)
Organic Disorders.....Structure..........Spiritual............Spiritual Disorders—Sin
(Organic Mental Disorders)   (Personality
                                                     Disorders)

Physical Disorders.......Development.......Maturity.........Spiritual Immaturity
Immaturity   (No DSM-III Category)
(Disorders Appearing in
Childhood or Adolescence)

Sensory Disorders	Sensation	Awareness	Perception	Perceptual Disorders
(Somatoform Disorders)		(States of Consciousness—Substance Use Disorders)		(Paranoid Disorders)
Learning Disorders	Learning	Intellect	Cognition	Thinking Disorders
(Phobic Disorders)		(Memory—Dissociative Disorders)		(Schizophrenic Disorders)
Motivational Disorders	Biological Motivation	Motivation	Cognitive Motivation	Selfishness
(Psychosexual Disorders)				(No DSM-III Category)
EMOTIONAL DISORDERS	PHYSIO-LOGICAL EMOTION	EMOTION	COGNITIVE EMOTION	EMOTIONAL DISORDERS
(ANXIETY STATES)				(AFFECTIVE DISORDERS)

these must at least be considered. Although some psychologists see them as a part of emotion itself, others see them as a byproduct of emotion.

Physiological. In addition to smiling, frowning, or clenching fists, internal physiological changes occur in an emotional state. In most of the emotions psychologists study, the sympathetic branch of the autonomic nervous system becomes dominant, and this brings about known changes. For example, if you are suddenly frightened by a loud noise, your heart rate increases, blood pressure rises, digestion stops, blood is sent to the skeletal muscles, sugar is released into the blood stream, breathing becomes more rapid and deeper, pupils in the eye dilate, salivation stops, sweating increases, and hairs stand on end, causing "goose bumps." Most of these physiological responses are valuable to help you respond to the emotional situation by making some bodily response (fight or flight). If you cannot make that response, the physiological responses may lead to illness.

These physiological changes are sometimes measured by the polygraph, or "lie detector," to detect the presence of emotion. The basic idea is that when people tell lies, they feel guilty, and physiological changes will reflect this. This fits into our Christian perspective in Figure 13:1 in that when people sin (spiritual disorder), they should experience guilt feelings (cognitive emotion), which will be expressed in physical responses (physiological changes) because humans are unified beings. Lie detector operators compare physiological changes following routine questions to the changes following questions related to the "crime."

Immaturity. Strongman (1978) emphasizes that the whole area of emotional development is confused. However, from observations psychologists have made, it does seem that emotional development depends on a combination of genetic and environmental factors. An increasing variety of emotions develops. Watson (1930/1958) observed only fear, rage, and love in children. Bridges (1932, as cited in Strongman, 1978) found only a state of undifferentiated excitement in infants.

Next, delight and distress developed. Gradually other positive emotions developed from delight and other negative emotions from distress.

Sensation. Sensations are involved in both producing and experiencing emotion. The sound of a horn as you step into the street can produce fear. In fact, any unexpected stimulus can produce a startle response and its emotion. We are also aware of the sensations brought about by physiological changes in our body during emotion. We have the sensations of a pounding heart, a dry mouth, perspiration, and hair standing on end. Some have even said that our experience of these sensations *is* the emotion.

Learning. Emotions can be learned through classical conditioning, as experiments by behaviorists in the 1920s demonstrated. Several of John Watson's early experiments involved learning the emotion of fear, and they showed that emotions can be learned. For example, when he showed an infant a white rat, the child showed no fear of it. Next, he paired the presence of the rat with a sudden loud sound, which produces a fear response in children. When the rat and the loud noise were paired repeatedly, the child learned to give the fear response to the rat alone. The fact that emotions can be conditioned, and therefore unconditioned, is the basis for systematic desensitization.

Furthermore, this fear response generalized to similar objects that previously had elicited no fear. The child may now fear not only the white rat, but also a white rabbit, and even a Santa Claus mask. As we counsel people in areas dealing with their emotions, we must be aware that emotional responses can be learned to many different stimuli. Through generalization, they may experience an emotional response to things they have never experienced before. The most common example is that responses learned to parents may generalize to others similar to their parents, either physically, or playing the same role (someone in authority).

Physiological Motivation. As was noted at the beginning of the chapter, emotion and motivation are closely related.

Sometimes the relationship is obvious. One person may strike out, either physically or verbally, in anger at another person. The emotion of anger is obviously the motivation for the striking. A child may run away from the school bully who beat him up yesterday. Fear is obviously the motive for running away. Numerous experiments have shown that animals can be taught to fear neutral stimuli, such as a white box.

Some of our counselees may seem to have unusual emotional responses motivating them to make odd actions, so we must be aware of their past reinforcement history. We must realize that they may have learned to fear or want some odd stimulus and this serves as a motive for many different behaviors. Consider the person who works many long hours for some green, wrinkled, old paper (money) or who leaps in elation at having found a piece of that dirty, wrinkled paper.

Like God

Our emotions are not only related to our animal-like aspects, but to our God-like ones as well. Let us now consider the aspects of people as created in the image of God, on the right side of Figure 13:1.

Spiritual. Earlier in this chapter, we saw that our spiritual condition influences our emotion. When we lie (sin), it causes us to feel guilty and is reflected in the responses of our body, which can be measured on a polygraph. Other emotions may be sinful as well. For example, people may sin in their anger or they may sin in their fear, although not all anger and fear are sinful. Secular psychologists have tended to emphasize the emotions that may be sinful, so let us concentrate on those that come from a right relationship with God.

Love is not only a motive and a behavior, but it is also an emotion. In the parable of the prodigal son, told to illustrate how God welcomes the sinner, we find the father running to the son, throwing his arms around him, and kissing him. That is emotion any way you look at it. Joy in heaven is one result of a sinner's repenting. Christ was characterized as having joy.

He said some of the things he had said were so that his joy might be in us and that our joy might be full. This is a joy that cannot be taken from us, and it is ours even when we face difficult situations. This joy does not depend on outward circumstances, so Christ even felt joy when facing the cross because he could look beyond it.

Two emotions seldom discussed by secular writers are peace and awe, perhaps because these emotions are so rare, or because they are not accompanied by physiological arousal. God is a God of peace. Christ gives us his peace. Probably the closest thing to awe is what Maslow (1968) calls "peak experiences." Whenever God visits his people, they stand in awe before him. Unfortunately many times the Hebrew word meaning "revere" is translated "fear." When the Bible says to fear God, it means to revere God. We should find these positive emotions in healthy Christians.

Maturity. At maturity we should find a fuller emotional life. As we saw earlier in the chapter, we start out with only one emotion (or a few), and more emotions develop from this. As we grow, we should experience a broader range of emotions. Unfortunately, we have come to associate maturity with emotional suppression, especially in men. Our culture tells us that while great emotional excitement at good news is all right in boys, men do not get too excited. Little boys may cry at bad news, but "big boys don't cry." Rather than experiencing a richer emotional life, many people try to suppress their emotions as they grow older. Although our emotions and their expression may change at maturity, we should not try to restrict them. We should become aware of them and evaluate them according to biblical standards.

Perception. The kind of emotion we experience and its intensity will depend on how we have perceived the stimulus. The same stimulus may lead to joy at one time and sorrow or anger at another. For example, if you took a test and thought that you failed it, seeing a "C" on your test paper may bring joy and relief. On the other hand, if you thought you wrote a nearly perfect answer to every question, the same "C" may bring sorrow or anger. Schachter and Singer (1962) injected subjects with epinephrine to bring about arousal of the sympathetic branch of the autonomic nervous system. They found that the emotion experienced depended on how the subjects perceived their arousal. Subjects told about the effects of the epinephrine did not become emotional. However, those who were not told about the effects of the epinephrine became either euphoric or angry, depending on how others in the room were acting.

Cognition. The emotion we experience also depends on our cognitions, on what we are expecting to see and how we are set to interpret it. Lazarus and Alfert (1964) showed subjects emotion-arousing films about puberty rites or bloody accidents. While watching the films, measures of arousal were taken as measures of emotion. One group heard a denial sound track before seeing the films, another group heard it during the films, and a third group heard no sound track. The question was whether or not the cognitions introduced in the sound track would influence physiological (emotional) arousal, and they certainly did. Those who watched the films with no sound showed the greatest arousal, those who heard the denial sound track during the films showed less, and those who heard the sound track before the films showed the least arousal of all.

Cognitive Motivation. We have already considered how guilt feelings may be a motive to perform some action. Such guilt feelings are cognitive emotions. Cognitive motivations may lead to emotions as well. Frustration and conflict have been studied primarily with animals, but they occur in humans as well, and at a cognitive rather than just a physical level. Frustration is the term psychologists use to apply to the blocking of a motive. It may arise as a result of something actually physically blocking your path, such as the door to your home being locked. It may also arise from internal factors when the person is not able to reach a desired goal, such as the person who wants to go to medical school, but can barely make passing grades in college. Emotions frequently arise in the face of such frustration. The person may become angry and attack, or apathetic and withdraw.

Conflicts may also arise. The most common and interesting are the approach-avoidance and multiple approach-avoidance conflicts. An approach-avoidance conflict involves both wanting to do and not wanting to do something. We experience this type of conflict every time we face a temptation. We both want to do the wrong thing (or it would not be a temptation) and want to do the right thing. Such conflicts can lead to emotional arousal. A multiple approach-avoidance conflict is simply a combination of approach-avoidance conflicts. This can be all at the cognitive level. For example, some women have both a need for achievement, a fear of failure, and a fear of success. This may lead to severe emotional stress. They want to succeed, but they are afraid that if they succeed they will not be asked for dates or their husbands will feel threatened.

As we counsel people, we must be aware that their emotional life has a multitude of causal factors influencing it, ranging all the way from physiological and spiritual factors to intellectual and motivational factors. We must try to determine the source of the inappropriate emotion.

Disorders

Emotion is obviously involved in some disorders, as is evidenced by the very language we use in talking about them. We talk about people being emotionally disturbed, having emotional problems, and being emotionally healthy. As we look at disorders of emotion in DSM-III, we find several categories that fit into our Christian perspective as shown in Figure 13:1. In general, anxiety states seem to fit in with the animal-like aspects of humans, while affective disorders fit in with the God-like aspects.

Anxiety Disorders

The term *emotional disorders* is often used to describe all of the disorders we have discussed, so we will find these disorders the least sharply defined. However, the category most directly related to emotion is the category of anxiety disorders. Anxiety may be characteristic of many of the disorders we have discussed, but in this section we will discuss those in which anxiety is the major symptom.

We have already discussed some of these anxiety disorders in other chapters. We saw that phobic disorders were learned fear reactions, and discussed them under "learning," even though their major symptom is fear (anxiety). Obsessive-compulsive disorders were discussed in the chapter on cognitive processes, since they are concerned with persistent thoughts. These disorders bring on attacks of anxiety if the person does not engage in some thought or behavior.

Anxiety States. Rather than being focused on some special stimulus occurring when a person does not do some particular thing, the anxiety may be unfocused and plaguing the person continually. It may also suddenly attack for no reason at all. Such anxiety disorders are relatively common.

The first type is the generalized anxiety disorder, in which people live in a constant state of tension, worry, and uneasiness, but cannot say what is causing their fear. They are always on edge, waiting for some calamity to occur. They have muscular tension, especially in the head, neck and shoulders. They get nervous twitches, clammy hands, tingling feelings, indigestion, and racing heart. They find it hard to concentrate or make decisions and they begin to forget things. Then they begin to develop anxiety about their anxiety, which only makes things worse.

The second type is the panic disorder, in which panic attacks occur periodically. In these attacks anxiety rises to an almost unbearable level. Sweating, heart pounding, trembling, and gasping for breath, the person has a feeling of inescapable doom. The attacks usually last for a few minutes, but may last for several hours, after which the person is exhausted. Since the occurrence of the attacks is unpredictable, people with this disorder are reluctant to go anywhere for fear that they will have an attack in front of everyone with no one present to help. Such people often become recluses.

Post-Traumatic Stress Disorder. Post-traumatic stress disorders are the great psychological reactions to very traumatic events, such as war, natural disasters, accidents, or assault. Although DSM-III classifies this as an anxiety disorder, anxiety is not always the major symptom, and the source of stress is a known external event. It is still appropriate for us to discuss this disorder here, because these people often have a sort of emotional anesthesia, a lack of responsiveness to others present. A soldier returning from battle may be unresponsive to his family when he returns home. Usually the symptoms appear shortly after the trauma, but they may appear days or even months later.

Christian counselors are more likely to encounter this disorder in reaction to civilian catastrophe, such as plane crashes, fires, floods, tornadoes, and individuals who have been attacked or raped. Although there is great variability in this disorder, it often follows a three-stage pattern called the *disaster syndrome.* In the shock stage the victims are stunned, dazed, and apathetic. They wander around aimlessly until someone tells them what to do. In the the suggestible stage they become deeply concerned over other people in the trauma and want to help, but their behavior is quite inefficient. At this time they are passive and willing to take orders from the rescue workers. In the recovery stage they become tense, apprehensive, and anxious. They seem to need to tell others about the event repeatedly. During this stage a counselor is most likely to be involved.

Related Emotional Disorders

Two other disorders are related to our emotional lives, and are much more common. They are the adjustment disorders and the psychological factors affecting physical conditions.

Adjustment Disorder. Adjustment disorders are the psychological reactions to more ordinary traumas, such as the death of a loved one or a heavy business loss. Of course, anyone has some adjustment following such a trauma, but if it is more severe than usual or goes on for an extended time, it may interfere with the person's life. This may include depression, anxiety, withdrawal, or interference with work and study.

Psychological Factors Affecting Physical Condition. These disorders were formerly called *psychophysiologic disorders* or *psychosomatic disorders,* and included a specific list of such disorders. However, DSM-III has dropped both the term and the list in recognition that psychological factors may affect a wide variety of physical conditions. This is the opposite of physiological psychology. Rather than looking at how anatomy and physiology affect behavior and mental processes, we are looking at how psychological factors can influence physical conditions. Let us now briefly consider a few of these factors.

An ulcer is any open sore in the wall of any part of the digestive system. Although we do not know all of the factors that cause ulcers, we do know that psychological stress is one. Hypertension, a chronic elevation of the blood pressure, can be caused by physical problems, but most often it has no known physical cause. In these cases it appears to be related to continuous stress brought on by environmental or psychological conditions. Headaches may be caused by stress. Most people have the usual tension headaches occasionally, but some people have migraine headaches, severe ones occurring on one side of the head. Apparently, what happens is that stress causes the blood vessels in the brain to constrict. When the stress is over, the arteries to the brain dilate and more blood than can be accommodated goes to the brain. The result of the great change in the flow of blood is the migraine, caused not just by stress, but by the relief after stress. Asthma is a disorder of the respiratory system. During an asthma attack the air passages narrow to cause coughing, wheezing, and general difficulty in breathing. Some asthmas are allergies, some are related to infectious conditions, and some can be triggered by stress.

Affective Disorders

By their very name, the affective disorders are emotional disorders. However, rather than the major symptoms being anxiety or physiological changes, they are changes in mood ranging from extreme elation to extreme depression. These affective disorders can be placed in our Christian perspective as shown in Figure 13:1. DSM-III distinguishes between two types of affective disorders, the major depression and the bipolar disorder.

Major Depression. People who experience only depression, either repeated episodes or only one episode, are said to have *major depression.* This does not mean that people just get sad (depressed), but that along with the depressed mood they have feelings of worthlessness and guilt; reduced motivation, energy, and activity; disturbances in appetite, sleep, sex, and thinking; and recurrent thoughts of suicide and death. This is a common disorder. About ten percent of the men in the U.S. and twenty percent of the women have at least one depressive episode at some time in their lives. About half of these people have only one episode, and only about a third require hospitalization. The other half have recurrent episodes in which the depression returns. Usually the person's adjustment between episodes is about normal, but about one-fifth of those with recurrent episodes do not return to normal. People suffering from major depression, either recurrent or single episode, are likely to be seen by Christian counselors. Depression is second only to schizophrenia in first and second admissions to mental hospitals, but is the most frequent diagnosis in outpatient clinics. In some cases one-third of the outpatients are depressives.

Bipolar Disorder. As is implied by the name, the major characteristic of this disorder is the addition of manic episodes. In a manic episode the person has not only an elevated mood, but is overactive, reckless, irritable, unable to sleep, overly talkative, and distractible. The pattern of manic and depressive episodes varies. There may be a manic episode, a depressive episode, and a normal period. There may be no normal periods at all, or there may be only manic episodes and normal periods. Bipolar disorders are different from major depressions in other ways too. They are less common, occur earlier in life, occur in men and women equally often, tend to run in families, and the episodes are usually briefer and more frequent.

Treatment

Once we have been able to diagnose the problem, we are in a position to choose a treatment appropriate for it. Of course, the most commonly used treatment for emotion disorders is the prescribing of mood-altering drugs: the antidepressants, tranquilizers, and antianxiety drugs. As was noted earlier, these treatments are not treatments based on correcting a known physiological disorder. No one knows why they work. There are questions about their side-effects, and questions about to whether they cure the disorder or only relieve the symptoms. Let us now consider each disorder.

Anxiety Disorders

Although mild tranquilizers provide some relief, they do not change a person's lifestyle. All types of psychotherapy are used to help people distinguish between real and imagined dangers, and to learn how to cope with them. People usually respond well to such treatment, or just to talking with a sympathetic friend. However, many such people still have some anxiety remaining.

Most cases of post-traumatic stress disorders respond quickly to the individual's being removed from the stressful situation. Victims of civilian catastrophes typically recover when given mild reassurance and proper rest. Although the victims may have recurrent nightmares and talk about the event repeatedly, these may be mechanisms to help the person to adjust. Most cases clear up in a few days or weeks, but a few individuals have problems for longer times.

Other Related Emotional Disorders

Adjustment disorders usually clear up after the counselee talks about the trauma, as is the case with anxiety disorders. When treating psychological factors affecting physical conditions, we must keep several factors in mind.

First, we must be sure a psychological problem is really causing the physical condition, and not a physical problem. For example, high blood pressure may be caused by kidney dysfunction, headaches may be caused by brain tumors, and asthma may be caused by allergies or infections. We must not try a psychological treatment when a physical one is needed.

Second, we may treat the disorders by reducing the symptoms. Through biofeedback training, we can learn to control many of these bodily functions. Migraine patients can be taught to dilate the blood vessels in their hands at the onset of an attack, thus taking the pressure off the blood vessels in the head. Hypertensive patients can be fitted with a device that beeps when their blood pressure rises. When given feedback about their bodily functioning, in some way (not yet understood) they begin to control the functioning. This has potential for treating hypertension, headaches, and ulcers.

Finally, the best treatment is to teach the patients how to handle their stress so that the physiological changes will not happen in the first place. That is, people can be taught to relax rather than get angry or anxious. If they can learn how to do this, they do not need to worry about biofeedback training.

Affective Disorders

The two most common treatments for the affective disorders are drugs and electroconvulsive shock. For example, lithium is commonly used to treat those who have manic episodes. Antidepressants are usually given to those with depression. Since many of the depressed patients are also anxious, antianxiety drugs are commonly used in combination with antidepressants. Since antidepressants usually do not take effect for a few days, electroconvulsive therapy is often used on patients in deep depression who are thought to be suicidal. Electroconvulsive therapy is also used if the antidepressants do not have the desired effect. Although electroconvulsive therapy was once used on a wider variety of disorders, it is now most frequently used on those with depressions. Usually drugs and shock combined with some type of psychotherapy help the patient make a better long-term adjustment. The cognitive therapy developed by Beck and his associates has been quite successful in the treatment of depression. Some evidence indicates that it is at least as successful as drugs.

We must realize that these treatments for the affective disorders are used to shorten the duration of the disorder or to make it more bearable while the patient has it. Most people who have affective disorders recover in less than a year without any formal treatment at all. Of course, those suffering from depression must be closely watched while they are in their depression and as they begin to come out of it, because they may commit suicide. Although they may assure you that they will not harm themselves, they may cut their wrists, overdose on drugs, or set fire to themselves. Unfortunately, depressions also tend to recur, so those who have had a depressive episode should be aware that they may have another one.

Suicide

Although suicide may occur with any disorder, it is most likely to occur with depression, so we will consider it here. It is one of the ten leading causes of death in the world and is most common in highly developed Western nations. Although we hear a great deal about adolescent suicides, most suicides are committed by people over forty years of age. The suicide rate remains relatively constant for nonwhites and for white females, but climbs steadily for white males as they get older. Although women attempt suicide more often than men, men succeed three times as often as women. There has recently been a rise in the number of adolescents committing suicide.

Christian counselors are likely to counsel potential suicides, and we need to be aware of several myths about suicide. First is the myth that people who talk about suicide do not actually do it. This is wrong, because nearly three-fourths of those who commit suicide have talked about it to someone before doing so. Any serious statement about suicidal thoughts should be considered a real danger signal. Second is the myth that people who have attempted suicide and failed were simply making a bid for sympathy and do not really want to die. This is also wrong, because about one in ten who attempt suicide actually succeeds within two years. Any attempt, even a superficial wrist-slashing, should be taken seriously. Last is the myth that suicide should not be mentioned when one is talking to depressed people. Most clinicians agree that such people should be encouraged to express their thoughts, and that talking about suicide helps discourage it.

Although there is a long Christian tradition condemning suicide, the Bible does not give any explicit statement concerning it. Most Christians believe that the basic commandment to do no murder extends to oneself. Killing yourself is still murder. Changing the victim does not change the act. Several suicides are recorded in the Bible, but none were given God's approval. The message of the Bible is one of life, not death. Jesus said that he was the life, and that he came that we might have abundant life.

Suicide prevention is very difficult, because most people who are depressed and thinking about suicide do not realize that their thinking is restricted and irrational. Currently the major preventive efforts focus on crisis intervention to help the individual deal with the immediate problem. Although it is imperative that we help in crisis situations, we must follow up on such people and help them make a long-term adjustment. For example, we can try to get them into a supportive Christian community.

Grief

One emotion many Christians have difficulty expressing is grief, or bereavement. The loss of a loved one has a profound effect on the survivors. We would expect an especially strong grief reaction to the death of a spouse. Two have become one, and there are repeated warnings about dividing what God has joined together. When this unit is broken by death, it is especially traumatic. Many studies have shown that the bereaved are much more likely to die through illness, accident, or suicide than are those who have not lost loved ones.

Those studying the mourning process have found from three to five phases in it. There is usually an initial period of shock, sometimes followed by anger, hostility, and appeals for help and support from others. Then there is an intense period of grief characterized by despair, withdrawal, and disorganization. Finally, there is the period of recovery and reorganization, which leads to the resumption of a normal social life.

As Christians, we are sometimes given the impression that we are not to feel grief in reaction to death, because death is to be a victorious time. However, numerous instances of grieving and mourning are recorded in the Bible, and we do not find the bereaved being reproved, but being comforted. Abraham mourned and wept over the death of Sarah, his wife. When Jacob thought that Joseph was dead, he felt such grief that he could not be comforted. Even when Absalom had been rebellious and caused him great anguish, David wept much for him and wished that he had died in his son's place. When Mary was weeping over the death of her brother Lazarus, Jesus did not rebuke her, but wept himself.

Of course, we are not to mourn like those who have no

hope, but we must remember that death was not God's original intention for humanity. Death entered through sin and is referred to as an enemy. As Christian counselors, we will work with people going through grief, and we must help them get through it.

Conclusion

We saw that emotion has both animal-like and God-like aspects, and that it is related to all other areas of psychology. Disorders can be in terms of anxiety states or the affective disorders. The most common way of treating these disorders is by means of mood-altering drugs, but this is not an adequate long-term solution. We need to teach our counselees how to cope with their feelings, both positive and negative.

Suggested Readings

Chapters on "Emotion" in general psychology textbooks and chapters on "Anxiety States" and "Affective Disorders" in abnormal psychology textbooks are recommended reading. Bootzin and Acocella (1980), Choron (1972), Coleman, Butcher, and Carson (1980), Glick, Weiss, and Parkes (1974), Izard (1977), Schuyler (1974), and Strongman (1978) expand on material presented in this chapter.

SOCIAL
PSYCHOLOGY

Social psychology considers the behavior of the individual in society. It studies the influence of the group on the individual and how the individual interacts with those in the group. Humans are social beings who spend most of their lives in the presence of others, so a knowledge of social psychology is crucial for those involved in Christian counseling. Relationships in the family, church, peer group, and other parts of society have a profound influence on our behavior.

Social psychology can be placed in our Christian perspective as shown in the lower central part of Figure 14:1 (Like Animals—Social—Like God). As created beings, like animals, we can find many parallels to our social relationships in animal societies. Psychologists have made comparisons between humans and animals in everything from family relationships to pecking orders. However, we are also created in the image of a social God. Knowing that it was not good for humans to be alone, God made us male and female in his image. Thus, social psychology considers us social beings similar to both animals and God. Now let us examine the subject areas of psychology listed above social psychology in Figure 14:1.

Structure

Our physical structure, ranging all the way from our appearance to unseen physiological changes within our bodies, plays a role in our social behavior. People's appearances may affect not only how others react to them, but how they think of themselves in a group situation. Sometimes the best counsel we can give is a lesson on basic neatness and cleanliness. As we have already seen, the level of thyroxin may influence a person's general energy level, and thus his or her energy for social interaction. Physical factors may also bring about dramatic changes in social behavior. In the 1960s, a man killed his wife and mother, then climbed to the top of a tower on the campus of the University of Texas at Austin. He began firing a rifle at people walking below. Before he was finally killed by police, he had killed fourteen people. An autopsy showed that he had a tumor near the part of his brain called the amygdala. This was probably the reason for his violent criminal behavior.

Spiritual factors also play a role in our social behavior. Sin brings separation between the sinner and the one sinned against. Of course, we are aware of this when it is sin against God, but separation also results when we sin against other people. We can sin against others, made in God's image, even though such sin is ultimately against God. Whenever we have sinned against others, there is always a barrier between us and them until the sin is confessed and forgiven.

Development

Our social behavior develops along with other aspects of psychology. Infants begin by playing just in the presence of others, then progress to forms of play in which they really interact with others. In early play, often the only interaction is when one child tries to take a toy away from another. However, social behavior develops until children actually play different, interacting roles, such as when they play house. Erikson (1963) has studied the development of psychosocial behavior throughout life.

Awareness

Sensation and perception are important factors in our social behavior. The amount of money we spend on our appearance

Figure 14:1 Social psychology and social disorders from a Christian perspective.

HUMANS

Created............in the..........Image of God
Like Animals   Like God

Overt Behavior......Definition..........Mental Processes

Understand...........Goals...............Make People
Creation   Like God

Psychoanalysis.......Systems............Humanistic
Behaviorism   Psychology

(DISORDER)   (DISORDER)

Experimental............Methods...........Descriptive

Organic Disorders............Physiological.........Structure...........Spiritual............Spiritual Disorders—Sin
(Organic Mental Disorders)   (Personality Disorders)

Physical Disorders...........Immaturity............Development.........Maturity............Spiritual Immaturity
(Disorders Appearing in   (No DSM-III Category)
Childhood or Adolescence)

Sensory Disorders..........Sensation..........Awareness..........Perception..........Perceptual Disorders

(Somatoform Disorders)   (States of Consciousness—Substance Use Disorders)   (Paranoid Disorders)

Learning..........Intellect..........Cognition..........Thinking Disorders
Learning
Disorders

(Phobic Disorders)   (Memory—Dissociative Disorders)   (Schizophrenic Disorders)

Motivational..........Biological..........Motivation..........Cognitive..........Selfishness
Disorders   Motivation   Motivation   (No DSM-III Category)
(Psychosexual
Disorders)

Emotional..........Physiological..........Emotion..........Cognitive..........Emotional Disorders
Disorders   Emotion   Emotion   (Affective Disorders)
(Anxiety States)

SOCIAL..........LIKE ANIMALS...SOCIAL..........LIKE GOD..........ABUSE OF OTHERS
MALADJUSTMENT

indicates that we all accept the fact that appearance is important. We use tooth pastes, mouthwashes, deodorants, and perfumes to remove some odors and add others. We cut, curl, straighten, and comb our hair. We straighten our teeth, wear clothes appropriate to the situation, drive the "right" kind of car, and so forth. We do all of these things to influence the way others perceive us. Much research demonstrates that our concern for our appearance is justified because appearance is important, especially in first impressions.

Intellect

People learn how to interact socially, and are rewarded or punished for their interactions with others. Reinforced responses tend to be repeated. Children who get attention or get their way for aggressive behavior will become more aggressive, while those who get attention for positive social contact will become more positive in their social behaviors.

Cognition is also important in social psychology. The theory of cognitive dissonance has been used to explain a variety of unusual social behaviors. Social psychologists have spent much time studying attitudes that have a cognitive component. If we are talking about our attitudes toward people of another race, our beliefs about them are a crucial part of that attitude.

Motivation

The satisfaction of even the physiological motives often has implications for our social behavior. We are all aware of the social restrictions on the satisfaction of the sex drive, but even the satisfaction of the hunger drive has social implications. In our culture, we eat with a knife, fork, and spoon. What would you think of people who picked up their peas, steak, or mashed potatoes with their fingers? Yet we use our fingers to pick up carrot sticks, chicken, and bread. In our culture it is impolite to burp, while in other cultures it is impolite not to do so. Meal times are social situations.

We have a variety of cognitive motives related to our social behavior, beginning with our basic need for affiliation, which is a reflection of the image of God in us. Social psychologists have also studied our motives toward both aggression and helpfulness.

Emotion

Emotion is strongly tied in with our social behavior. In fact, it is usually another person who evokes the strongest emotions in us. Although we may feel positively toward our dog or our car, love is strongest between two persons. Although a machine that does not work as we think it should may arouse our anger, other people who do not behave as we think they should are more likely to arouse it.

Relevant Research in Social Psychology

Social psychology has investigated some topics quite relevant to counseling. Let us now consider a few of these.

Conformity. We must remember that human beings have a strong tendency to conform to those around them. Asch (1955) found that even in as simple a task as judging the length of lines people would conform to what the group said. If the group gave the wrong answer, the one member of the group who was being tested was under great pressure to give the wrong answer as well. Some persons conformed little and others conformed much, but overall they gave the group's answer about one-third of the time when it was wrong.

The situation is important as well. For example, everyone tends to conform more when the task is more difficult or ambiguous and when they feel less competent than the other people in the group. The group does not have to be very large. A mere five or six people can exert great pressure on the remaining one. However, the group must be unanimous. If one other member differs with the group, the power of the group is broken, especially if a respected member disagrees. As we counsel people, we must remember this power of the group, and make use of it whenever possible. This need for conformity can be used in group therapy. We can place people in groups selected to help them if they conform.

Obedience. Milgram (1963) showed that there was a strong tendency for people to comply with the explicit commands of a person in authority. Compliance with parents, teachers, and the law is essential for society to function, but many people show an unquestioning obedience to any authority. This is especially true of people in Kohlberg's (1973) authority and social order orientation. Christians are no exception. Milgram found that nearly two thirds of the subjects would obey the person in authority even when they thought they were actually hurting others.

Many factors influence the extent to which people will obey authority. People wearing a uniform are more likely to be obeyed than those not wearing one. We are more likely to obey people who are physically present than we are to obey those who are absent. Finally, we are less likely to obey when we see someone else defying the authority. We must remember that our counselees will view us as people in authority. They will often obey us unquestioningly.

Disorders

Disorders can arise from social factors as well as from the other factors we have discussed. Although psychologists usually do not classify most of these as mental disorders, they are disorders we need to treat. These disorders can occur on either side of our Christian perspective as shown in Figure 14:1. On the left side, social maladjustment refers to situations in which the person is making a maladaptive response. On the right side of the perspective we will consider the situations where the person is making an intentional effort to harm others.

Social Maladjustment

Some individuals have social disorders simply because they have never learned how to get along with others and have withdrawn from society. Ellison (1980) notes that most people have experienced loneliness at one time or other in their lives. It is a common reason for seeking psychiatric help. In fact, most college students going to the counseling center go not because they think they are mentally ill or seriously disturbed, but because they have trouble breaking down barriers separating them from others.

Middlebrook (1974) points out that loneliness can have a variety of causes. Some existential writing emphasizes anxiety about death and the meaninglessness of life, and these questions and anxieties can lead to loneliness. Loneliness can be caused by largely unavoidable losses, such as death or divorce. People who try to save their marriage, and even those who do not, report loneliness after the divorce. Some people feel lonely because they believe they are failures, and that sets them apart from others. Other feel lonely because they only play roles, rather then entering into significant human interactions in which they really share themselves with other people. Still others feel lonely because they lack the social skills necessary to interact successfully with other people.

Zimbardo (1977) has more recently looked at shyness as a social disorder. Most individuals who are shy do not like being shy and wish they could get over it. Such individuals report a variety of consequences associated with shyness. They have difficulty in meeting new people and making new friends. This is accompanied by depression, feelings of isolation, and loneliness. They become self-conscious and preoccupied with their own reactions. They have problems in thinking clearly and communicating what they are thinking when they are with others. They find it hard to assert their opinions and values to others. This results in others' making wrong evaluations, thinking of the shy person as snobbish, unfriendly, stupid, or weak.

Abuse of Others

The other type of disorder occurs when one intentionally hurts others. This can range all the way from the behavior of the sociopath discussed in a previous chapter to cutting remarks said primarily to hurt others.

Spouse Abuse. Until a few years ago this would have been called wife abuse. It was widely known that some husbands beat their wives. The wives frequently tolerated the beatings and explained away the bruises they had. Recently, however, we have realized that some wives beat their husbands, so the disorder is now called spouse abuse. Of course, such abuse is not limited to physical beatings. It may include the more damaging verbal abuse which is even more frequently found in unhappy marriages.

Child Abuse. There is a growing concern about child abuse. In the United States more than 200,000 cases are reported each year, and there are undoubtedly many more cases than this. About one-third of the children in reported cases are seriously injured. Although children of all ages are physically abused, children under three years of age are the ones most frequently abused. Parents caught abusing their children tend to be young, and have more frustrating circumstances in their lives than most. They tend to be from lower socioeconomic levels, have marital problems, unemployment, high use of alcohol, and come from abusive families themselves. Individuals who abuse children tend to be aggressive, selfish, and nonconforming.

Crime. Criminal behavior in the United States is at a high level and rising rapidly. Official figures show that the United States has one of the highest crime rates in the world, and it is estimated that from one-third to one-half of all serious crimes are not reported to the police. Violent crimes (murder, rape, robbery, assault) increased eleven times as fast as the population during the 1960s and fifteen times as fast during the first half of the 1970s. Crime rates vary considerably, but are generally much higher in metropolitan centers than in smaller cities and rural areas. Blacks are more likely to be victims of crimes of violence. Although most people believe otherwise, criminals usually strike in the area where they live and often know their victims personally. Although most offenders are male, the crime rate of females is currently rising at a faster rate than that of males. Nearly one-third of all murders are committed by people between 18 and 25 years of age.

Discrimination. A person's prejudices are often expressed in actual discrimination against people in that particular group. We are well aware of many different types of discrimination, such as racial, religious, or sexual discrimination. Belonging to a given group may mean that a person is unable to find housing, unable to get a job, or more likely to be arrested because of someone else's prejudice. We often do not even recognize our discrimination. Until the mid-twentieth century it was simply accepted throughout the South that blacks would go to one school, whites to another; blacks would use one drinking fountain or restroom, whites another; blacks would ride in the back of the bus, whites in front, and so forth. Christians discriminate against other denominations or certain factions within their own.

Cutting Remarks. Much abuse of others comes in the form of verbal attacks. Such remarks can leave longer-lasting damage than physical attacks. Physical damage heals in a few days or weeks, but an attack on a persons's self-concept may leave lifelong damage. Parents who convince their children that they are no good may leave their children with that concept for years. Christian psychologists have to deal with much of the damage brought about in this way. The Bible says much about controlling the tongue.

Treatment

As before, we must decide what is the cause of the disorder and get at that cause. We must also remember that secondary disorders may have developed and treat them as well. Frequently, Christian counselors can help those with social maladjustment by dealing with the problem. If abuse of others is a problem, legal authorities are likely to be involved and Christian counselors may not have as much opportunity to get involved unless they are working in an institution such as a juvenile home, jail, or prison. Finally, social relationships are found in many types of therapy, therapy for problems other than social ones.

Social Maladjustment

We must determine the causes of the loneliness or shyness, then work to remove them. If the counselees have an existential loneliness and are questioning the meaningfulness of life, we need to answer their questions about meaning in life. To do this we will have to bring in a Christian world-view and attempt to show them how meaning can be found in it.

If the loneliness is caused by some unavoidable loss, the counselees may simply need comfort until they can rebuild their lives in face of the loss. Following death and divorce, it takes time for them to begin to put their lives together again. If the problem is a failure on their part, we must help them to see that failing in one or two things does not make them "failures" as people.

If the shyness or loneliness is a result of the lack of interaction with others, we need to help with that. Some people have learned their social roles so well that all they can do is play those roles. They seldom act spontaneously and need help in relaxing and acting naturally, and not playing a role. Some have not learned their social roles and general social skills well enough. These people need to be taught basic manners, how to carry on a conversation, how to make others feel at ease, and so forth.

Abuse of Others

Although legal authorities may do most of the treatment, Christian counselors must be alert for abuse of others.

Although we may think that child abuse or spouse abuse is not perpetrated by church members, it is. When we discover it, we are faced with making the judgment of how badly the one being abused is likely to be hurt while we are treating the abuser. This is a serious and difficult decision. It is serious because a wrong judgment may mean serious injury to an innocent individual, while reporting the abuser will result in a loss of confidence in the therapist. It is a difficult decision because it is hard to tell how bad the abuse has been and to predict how bad it will get during counseling. In many areas of the country, the law requires counselors to report cases of child abuse to authorities.

The question of how to treat criminal behavior is still an open one. Tradition stressed punishment of the offenders for their crimes. Recently, emphasis has been placed on rehabilitation—the idea being that the criminals needed some type of treatment—so many types of therapy were used on them. However, attempts at rehabilitation have not been successful. The nationwide rate of people's being rearrested for new crimes after release from prison is over two-thirds, and as high as 90% in some areas of the country.

As a result of the ineffectiveness of treatment programs and the questions about prisoner's rights, the trend is back toward punishment. In 1973 and 1974, the American Civil Liberties Union filed a lawsuit to abolish the use of an experimental behavior modification program for aggressive inmates. The moral-ethical issue was that the behavior-modification was used as a management technique, not as a therapeutic tool. The program was discontinued, as was support for other, similar programs. The fact is that we do not know how to change criminals, and we must lock up some people to protect society in general.

Although many types of discrimination have been made criminal offenses, as Christian counselors we must be alert for other prejudices and their resultant discrimination. We find such discrimination even in Christian circles. We must watch for statements implying prejudice against "charismatics," "fundamentalists," or "liberals." Simply attaching such a label may result in real discrimination against Christian brothers and sisters.

We must also counsel against hurting others with words. Many times the people we are counseling are not even aware that their remarks are hurting others. Joking remarks, laughed at by everyone, may do much more actual harm than anyone realizes. We must caution our counselees about their use of words, intentional or unintentional.

Group Therapy

Many types of psychotherapy have been developed involving the interaction of several people. Of course, even one-on-one psychotherapy is a social situation, but in this section we will consider some of the types of therapy using larger groups. The group therapy movement received its major impetus during World War II, when therapists were in short supply. Such therapy typically involves a relatively small number of patients, led by a therapist, and using any of the types of therapy discussed throughout this book as individual methods of therapy.

Since 1945 the group therapy movement has mushroomed, with many different types being proposed, used, and written about. Of course, it has the obvious advantage of saving time and money. Since one therapist can see eight or ten people an hour instead of one, more people can receive help. Because several people are seeing the therapist at once, each has to pay for only a part of the therapist's time, so it is cheaper per person. However, economy alone is not the major reason for the popularity of group therapy. Since many disorders are believed to be caused by interpersonal difficulties, it follows that these should be worked out in an interpersonal context. That is, if a married couple is having a problem, it seems reasonable to talk to both of them rather than to just one.

There are many different kinds of groups. Some groups are organized around methods of treatment: such as psychoanalytic groups, behavioral groups, and humanistic groups. Some groups are for people who have specific kinds of problems, such as alcoholics, spouses of alcoholics, delinquents, parents of delinquents, married couples, unmarried couples, and so forth. The most common types of groups are ones organized by therapists for anyone they believe will be helped by the group setting. The groups usually consist of seven to ten people who meet two or more times each week. The group members rarely know each other before they meet in the group. In some smaller communities, patients may be concerned about being put in a group with someone they already know. The interaction in the group is primarily verbal, although nonverbal communications such as body posture, facial expression, and seating arrangements are all noted as well. Let us now consider some special types of group therapy.

Psychodrama. Although psychodrama has never become part of the mainstream of psychotherapy, its founder was one of the first to use the term "group therapy." In Vienna, Moreno had worked with a "theatre of spontaneity" in which he began to use role-playing techniques. In psychodrama the participants get up on an actual stage and act out their emotional conflicts. The stage is intended to be an extension of life, but beyond the reality of life. It is to give the counselee a "space for living."

The participants are asked (at least at first) to be themselves, to share their thoughts and emotions as they respond to other actors. They are not to "perform," but to respond spontaneously as things come to mind. The emphasis is not on being a good actor, but on being spontaneous. The psychotherapists are directors, producers, and analysts. As directors, they may joke with or attack the patients, or even decide to be completely passive and let the patients dominate the session. As producers, they keep the action going, maintaining rapport with the audience, an integral part of the psychodrama. As analysts, they integrate into their interpretation of the psychodrama information obtained from the patient's family, friends, and even members of the audience.

For example, a woman who had difficulties with her father may be asked to act out a childhood scene playing herself with a male member of the group playing her father. Other members of the group may play the roles of her mother, brothers, and sisters, while others are the audience. Presumably the sources of the conflict will emerge in the drama. This typical pattern may be varied in many ways. One popular variation is role reversal, in which the actors switch parts, so the woman may play the role of her father, while someone else plays her part. Another variation is the double technique, in which the therapist gets on stage and acts out the counselee's part at the same time the counselee does. Still another variation is mirroring, in which group members portray each other on stage.

Moreno (1946) claims several advantages for psychodrama over therapies involving mainly talking. First, an individual may be able to act out feelings otherwise indescribable or inexplicable, so that counselees can express themselves more fully. He also believes that the role playing in therapy helps prevent the patients from acting out such things in real life, and that it encourages counselees to reveal the deepest roots of their problems. Finally, it enables counselees to learn from one another, like all other forms of group therapy.

Encounter Groups. More recent types of therapy are the encounter group and the T-group. The sensitivity-training group, or T-group movement, was first used in the late 1940s to help train group leaders and help executives improve relationships with their co-workers. During the 1960s and 1970s the encounter group movement originated in the humanistic psychology movement, emphasizing personal growth, openness, and honesty in interpersonal relationships. Originally the T-group limited itself to verbal interchange, while the encounter group encouraged more radical things such as touching exercises, yelling, and weeping. However, the distinctions have blurred in recent years.

The goals and formats of encounter groups vary greatly. Some groups are directed toward treating people with personal problems, while others are directed toward helping normal individuals learn about their feelings and personal interaction. Schutz (1973) gives a list of twenty-seven "rules of encounter," but many groups function with few rules. The basic premise is that one must be open and honest in all interactions with members of the group. The leader-participant tries to establish a climate in which members will be able to drop their masks and express their real feelings.

Sometimes "warming-up" exercises are used to encourage openness and closeness. Some use "eyeball-to-eyeball," in which two persons stare into each other's eyes for a minute or two. Others use the "blind mill," in which group members close their eyes and walk around communicating only by touch. Still others use "trusting exercises," in which group members take turns being lifted and passed around a circle formed by other group members. Some encounter groups use the marathon format, in which the group meets for a whole weekend, breaking only briefly for sleep.

Some Christians have been quite critical of encounter groups because of some of the excesses that have occurred. For example, Schutz' (1973) rules nine and ten say that if something can be expressed either physically or verbally, one should do so physically, whether this means a hug or a fight. If it is a fight, other group members should stand in front of windows, sharp objects, hard objects, or anything that might cause damage. Each person is responsible for himself or herself, so physical injury is each person's own responsibility. Schutz goes on to say that we should accept members' taking off clothing whenever it is valuable to the activity of the group. Some encounter leaders encourage total nudity on the part of all participants.

Although as Christians we may not approve of fighting and nudity, we certainly want our counselees to reach the goals of openness and honesty in their personal relationships. As with other methods of treatment, we can use many of the techniques of encounter groups to help people learn how to interact. However, if we use these techniques, we must be careful that we do not produce encounter-group casualties. Some people who are unable to handle the pressure to open up and the intensive emotional stimulation, may leave the group hurt rather than helped. We must also help people in the groups reenter their everyday world where they cannot be completely open and honest in their relationships.

Family Therapy. Family therapy is group therapy with a naturally formed group, rather than one convened by the therapist. Family therapists believe that the disorder shown by the person (adult or child) identified as the patient is only a symptom of a larger family problem. Therefore, the whole family needs to be involved in the treatment. This movement began when it was noticed that some people released from institutions had a relapse when they returned home.

One approach to family therapy emphasizes communication and interaction among the family members. Sometimes family members receive conflicting communications, such as the children who are urged to express themselves and then punished for talking back. Another example is spouses who claim an interest in sex, but have a headache whenever it seems like sexual activity is in the offing. Therapists encourage family members to be open about what they really want. Therapists try to overcome faulty communication systems.

Another approach is the systems approach or structured family therapy. This approach assumes that the whole family system is more important than any individual personality in producing abnormal behavior. Family members create roles for each other, so the family is analyzed as a set of interlocking roles. The misbehaving child may have created the role of the disciplinarian, or the disciplinarian may have created the role of the misbehaving child. The helpless individual may have created the role of the helping individual, or the helping individual (rescuer) may have created the helpless one.

These roles may interfere with what the other person wants to do, but family members go on fulfilling their roles, even when they should change. For example, the mother may learn the role of helper when her children are infants. She gives them baths, dresses them, and so forth. However, as the children grow, the mother may not be able to change her role, so that she goes on being too much of a helper even when the children grow up. When the children try to become independent, they meet with great resistance from the mother and even other members of the family.

According to systems theory, these roles are the key to family disturbances. Some even believe that one family member becomes disordered because the role system in that family requires that one member be "sick." Thus, therapists gather information about the family, analyze the roles, determine the purposes these roles serve, and encourage family members to develop more comfortable and flexible roles. Therapists may gather the information by participating in the family interactions as a part of the family and then begin to produce changes by using themselves as "change mediums" to alter the interactions among family members.

Marital therapy or couple counseling, counseling in which the group consists of only a married couple, is really a subtype of marital counseling. The most common problem here is lack of communication or unclear communication. Marriage therapists nearly always try to get the couple talking openly to each other, expressing their needs, and then meeting each other's needs. Spouses often have different expectations about the role each is to play. Since they do not communicate, each never realizes what the other expects. Christian counselors are very likely to be involved in some form of marital therapy.

Conclusion

We have seen that our social behavior is related to all other areas of psychology, even our anatomy, physiology, and sensory processes. We are like both God and animals in that we are social beings. Disorders can range from social maladjustment, in which we withdraw from social interaction, to the abuse of others. Many kinds of treatment have developed involving the use of groups of other people, although most of them are not directly involved with the treatment of social disorders.

Suggested Readings

Chapters on "Social Psychology" in general psychology textbooks are recommended reading. Bootzin and Acocella (1980), Coleman, Butcher, and Carson (1980), Corsini (1973), Goldenberg and Goldenberg (1980), Koteskey (1980), Levine (1979), Middlebrook (1974), Milgram (1973), Starr (1977), and Zimbardo (1977) expand on material presented in this chapter.

CONCLUSION

Readers familiar with general psychology look at the title of this chapter and undoubtedly think that it is too soon to come to the conclusion. Too many chapters usually found in general psychology books are missing. There are no chapters on personality, adjustment, abnormal psychology, and psychotherapy. Although there are no chapters on these topics, the material has been covered in other chapters. The whole book is an approach to personality from a Christian perspective. Each chapter began with a section on the normal person, included a section on disorders, and concluded with a section on treatment.

Integration of Psychology

Christian psychologists have come through a long period in which they talked at length about the integration of psychology and Christianity. The basic idea seemed to be that we had psychological concepts on the one hand and theological concepts on the other and our task was to interrelate the two. Psychologists were seen as working at one level with one vocabulary and theologians at another level with a different vocabulary, but it was assumed that they were really talking about the same things.

The approach taken in this book is not that psychology and Christianity need to be integrated, but that psychology itself is fragmented, and when viewed from a Christian world-view it can be unified. This book has attempted to present a unified view of psychology, showing how all areas of it are interrelated. One major attempt at unification has been to show how the clinical-counseling topics of psychological disorders and treatment are intimately related to the subject areas often considered to be academic or experimental psychology. A Christian perspective thus enables us to make an integration of the scientist and the professional as secular psychology has been unable to do.

In making the integration between academic-experimental psychology and clinical-counseling psychology, I relied heavily on the diagnostic categories found in DSM-III. I did this simply because they are the most widely used categories, not because I believe that they are correct in any absolute sense. In the figures in each chapter these specific diagnostic categories were enclosed in parentheses to indicate that they were examples of the types of disorders to be considered there. This book is not a handbook attempting to list every diagnostic category in every place it could be considered. It is a book to present a basic framework, with a few specific examples included. In some instances there were simply no DSM-III categories to fit into our Christian perspective, but that did not mean that there were no disorders. Since DSM-III does not consider sin a disorder, it does not have diagnostic categories for some forms of sin.

This approach is an eclectic one, taking material from many different approaches. However, it is different from many eclectic approaches. It not only takes concepts from different systems of psychology, but also integrates them in a systematic way. It is a systematic eclecticism rather than a bits-and-pieces eclecticism. Thus, it does not have the major fault of most eclectic approaches. It is an eclectic approach, but still not all-accepting, without critical selection.

Other Disorders and Treatment

As Christian counselors, we must not confine our thinking only to disorders and treatments considered by contemporary psychologists. Several times in this book I have discussed disorders that secular psychologists would not consider to be disorders. The subject matter of psychology changes periodically, and we must not be bound by a given time frame. For example, as discussed in a previous chapter, at the turn of the century, the will (volition) was a subject area discussed in most general psychology texts. This whole subject area is largely missing from contemporary texts.

Odd as it may seem, one of the most successful treatments of all types of disorders—moral treatment, used widely during the early part of the nineteenth century—is no longer used. In France, Philippe Pinel began treating patients with kindness and consideration rather than treating them as animals or criminals. The noise and filth of asylums and prisons were replaced by order and peace, and people began to recover. William Tuke, an English Quaker, established the "York Retreat" where patients lived in a religious atmosphere and were treated with kindness. Patients there also recovered.

The users of moral treatment never clearly defined their practices, but they included kindness, compassion, and understanding of the innocent sufferers, and even those not so innocent. Moral therapists expected their patients to recover and went at their work with zeal, hope, and confidence. Punishment and shock treatments were forbidden. Patients read, played games, ate with ordinary silverware, and worked with the tools of their trade. The superintendent and his family lived and ate with the patients, who were considered part of his family. Moral treatment was very effective, with hospitals reporting discharge rates higher than for previous or subsequent times.

In spite of its success, the use of moral treatment declined during the second half of the nineteenth century. Probably as a result of the Industrial Revolution, the average size of the mental hospital increased greatly. Hospitals with 200 patients were not as efficient to run as one with several thousand patients. Increases in staff did not follow the increase in the number of patients; and soon, rather than helping the patients get ready to leave the hospital, the staff concentrated on keeping the patients clean, quiet, and peaceful. Another factor in the decline of moral treatment was the emergence of the "medical model" of mental "illness." The success of medicine led to its adoption as a model for the treatment of mental disorders, which were now assumed to be caused by some brain pathology. Thus patients were given custodial care, rather than expected to recover.

The results were disastrous. The recovery rate of 70% (between 1833 and 1846) at Worcester State Hospital using moral treatment, dropped to 5% by the end of the century. Only one person out of twenty admitted recovered. It is easy to see why great fear of becoming mentally ill and being committed to a mental hospital became commonplace during the first half of the twentieth century.

We need to seriously consider techniques used in the past, techniques that were largely successful, such as moral treatment. We must examine past methods for principles that may still be effective. Although we might not want to reinstitute the treatments in full, they may give us clues to help those with disorders.

Holistic Treatment

As Christian counselors, we must treat not only one area of the person's disorder, but the whole person. In this book, each disorder and treatment has been presented individually to show how many of the disorders fit into our basic Christian perspective, and to show that our perspective points out some disorders secular psychologists have not considered. However, we must not think of treating only one area of an individual. People are wholes. We cannot divide them up into sensation, learning, physiological motives, and so forth. Disorders beginning in one area are likely to spread to other areas of the person's life, and we need to treat them all.

A Christian counselor must not be a specialist in only one kind of treatment, but be able to use a variety of treatments and be able and willing to refer counselees to appropriate specialists for parallel treatment of problems the counselor is not qualified to treat. In one case, confession, repentance, and forgiveness may be needed; in another, behavior modification may be needed; in another, chemicals; and in still another, cognitive therapy. A Christian counselor must be able to use many different therapies, depending on what is the nature of the disorder in the counselee. If the counselor is not able to use the necessary type of treatment, he or she should at least be able to refer the counselee to someone who can treat that disorder.

The Absent Church

The role of the church in the treatment of mental disorders has varied over the years, but Christianity in general does not have a consistently good record. Emphasis on demonology had declined with the Greek and Roman civilizations, but returned again in the Middle Ages. At this time treatment of the disturbed was left largely to the clergy, and the mentally ill were usually treated with considerable kindness. However, as theological beliefs about such behavior became more fully elaborated and widely accepted by the secular world, treatment became harsher. The treatment then was to make the body such an unpleasant place to reside that the demon would leave. People were whipped, starved, chained, and immersed in hot water—anything to drive the devil out of them. Then came the widespread beliefs about attributing all kinds of things to witches, individuals (mostly women) who had supposedly made a pact with the devil and been given supernatural powers. Individuals tortured until they confessed were usually burned after further torture. Both Roman Catholic and Protestant churches were widely involved in the death of millions of people all over the world.

The church was somewhat involved in the moral treatment movement. As moral treatment declined, the church withdrew and left the treatment of mental disorders to the state.

During the first half of the twentieth century, the church had virtually no direct involvement in the treatment of the mental disorders. There were a few isolated individuals and institutions, but no general movement. The colony of Geehl in Belgium has continued its treatment of the mental disorders with kindness and love from the thirteenth century to the present. The Christian Reformed Church founded Pine Rest Christian Hospital in Grand Rapids, Michigan. But until the mid-twentieth century there were few bright spots in the involvement of Christians in treatment.

In general, the inclination within the church in this century has been to care for the physically ill and ignore the mentally ill. In my own area in central Kentucky, we have a Roman Catholic hospital, a Methodist hospital, and a Baptist hospital—all caring for the physically ill. However, there are no church-related facilities for caring for the mentally ill, other than a psychiatric unit on one floor of one hospital. Granted that there is a Christian counseling center, and pastoral counseling is available; but if someone becomes too seriously disturbed, we turn the patient over to the local state hospital.

The only denomination that has an organized national system to care for people with mental disorders is the Mennonite church, and this was not started until after World War II. During the war, about 1,500 Mennonite young men served in twenty state mental hospitals and six training schools as conscientious objectors to military service. These individuals were impressed by the mental health needs that existed and became convinced that the church should do something to meet those needs. In the late 1940,s the Mennonite Central Committee agreed to establish three mental health facilities, one each in the eastern, central, and western regions of the United States. This was accomplished by 1953. By the early 1970s, this network had expanded to seven institutions across the United States and Canada.

Other than the Mennonites, I have been able to find no other Protestant denomination that has made any large-scale attempt to deal with the seriously mentally disturbed. Christians often point to the fact that psychologists can show little evidence of helping people recover (over the spontaneous recovery rate). However, when asked what their church is doing, they have nothing to say. At least psychologists are trying, while the church has done virtually nothing.

An encouraging sign is the recent growth in Christian psychology. The Christian Association for Psychological Studies, founded in 1955, grew to well over 1,000 members in the 1970s. Graduate education in psychology from a Christian perspective begun at Fuller Theological Seminary in 1965, has since emerged in a variety of settings. The *Journal of Psychology and Theology* and the *CAPS Bulletin* (now the *Journal of Psychology and Christianity*) begun in 1973 and 1975 now provide a means of communication among Christian psychologists. Since the mid-1970s, a number of books have appeared integrating psychology and Christianity. Churches now sponsor Christian counseling centers in most major cities. In addition, a number of independent Christian counseling centers have been organized.

Even with all this activity among Christians in psychology, much remains to be done. Most Christian psychologists spend the bulk of their time with the least seriously disturbed people. We spend most of our time working with the disorders on the animal-like side of our perspective, largely ignoring the disorders on the God-like side. Although psychology alone may not have adequate answers for these disorders, as Christians we should be able to bring to psychology a unifying perspective with new clues for answers.

R E F E R E N C E S

Adams, J. E. *Competent to Counsel.* Nutley, N.J.: Presbyterian and Reformed, 1970.

Agranowitz, A., & McKeown, M. R. *Aphasia Handbook for Adults and Children.* Springfield, Ill.: Charles C. Thomas, 1964.

Asch, S. E. "Opinions and Social Pressure." *Scientific American,* 1955, *193* (5), pp. 31-35.

Baddeley, A. D. *The Psychology of Memory.* New York: Basic Books, 1976.

Balagura, S. *Hunger.* New York: Basic Books, 1973.

Bartley, S. H. *Principles of Perception* (2nd ed.). New York: Harper & Row, 1969.

Beck, A. T. *Cognitive Therapy and the Emotional Disorders.* New York: International Universities Press, 1976.

Berkhof, L. *Systematic Theology.* Grand Rapids, Mich.: Eerdmans Publishing Co., 1946.

Bernheim, K. F., & Lewine, R. R. J. *Schizophrenia.* New York: W. W. Norton & Co., 1979.

Birren, J. E. *The Psychology of Aging.* Englewood Cliffs, N.J.: Prentice-Hall, 1964.

Blake, R. R., & Ramasey, G. V. *Perception: An Approach to Personality.* New York: Ronald Press, 1951.

Bootzin, R. R., & Acocella, J. R. *Abnormal Psychology* (3rd ed.). New York: Random House, 1980.

Brecher, E. M. *Licit & Illicit Drugs.* Boston: Little, Brown, 1972.

Breggin, P. R. *Electroshock.* New York: Springer Publishing Co., 1979.

Brown, J. W. *Aphasia, Apraxia, and Agnosia.* Springfield, Ill.: Charles C. Thomas, 1972.

Brown, T. S., & Wallace, P. M. *Physiological Psychology.* New York: Academic Press, 1980.

Bruch, H. *Eating Disorders.* New York: Basic Books, 1973.

Bufford, R. K. *The Human Reflex.* New York: Harper & Row, 1981.

Cameron, N. "Perceptual Organization and Behavior Pathology." In R. R. Blake & G. V. Ramasey (eds.), *Perception: An Approach to Personality.* New York: Ronald Press, 1951.

Cerling, C. E. "Anger: Musings of a Theologian/Psychologist." *Journal of Psychology and Theology,* 1974, *1,* pp. 12-17. (a)

Cerling, C. E. "Some Thoughts on a Biblical View of Anger: A Response." *Journal of Psychology and Theology,* 1974, *2,* pp. 266-268. (b)

Choron, J. *Suicide.* New York: Scribner's, 1972.

Coleman, J. C., Butcher, J. N., & Carson, R. C. *Abnormal Psychology and Modern Life* (6th ed.). Glenview, Ill.: Scott, Foresman, 1980.

Corsini, R. (ed.), *Current Psychotherapies.* Itasca, Ill.: Peacock, 1973.

de Becker, R. *The Understanding of Dreams* (M. Heron, trans.). New York: Hawthorn, 1968. (Originally published 1965.)

Diagnostic and Statistical Manual of Mental Disorders (3rd ed.). Washington, D. C.: American Psychiatric Association, 1980.

Ellis, A. "Rational Psychotherapy." *Journal of General Psychology,* 1958, *59,* pp. 35-49.

Ellis, A. "Rational-Emotive Therapy." In R. Corsini (ed.), *Current Psychotherapies.* Itasca, Ill.: F. E. Peacock Publishers, 1973. (a)

Ellis, A. *Humanistic Psychotherapy: The Rational-Emotive Approach.* New York: Julian Press, 1973. (b)

Ellison, C. W. (ed.). *Self Esteem.* Oklahoma City: Southwestern Press, 1976.

Ellison, C. W. *Loneliness.* Chappaqua, N.Y.: Christian Herald, 1980.

Erikson, E. H. *Childhood and Society* (2nd ed.). New York: W. W. Norton & Co., 1963.

Erwin, E. *Behavior Therapy.* Cambridge: Cambridge University Press, 1978.

Fairlie, H. *The Seven Deadly Sins Today.* Washington, D. C.: New Republic, 1978.

Fantz, R. L. "The Origin of Form Perception. *Scientific American,* 1961, *204* (5), pp. 66-72.

Festinger, L. *A Theory of Cognitive Dissonance.* Stanford, Calif.: Stanford University Press, 1957.

Forrest, G. G. *The Diagnosis and Treatment of Alcoholism.* Springfield, Ill.: Charles C.Thomas, 1975.

Freud, S. *The Standard Edition of the Complete Psychological Works of Sigmund Freud* (J. Strachey, ed. and trans.). London: Hogarth, 1886-1939.

Garfield, S. L., & Bergin A. E. (eds.). *Handbook of Psychotherapy and Behavioral Change* (2nd ed.). New York: Wiley, 1978.

Glick, I. O., Weiss, R. S., & Parkes, C. M. *The First Years of Bereavement.* New York: John Wiley & Sons, 1974.

Goldenberg, I., & Goldenberg, H. *Family Therapy.* Monterey, Calif.: Brooks/Cole Publishing Co., 1980.

Gregory, R. L. *Eye and Brain.* New York: McGraw-Hill, 1973.

Harlow, H. F. *Learning to Love.* San Francisco: Albion Publishing Co., 1971.

Heron, W. "The Pathology of Boredom." *Scientific American,* 1957, *196* (1), pp. 52-56.

Hilgard, E. R., Atkinson, R. C., & Atkinson, R. L. *Introduction to Psychology* (6th ed.). New York: Harcourt Brace Jovanovich, 1979.

Hjelle, L. A., & Ziegler, D. J. *Personality Theories* (2nd ed.). New York: McGraw-Hill, 1981.

Hutt, M. L., Isaacson, R. L., & Blum, M. L. *The Science of Interpersonal Behavior.* New York: Harper & Row, 1966.

Izard, C. E. *Human Emotions.* New York: Plenum Publishing Corp., 1977.

Kanfer, F. H., & Phillips, J. S. *Learning Foundations of Behavior Therapy.* New York: John Wiley & Sons, 1970.

Kaplan, H. S. *The New Sex Therapy.* New York: Brunner/ Mazel, 1974.

Kazdin, A. E. *History of Behavior Modification.* Baltimore: University Park Press, 1978.

Kelly, G. A. "Sin and Psychotherapy," in O. H. Mowrer (ed.), *Morality and Mental Health.* Chicago: Rand McNally, 1967.

Kohlberg, L. "Stages and Aging in Moral Development— Some Speculations." *The Gerontologist,* 1973, *13,* pp. 497-502.

Korchin, S. J. *Modern Clinical Psychology.* New York: Basic Books, 1976.

Korman, A. K. *The Psychology of Motivation.* Englewood Cliffs, N.J.: Prentice-Hall, 1974.

Koteskey, R. L. *Psychology from a Christian Perspective.* Nashville: Abingdon, 1980.

LaHaye, T., & LaHaye, B. *The Act of Marriage.* Grand Rapids, Mich.: Zondervan, 1976.

Lashley, K. S. "In Search of the Engram." *Symposium of the Society of Experimental Biology.* (No. 4). Cambridge: Cambridge University Press, 1950, pp. 454-82.

Lazarus, R. S., & Alfert, E. "Shortcircuiting of Threat by Experimentally Altering Cognitive Appraisal." *Journal of Abnormal and Social Psychology,* 1964, *69,* pp. 195-205.

Leukel, F. *Introduction to Physiological Psychology* (3rd ed.). St. Louis: Mosby, 1976.

Levine, B. *Group Psychotherapy.* Englewood Cliffs, N.J.: Prentice-Hall, 1979.

Lewis, C. S. "The Humanitarian Theory of Punishment," in W. Hooper (ed.) *God in the Dock*. Grand Rapids, Mich.: Eerdmans, 1970. (Reprinted from *20th Century: An Australian Quarterly Review,* 1949, *3.*)

Lewis, G. R. *What Everyone Should Know About Transcendental Meditation.* Glendale, Calif.: Regal Books, 1975.

Linn, D., & Linn, M. *Healing of Memories.* Ramsey, N.J.: Paulist Press, 1974.

Luce, G. G., & Segal, J. *Sleep.* New York: Coward, McCann & Geoghegan, 1966.

Luce, G. G., & Segal, J. *Insomnia.* Garden City, N.Y.: Doubleday & Co., 1969.

Lundin, R. W. *Theories and Systems of Psychology* (2nd ed.). Lexington, Mass.: D. C. Heath & Co., 1979.

Luria, A. R. *The Mind of a Mnemonist.* (L. Solotaroff, trans.) New York: Basic Books, 1968.

Lyman, S. M. *The Seven Deadly Sins.* New York: St. Martin's Press, 1978.

Maslow, A. H. *Motivation and Personality.* New York: Harper & Brothers, 1954.

Maslow, A. H. *Toward a Psychology of Being* (2nd ed.). New York: Van Nostrand Reinhold, 1968.

Masters, W. H., & Johnson, V. E. *Human Sexual Inadequacy.* Boston: Little, Brown, 1970.

Masters, W. H., & Johnson, V. E. *Homosexuality in Perspective.* Boston: Little, Brown, 1979.

Matheson, D. W., Bruce, R. L., & Beauchamp, K. L. *Experimental Psychology* (3rd ed.). New York: Holt, Rinehart and Winston, 1978.

May, R. *Love and Will.* New York: W. W. Norton & Co., 1969.

McCary, J. L. *Human Sexuality* (3rd ed.). New York: Van Nostrand Reinhold, 1978.

Mendelson, J. H., & Mello, N. K. (eds.). *The Diagnosis & Treatment of Alcoholism.* New York: McGraw-Hill, 1979.

Menninger, K. *Whatever Became of Sin?* New York: Hawthorn Books, 1973.

Middlebrook, P. N. *Social Psychology and Modern Life.* New York: Alfred A. Knopf, 1974.

Milgram, S. "Behavioral Study of Obedience." *Journal of Abnormal and Social Psychology,* 1963, *67,* pp. 371-78.

Mintz, S., & Alpert, M. "Imagery Vividness, Reality Testing and Schizophrenic Hallucinations." *Journal of Abnormal Psychology,* 1972, *79,* pp. 310-16.

Minuchin, S., Rosman, B. L., & Baker, L. *Psychosomatic Families: Anorexia Nervosa in Context.* Cambridge, Mass.: Harvard University Press, 1978.

Mischel, W., & Mischel, H. N. *Essentials of Psychology* (2nd ed.). New York: Random House, 1980.

Moreno, J. L. *Psychodrama* (vol. 1). Boston: Beacon Press, 1946.

Mowrer, O. H. "Some Constructive Features of the Concept of Sin." *Journal of Counseling Psychology,* 1960, *7,* pp. 185-88.

Mowrer, O. H. "Abnormal Reactions or Actions? (An Autobiographical Answer)," in J. A. Vernon (ed.), *Introduction to Psychology.* Dubuque, Iowa: Wm. C. Brown Group, 1966.

Munsey, B. *Moral Development, Moral Education, and Kohlberg.* Birmingham, Ala.: Religious Education Press, 1980.

Narramore, S. B. "Guilt: Where Theology and Psychology Meet." *Journal of Psychology and Theology,* 1974, *2,* pp. 18-25.

National Institute of Mental Health. *Alcohol and Alcoholism* (Public Health Service Publication No. 1640). Washington, D. C.: U. S. Government Printing Office, 1968.

Oates, W. E. *The Psychology of Religion.* Waco, Tex.: Word, 1973.

O'Brien, P. *The Disordered Mind: What We Now Know About Schizophrenia.* Englewood Cliffs, N.J.: Prentice-Hall, 1978.

Pavlov, I. P. *[Conditioned Reflexes]* (G. V. Anrep, ed. and trans.). New York: Dover, 1960. (Originally published 1927.)

Pederson, J. E. "Some Thoughts on a Biblical View of Anger." *Journal of Psychology and Theology,* 1974, *2,* pp. 210-15.

Perry, N. *Teaching the Mentally Retarded Child.* New York: Columbia University Press, 1974.

Physicians' Desk Reference (33rd ed.). Oradell, N.J.: Medical Economics, 1979 (updated yearly).

Piaget, J., & Inhelder, B. *[The Psychology of the Child.]* (H. Weaver, trans.), New York: Basic Books, 1969. (Originally published 1966.)

Rank, O. *Will Therapy* (J. Taft, trans.) New York: W. W. Norton & Co., 1936. (Originally published 1931.)

Rogers, C. R. *Client-Centered Therapy.* Boston: Houghton Mifflin, 1951. (a)

Rogers, C. R. "Perceptual Reorganization in Client-Centered Therapy," in R. R. Blake and G. V. Ramsey, *Perception: An Approach to Personality.* New York: Ronald Press, 1951. (b)

Rogers, C. R. "A Theory of Therapy, Personality, and Interpersonal Relationships, As Developed in the Client-Centered Framework," in S. Koch (ed.), *Psychology: A Study of a Science* (vol. 3). New York: McGraw-Hill, 1959.

Sall, M. J. "Demon Possession or Psychopathology?: A Clinical Differentiation. *Journal of Psychology and Theology,* 1976, *4,* pp. 286-90.

Schachter, S., & Singer, J. "Cognitive, Social, and Physiological Determinants of Emotional State." *Psychological Review,* 1962, *69,* pp. 379-99.

Schaeffer, F. A. *The God Who Is There.* Downers Grove, Ill.: Inter-Varsity Press, 1968.

Schell, R. E., & Hall, E. *Developmental Psychology Today* (3rd ed.). New York: Random House, 1979.

Schoeck, H. *[Envy: A Theory of Social Behavior]* (M. Glenny, & B. Ross, eds. and trans.). New York: Harcourt Brace & World, 1969. (Originally published 1966.)

Schultz, D. *A History of Modern Psychology* (3rd ed.). New York: Academic Press, 1981.

Schutz, W. C. Encounter. In R. Corsini (ed.), *Current Psychotherapies*. Itasca, Ill.: F. E. Peacock Publishers, 1973.

Schuyler, D. *The Depressive Spectrum*. New York: Jason Aronson, 1974.

Seamon, J. G. *Memory & Cognition*. New York: Oxford University Press, 1980.

Shedd, C., & Shedd, M. *Celebration in the Bedroom*. Waco, Tex.: Word Books, 1979.

Skinner, B. F. *Beyond Freedom and Dignity*. New York: Alfred A. Knopf, 1971.

Small, D. H. *Christian: Celebrate Your Sexuality*. Old Tappan, N.J.: Fleming H. Revell, 1974.

Solomon, C. R. *Handbook of Happiness*. Denver, Colo.: House of Solomon, 1971.

Starr, A. *Psychodrama*. Chicago: Nelson-Hall Publishers, 1977.

Stephenson, F. D. *Gestalt Therapy Primer*. Springfield, Ill.: Charles C. Thomas, 1975.

Strongman, K. T. *The Psychology of Emotion* (2nd ed.). New York: John Wiley & Sons, 1978.

Tozer, A. W. *The Knowledge of the Holy*. New York: Harper & Brothers, 1961.

Valenstein, E. S. (ed.). *The Psychosurgery Debate*. San Francisco: W. H. Freeman & Co., 1980.

Walen, S. R., DiGiuseppe, R., & Wessler, R. L. *A Practitioner's Guide to Rational-Emotive Therapy*. New York: Oxford University Press, 1980.

Watson, J. B. ["Psychology as the Behaviorist Views It"] In W. S. Sahakian (ed.), *History of Psychology*. Itasca, Ill.: F. E. Peacock Publishers, 1968. (Reprinted from *Psychological Review,* 1913, *20.*)

Watson, J. B. *Behaviorism* (rev. ed.). Chicago: University of Chicago Press, 1930. (Phoenix Edition, 1958.)

Wertheimer, M. *Fundamental Issues in Psychology*. New York: Holt, Rinehart and Winston, 1972.

REFERENCES

Wesley, J. "A Plain Account of Christian Perfection," in J. A. Wood (ed.), *Christian Perfection As Taught by John Wesley*. Chicago: Christian Witness Co. 1921. (Originally published 1777.)

Wheat, E., & Wheat, G. *Intended for Pleasure*. Old Tappan, N.J.: Fleming H. Revell, 1977.

Zimbardo, P. G. *Shyness*. Reading, Mass.: Addison-Wesley Publishing Co., 1977.